Fight To The Finish
"Gentleman" Jim Corbett, Joe Choynski, and the Fight that Launched Boxing's Modern Era

By Ron J. Jackson, Jr.

EAKIN PRESS ⊽⧉ Fort Worth, Texas
www.EakinPress.com

Copyright © 2019
By Ron J. Jackson, Jr.
Published By Eakin Press
An Imprint of Wild Horse Media Group
P.O. Box 331779
Fort Worth, Texas 76163
1-817-344-7036
www.EakinPress.com
ALL RIGHTS RESERVED
1 2 3 4 5 6 7 8 9
ISBN-10: 1-68179-126-9
ISBN-13: 978-1-68179-126-5

In loving memory of
Joseph James-Paul Jackson
(1991-2017)

My firstborn, best friend, and confidante in life and literature – an epic
reader who blossomed into a soulful master of the written word …

"We were born to clash."

Joe Choynski on rival James J. Corbett

Contents

Foreword

By Gerry Cooney

I wish I had been there June 5, 1889.

I wish I had been standing on the barge that day, against the ropes of the makeshift ring, watching "Gentleman" Jim Corbett and Joe Choynski battle courageously for twenty-seven rounds in their legendary fight to the finish. The fury of the punches . . . the raucous fans . . . two young fighters in the battle of their lives . . . What a sight it would have been.

Corbett and Choynski grew up a mile apart on the tough streets of early San Francisco, dedicated themselves to the life of prizefighting, and in the process, became fierce rivals. They were seemingly two young men destined to clash, and thanks in large part to outside forces, found themselves engaged in a ballyhooed, illegal finish fight near Benicia, California, in 1889. Some of San Francisco's most powerful and influential residents clamored for the fight, which resulted in an epic bloodbath — a bout that instantly became enshrined in boxing lore.

Like most legends, however, the memory of the Corbett-Choynski barge battle has faded with the passage of time. Participants and eyewitnesses died. Eventually, so did many of boxing's early storytellers — pioneer historians like Nat Fleischer. Now, 130 years later, the valor and courage displayed on that memorable day has been all but forgotten. But boxing fans have once again a chance to step back in time and relive the glory of that day.

In *Fight to the Finish,* author Ron J. Jackson, Jr. salvaged this legendary story from the shadows of time. He invested years of research, meticulously pouring over period documents, memoirs, letters, maps, and eyewitness accounts to piece together a classic boxing tale for a new generation to experience. *Fight to the Finish* also reaches far beyond the heroics in the ring to create thoughtful portraits of Corbett and Choynski in all their vulnerability.

In reality, Corbett and Choynski were two gritty, young boxers trying to find their footing in a sport they loved. They quickly found themselves on a collision course, and caught in the whirlwind of pre-fight hype. That spotlight was intensified by family, friends, promoters, gamblers, and strangers who coveted their own agendas.

Corbett and Choynski became pawns for many who viewed their fight as an ethnic showdown between a Jew and an Irishman, or a battle between the city's white-collar and blue-collar communities. Corbett represented the high-brow Olympic Club, while Choynski carried the banner for the gritty California Athletic Club. The truth is Corbett and Choynski were far more similar than different. They were both smart, tough, and ambitious competitors who desperately wanted to win the big fight — the biggest of their young careers. Race and ethnicity played no role in their ambitions.

I too became familiar with the glare of the spotlight during my career in the ring. Everyone handles the glare differently. In the days leading up to my fights, I liked to surround myself with my closest friends — the guys I grew up with. We would hang out just like we did in the old days. That's how I used to deal with the pressure of an upcoming fight, but you still couldn't wait for the bell to ring.

In *Fight To The Finish*, readers will discover how Corbett and Choynski dealt with the pre-fight hype.

Each week I have the privilege of addressing an international audience on a SiriusXM radio show I co-host with Randy Gordon called *Monday and Friday Night at the Fights*. I do a segment — *This Day in Boxing* — where I tell a lot of the old stories. These stories are the lifeblood of our sport, and I think it's important to keep them alive.

Throughout my career in boxing I have been honored to hear a lot of these stories firsthand from the fighters themselves — legends like Willie Pep, Gene Fullmer, "Sugar" Ray Robinson, Joe Louis, and Jake LaMotta. I have personally met these men, and heard them tell amazing stories. Jake LaMotta, for instance, fought Ray Robinson twice in three weeks. Unbelievable.

Every once in a while we also see a great rivalry come along in boxing — storied rivalries like Ali-Frazier or Gatti-Ward. They are rare and special. The Corbett-Choynski rivalry was the type of rivalry we just don't see nowadays — two fighters laying it all on the line in the fight of their lives.

The Corbett-Choynski bout is worth celebrating and remembering. What would Corbett and Choynski have told us? What did they remember most? What did they learn? What, if anything, did they regret? This book offers us a glimpse into their memories of that classic showdown long ago.

Fight to the Finish also delivers a message of humanity, but I don't want to give away the ending. Let me just say this gripping story of the Corbett-Choynski fight will inspire readers with its showcase of determination, stamina, and courage, and will ultimately leave them cheering long after the final bell.

Acknowledgements

For an author, the completion of a book is akin to summiting a great mountain. In some cases, I imagine that mountain might even feel like Mount Everest. The sense of accomplishment is nirvana for one like myself who writes historical narratives, having persevered years of tedious research, sifting through reams of books, newspapers, letters, and other documents in special collections, libraries, courthouses, and museums to piece together a story. Let me leave no doubt that the hunt for history can be adventurous, although not always glamorous. The journey is all too often filled with various roadblocks, which only adds to the luster of victory when a manuscript is finally completed. Then, and only then, can an author truly take a moment to savor the magnitude of their accomplishment.

And while they are deserving of a victory lap, I dare say none of them have ever done it alone. I haven't.

Fight To The Finish is the culmination of four years of research and writing, although the idea for the book has existed in my imagination for three decades. Along the way I sent countless emails, made untold calls, and scoured over thousands of pages of historical information for this book. I walked in the footsteps of my two protagonists — James J. Corbett and Joe Choynski — in their hometown of San Francisco, as well as the scenes of their 1889 encounters in neighboring Marin and Solano counties. I stood on the very spot where they first brawled in May 1889 in a barn in Fairfax, California and walked the length of Dillon's Point, which overlooks Benicia's Southampton Bay — site of their fateful June 5, 1889, barge fight. And nearly each step of the way there was someone present who lent a helping hand in some manner — enough, I'm sure, to fill another book.

My father Ronald Joseph Jackson, Sr. is high on that list. In addition to his years of moral support ("How's the boxing book coming, Ronnie? Now I'm looking forward to that one . . ."), he served as my loyal companion on our road trips into San Francisco, Fairfax, and Benicia. He too walked in Corbett and Choynski's footsteps by my side, and unknowingly made me delve much deeper into their lives beyond the ring as I shared stories about their earliest days in San Francisco.

My research trips to California provided access to a wealth of information at various institutions such as the California Historical Society in San Francisco; the Bancroft Library at the University of California, Berkeley; the San Francisco Maritime National Park; the Marin County Museum; and the Benicia Historical Museum at the Camel Barns. Staffs at each institution freely gave of their time to ensure I obtained the information I needed. A few, like the Benicia Historical Museum's curator Beverly Phelan, have even stayed in touch to inquire about the book's release date.

I also owe a great debt of thanks to David and Mortimer Feishhacker, the great-grandsons of I.N. and Harriet Choynski. David and Mortimer graciously welcomed me to their family estate, and allowed me to copy the original letters of I.N.'s journey to the California gold fields. The letters offer an invaluable insight into I.N. and Harriet's relationship, and thus a foundation for understanding Joe's childhood home. Thankfully, the letters were preserved by David and Mortimer's mother, Janet — Herbert Choynski's only child. Herbert was Joe's oldest sibling.

Author Christopher J. LaForce also deserves much thanks for hooking me up with some Choynski family images. We first became aware of one another years ago through the Fleishhackers. At the time, LaForce was writing the first – and long overdue — biography of Joe Choynski, *The Choynski Chronicles: A Biography of Hall of Fame Boxer Jewish Joe Choynski*. I highly recommend *The Choynski Chronicles* to anyone interested in the early history of America, let alone the life of one its greatest pioneering pugilists. His work is the definitive account of Choynski's life from cradle to grave.

Lee White, my long-time friend and co-author of *Joe, the Slave Who Became an Alamo Legend*, also deserves praise for keeping my spirits buoyed at all times. Lee is one of the best historical researchers in the business, and was always ready for a brainstorming session whenever I found myself against the ropes.

Of course, no book of this nature is possible without the historical pathfinders like boxing historians Nat Fleischer and Jack Fiske. Fleischer wrote *Gentleman Jim, The Story of James J. Corbett* in 1942, and Fiske – the *San Francisco Chronicle's* late boxing columnist — shared details of Choynski's life to a then-young sports reporter from Vacaville, California.

Former No. 1 heavyweight contender "Gentleman" Gerry Cooney proved once again that some of the friendliest people in the world can be found in the fight business. Cooney, a childhood sports idol of mine, graciously agreed to write this book's foreword despite not knowing me previous to my request. Elements of the historic Choynski-Corbett bout reminded me of Cooney's titanic fight with Heavyweight Champion Larry Holmes in 1982, and therefore I thought the famed slugger was a perfect fit. Cooney knows boxing history intimately, as well as the glare of the sport's brightest spotlight. "Yeah, Ron," Cooney said in our first conversation. "Count me in." Class. All class.

Readers will also see the names of legendary cutman Jacob "Stitch" Duran grace the back cover of this book with an endorsement. Duran and I used to run in the same boxing circle back when I was a young sports writer in California. Duran has since achieved great success in the boxing business, and agreed to lend a hand when asked without hesitation. Such generosity means more than I can articulate with words.

Naturally, my publisher Billy Huckaby at Wild Horse Media Group in Fort Worth deserves much credit for taking this project. Huckaby is fearless when it comes to publishing. A few years ago he purchased the once-great, independent publishing house, Eakin Press, and thanks to him, a number of its memorable titles will live on for future generations to enjoy.

My support team extended to a parade of family and friends — many of whom probably don't even remember their contribution to this project over the years. Some of those folks include my first sports editor Chuck Barney; boxing trainer and friend Al LaGardo; fellow author Jay "Mr. Sweet Tea" Grelen; my niece Stephanie Trujillo; my late mother-in-law Darlene Giblet; *Vallejo Times-Herald* reporter Richard Freedman; former managing editor Robin Miller of *The Reporter* in Vacaville, California; and friends Andy Grima, Aaron and Laura Prien, Cecil Conley, Chuck Barney, Sean Gibbons, and Hall of Fame matchmaker Bruce Trampler. Sometimes, their contribution was as profound as a kind word of support.

Last on this list, but not in my heart, is my wife, Jeannia, and my four children — Joseph, Ashley, Tristan, and Missouri. Throughout their lives they have made sacrifices so that I might pursue my dream of writing books. They have surrendered time with me, as well as an occasional vacation so that I might finance another research trip. They have done so without complaint, and have even become my most ardent fans. All I can say is I love each of you bigger than the sky.

Sadly, we lost Joseph in January 2017. He was twenty-five. Joseph was unquestionably my biggest fan. He was also a voracious reader and master student of literature. Joseph always read my books, and bestowed upon me advice that I grew to cherish. I miss him more and more with each passing day, but he would want me to fight until the final bell. So I press on in search of other soulful stories to tell in his honor. Thank you, son. And know I will love you until the end of time.

Introduction

The origins of *Fight To The Finish* can be traced back thirty-four years to my senior year of high school in my hometown of Vacaville, California. I suppose one might credit Drew Wyant — our stud quarterback and my catcher on the baseball diamond — for unknowingly planting the seeds of this book.

Wyant watched with amusement one day as my best friend, Andy Grima, and I passed time before baseball practice with a mock boxing match. Epic air punches were being thrown with fast and furious precision that day, and I was caught somewhere between my best "Gentleman" Gerry Cooney and "Terrible" Tim Witherspoon when Wyant interrupted the clowning.

"Hey, 'Goose,'" chimed Wyant, calling me by a nickname bestowed upon me because I was a junk-ball pitcher who threw nothing like Yankee flame-thrower Goose Gossage. "Ever heard of 'Gentleman' Jim Corbett?"

Smirking, I replied, "Well, yeah. Corbett defeated John L. Sullivan to become the first gloved World Heavyweight Champion. He was from San Francisco."

Back in the day, I was a full-fledged sports nerd. If you gave me a year, I could tell you who played in the World Series that year and who won. Yes, it was bad. I also prided myself on being an avid boxing fan. I read *Ring Magazine* and Jack Fiske's boxing column in the *San Francisco Chronicle* religiously, and reveled in boxing's colorful history and characters. I could even tell you the lineage of the true heavyweight titleholders dating back to Sullivan. You know, the man who beat the man who beat the man. But Wyant taught me something that day I didn't know – something, in fact, I was ashamed I didn't know given my nerdy side for all things sports and boxing.

"Did you know Corbett once fought some dude over in Benicia?" he asked.

Wyant's question stopped me in my tracks. I immediately ceased the clowning to hear more. If Grima and I had been boxing for real, he would have knocked me out at that moment with a haymaker. Benicia was a quaint, bedroom community a half hour from my hometown, and I never knew it once hosted a Corbett boxing match. I remember thinking: "Corbett fought in my backyard? Why hadn't I heard this story before?"

"Really?" I replied. "Who did he fight?"

"I don't know," Wyant said, "but they fought out on the water on a big barge."

"Where did you hear about this?" I pressed.

Wyant confessed with a sly grin, "I saw a painting of the fight one night in a Benicia pub. The bartender told us all about the fight."

The illegalities of Wyant's teenage escapade aside (He is now a well-respected member of Sacramento's dedicated law enforcement community), I wanted to learn more about the Corbett fight and his opponent. I also wanted to know how a waterfront hamlet like Benicia came to host a bout featuring the heavyweight champion. Was it an exhibition or a real fight?

My curiosity survived my high school graduation, summer vacation, and even my first year as a part-time sports writer for my hometown newspaper, *The Reporter*. Then, one day, I finally decided to journey to the California State Library in Sacramento to learn the facts of Corbett's Benicia adventure. Since this was the pre-Internet days, I first surveyed a copy of *The Ring Record Book and Boxing Encyclopedia*. I learned Corbett fought June 5, 1889, in Benicia against fellow San Franciscan Joe Choynski — the "dude" from Wyant's story. Choynski had carved out his own Hall-of-Fame boxing career as a phenomenally rugged, undersized heavyweight contender and was arguably the best Jewish big man of all-time. I was further intrigued, and soon began searching the microfilm of the local newspapers that covered the fight — the *San Francisco Chronicle, San Francisco Examiner,* and *Daily Alta California.*

Each newspaper gave its own blow-by-blow account of this unique fight, from the clandestine actions of the participants engaging in an illegal "fight to the finish" to the desperate brawl waged by two young, San Francisco rivals. What unfolded before my eyes was an epic contest of courage. Corbett and Choynski waged a twenty-seven-round war on the deck of a blood-soaked barge under a blistering sun, and neither man would dare quit. I was hooked, and in the months and years that followed, gathered information and eyewitness accounts related to the fight for a book I knew I would someday write. I discovered a strong undercurrent of ethnic and social tension associated with the fight, and a rivalry often fanned by the selfish motives of others.

But I also discovered something much more profound than a legendary fight from boxing's bygone days. I stumbled upon two young men in Choynski and Corbett locked in an intense struggle to emerge from San Francisco's hard streets with their own version of the American Dream. And they did so on their own terms, often against the blessings of loving and protective parents.

Corbett and Choynski were simply destined to fight. They were on the same path at the same moment in time. They lived only a mile apart, but ran in different circles. They even brawled once on the streets, and quickly developed a blood feud. Ironically, despite their rivalry, they probably shared much more in common than even they would have admitted. Both youngsters were highly intelligent, inquisitive, and quick students in the ring. They were also extremely ambitious, tough, and prideful. Frankly, it's no wonder both enjoyed great careers in the fight game long after their Benicia showdown. The barge fight simply proved to be the springboard to greatness.

As is the fate with most great stories, though, this one too faded with time. History is filled with such examples. First, eyewitnesses die. Then the historians who carried the torch. Eventually, the story is retold with less frequency and historical facts until myth and reality blur. This has been the fate of the Corbett-Choynski barge affair.

Amazingly, this legendary boxing match never became the sole focus of a book. *Fight To The Finish* attempts to preserve this epic battle — and all its social and cultural ramifications in 1889 San Francisco — for future generations. I've drawn on every known primary source available to reconstruct Corbett and Choynski's earliest years in this lively, historical narrative, as well as the intimate details that eventually placed them on a collision course. Along the way readers will be introduced to a parade of colorful San Francisco socialites, gamblers, newsmen, and sporting hacks who helped secure the clandestine match.

Alas, you too will stand ringside on the barge June 5, 1889, with the sea air in your lungs and the smell of blood in the air. The fighters will appear on deck to the raucous cheers of their loyal followers, and wagers of new bets will be made on the spot. Your adrenaline will flow because what you are about to experience is boxing history.

Chapter One
The Legend
— —

Old-timer John Carty could still see the blood flow forty-four years later, running like a red river somewhere in the deep reservoir of his mind, where unimaginable feats sometimes become legendary with time.

Carty never needed time to season his perspective, though.

The former shipyard apprentice realized he had witnessed an epic scene June 5, 1889, on a blistering summer morning west of Benicia, California. On that day, from a teetering skiff in Southampton Bay, a teenage Carty watched two young San Francisco boxers — "Gentleman" James J. Corbett and Joe Choynski — wage a brutal "fight to the finish" aboard a grain barge anchored in the bay.[1]

The two boxers fought relentlessly for twenty-seven rounds.

Carty was one of about 300 people who could attest to the extraordinary courage and grit displayed by Choynski and Corbett. Now, more than four decades later, Carty hearkened back to that legendary fight at the request of *Benicia New Era* publisher William Dykes.[2]

News of Corbett's death reached Carty's Benicia home Feb. 18, 1933, through Dykes, who planned to write a memorial to the former World Heavyweight Champion and record his link to the sleepy waterfront community for posterity. Carty didn't disappoint.

Images from the Corbett-Choynski fight remained starkly

1

etched in his mind as if he had taken the blows himself from the bloody footing of that barge long ago. Now, at age sixty-one, Carty turned his memory loose in recounting the colorful scene: The tugboats plowing into the bay, loaded with anxious supporters from some of San Francisco's wealthiest quarters . . . Corbett's speedy footwork . . . Choynski's enormous shoulders . . . their violent, fistic collisions . . . [3]

Boxing matches were forbidden outside of organized athletic clubs in California in those days. All of which added to the allure of the illegal match. Spectators were enticed by the romantic notion of alluding police, an adrenaline rush that an adventurous youngster like Carty could especially appreciate.

Carty's story eventually trailed back to the one image that always dominated his recollections of that scrap — the blood.

"The men were very bloody," Carty told Dykes as he scribbled notes. "After the twentieth round they were so bloody that buckets of water were thrown on them to wash off the blood . . . "[4]

Corbett and Choynski were motivated by a bitter feud.

Borne on the tough streets of a diverse San Francisco, their rivalry grew to local prominence, climaxing with their showdown on the barge. The bad blood was real. Corbett and Choynski harbored disdain for one another. Still, there was no shortage of hype to stir the city's sporting hacks and gamblers into a frenzy.

The exclusive Olympic Club (Corbett) vs. The blue-collar California Athletic Club (Choynski).

The Amateur (Corbett) vs. The Professional (Choynski).

The Hayes Valley gang (Corbett) vs. The Golden Gate Avenue boys (Choynski).

The Irishman vs. The Jew.

For some, a Corbett-Choynski battle was strictly a matter of ethnic pride. For the fighters themselves, it was simply a matter of pride. Who was the best fighter in San Francisco? Corbett or Choynski? Plain and simple.

The feud resulted in arguably the most savage fight ever contested in the annals of boxing history, and surprisingly, a profound story about two good men destined to spill each other's blood.

This is their legend . . .

Chapter Two
The 'Dude'

— —

San Francisco, California: Circa 1884

Enchanting and mysterious. Worldly and wholesome. Sophisticated and barbaric. San Francisco offered a little of everything for those who explored its electric-lighted streets during the decade of the 1880s. The city rewarded tenacity, creativity, and grit in those days, but could also swallow dreams as swiftly as a riptide in its golden bay.

San Franciscans grew to understand that thin line between prosperity and despair. Decades of hard knocks taught them well. Those who resided on its hilly banks were generally a hardy lot whose city was molded during the wild days of '49, back when dreamers flocked to a rocky shoreline en route to the gold fields along the Sacramento River and beyond.

Less than 1,000 people lived in San Francisco in 1848 when the first reports of gold began to filter out of California. Within two years, city forefathers boasted a population of more than 25,000 people and the most prominent port on the Pacific Coast. By 1880, San Francisco's permanent populous numbered nearly 234,000 souls.

As if overnight, through the shifting tides of fate, the city became a breeding ground for survivors. The Gold Rush dashed countless dreams, prompting disenchanted prospectors to sail away and never look back. Other folks, through either good fortune or hard work, remained behind to build a future and a city.

They would build something special.

Shrouded almost daily by a blanket of fog, San Francisco often appeared mystical or magical from a distance. And in many ways, the city was both. By 1884, streetcars glided effortlessly up its steep cobblestone streets, as if climbing to the heavens. Yet beneath the cobblestone ran a grinding operation of steel cables — the guts and ingenuity of the city's world-famous cable car system. Locals cleverly called it "riding the rope."

Four separate cable car lines converged at the city's Ferry Building, a low, wooden shed with twelve open bays and a squat wooden tower that served as a beacon to passengers. The Ferry Building sat sturdily on the waterfront at the foot of Market Street, an unusually wide, untidy thoroughfare that became the epicenter of traffic and commerce for San Francisco.[5]

Engineers designed Market Street to cut a wide, 120-foot swath through the city, inadvertently dividing it into primarily two distinct sections — residential to the north and industrial to the south.

Pandemonium reigned daily on Market Street. Horse-drawn streetcars and cable cars constantly rang their bells as they clattered down the street loaded with clinging passengers. Along the storefronts, vendors aggressively peddled their goods.

"Everywhere ambulant peddlers make their way through the multitude, laying insolent siege to pocketbooks," one visitor wrote. "They have trays of flowers; handcarts full of peanuts and oranges; pen-knives, buttons, neckties, lemonade and soda pop in boxes on tripods . . . Between a jeweler and a milliner, sellers of fruits, celery, conserves, soaps and shoes invade the sidewalk. Rows of shawls, cashmeres, and parasols are broken by legs of beef and mutton that hang from their pegs and catch the scarf of the passerby."[6]

San Francisco exported and imported an exotic variety of merchandise and foods that reflected its prominence as an international port city. Stacks of lumber cluttered the waterfront, where drays and wagons crisscrossed in a hectic maze of activity and noise. The lumber, including planks cut from California's mighty redwoods, would eventually be shipped abroad to build houses in places as far away as Scotland and Australia.[7]

Elsewhere, sat stacks of hay, crates of fruits and vegetables, and wooden barrels of fish packed in salt.

Bottled wines also circulated city streets from remote regions in the East, Central America, Mexico, and islands rumored to be located in the Pacific. A goodly number of those bottles would end up in the dining rooms of some of the city's finest hotels.

Two such luxurious establishments — the Palace Hotel and the Grand Hotel — were located across the street from one another on New Montgomery Street, at the junction of Market Street. The Palace Hotel stood as a testament to San Francisco's place in the civilized world, presenting a portrait of opulence and grandeur upon its completion in 1875. The seven-story hotel offered guests a choice of 800 rooms with a myriad of bay windows that could be seen for miles in any direction. From the main entrance, one could gaze at the hotel's elaborate, brick facade and into its spacious Grand Court, where carriages delivered guests through one of three mammoth open bays. Inside, guests mingled about marble-lined halls beneath the glow of bright electrical lights and discussed the news of the day.[8]

Most other desires could be satisfied a few paces away on Market Street. The street merged San Francisco's residential and commercial districts with the waterfront, where the Ferry Building hummed with chatter from travelers coming and going from its terminals. Ferryboats shuttled passengers hourly across the bay to Oakland, another burgeoning port city built on the good fortune of its locale and the sweat of its founders.

Beyond the Ferry Building, in the choppy, chilly waters of the bay, existed a frenzy of coal-burning tugboats, steamboats, yachts, fishing skiffs, whaling schooners, and mighty Clipper ships. Each cruised through the water in a steady rhythm of organized chaos, feeding the economy as well as the imaginations of those who beheld its scene.

Collectively, these maritime vessels were the bloodline of San Francisco.

Still, the city's heartbeat remained its people, mostly a melting pot of industrious first and second-generation immigrants from Ireland, England, Italy, Germany, China, and Prussia. Of these ethnic groups, only the Chinese suffered an exorbitant amount of racism at this time because they offered cheap labor and were few in number. Yet each group — even the steadfast Chinese—maintained one thread of commonality: A sense of freedom and independence.

One annoyed visitor mused at this free-spirited attitude while checking into the Palace Hotel:

> When the hotel clerk—the man who settles your room for you and who is supposed to give you information— when that resplendent individual stoops to attend to your wants he does so whistling or humming, or picking his teeth, or in the pauses of conversation with someone he knows. These performances, I gather, are to show you that he is a free man and your equal. From his general appearance and the size of his diamonds, he ought to be your superior.[9]

Samuel Williams, a San Francisco newspaper writer from the period, may have explained that sense of independence best by describing the city's social structure. "The lines of class and caste are often vague and shadowy," Williams wrote. "Your coachman of yesterday may be your landlord tomorrow."[10]

And perhaps no one coveted that freedom more than the immigrant.

The immigrant sailed from distant shores and likely endured numerous hardships for a mere taste of American freedom. Whether Irish or Jewish or Chinese, their path was generally a shared experience from their homeland and each would find refuge in San Francisco neighborhoods of their own ethnicity. The Irish harbored the Irish . . . the Jews cared for the Jews . . . the Chinese found safe haven in Chinatown . . . There, among their native people, they found strength in numbers and re-enforcement for their common dreams. Harriet Lane Levy recalled that unspoken bond from her childhood neighborhood:

> *At nine o'clock every morning the men of O'Farrell Street left their homes for their places of business downtown; dressed in brushed broadcloth and polished high hats, they departed soberly as to a funeral. The door of each house opened and let out the owner who took the steps firmly, and, arriving on the sidewalk, turned slowly eastward toward town. A man had not walked many yards before being overtaken by a friend coming from the avenue. Together they walked with matched steps down the street.*
>
> *All the men were united by the place and circumstances of their birth. They had come to America from villages in Germany, and they had worked themselves up from small stores in the interior of California to businesses in San Francisco.*[11]

So went the working-class heroes of San Francisco each day at sunrise. They scattered about the city to service their fellow citizens by manning the banks, blacksmith shops, hotels, cafes, bakeries, and so forth. Ultimately, they represented everything that was honest and decent about life in young San Francisco.

By nightfall, another city dweller surfaced.

One observer noted how, in the dim fog of night, a "thousand tricksters, sharpers and charlatans display their wares by torchlight" along the city's main thoroughfares. Beyond one hustler would stand a sage who "operates an electrical device for treating hemorrhage, rheumatism, dyspepsia, and every scourge of unhappy mankind." Further down the street, "a gypsy tells fortunes to some rustics, and a spiritualist relates conversations with the shade of Santa Ana's [*sic*]widow or of Lincoln's assassin, Booth . . . "[12]

Tucked in the back alleys and dives one might also encounter young gangs of ruffians. The reporter Williams referred to this societal scourge as "Hoodlums," noting with no pride whatsoever that "The Hoodlum is a distinctive San Francisco product . . . He drinks, gambles, steals, runs after lewd women, sets buildings on fire, rifles the pockets of inebriated citizens going home in the small hours, parades the streets at night singing obscene songs, uttering horrid oaths, and striking terror to the heart of the timid generally."[13]

Nowhere did life mean so little than in the haunts of San Francisco's Barbary Coast, a seamy district of bordellos, saloons, gambling dens, and dives. A local reporter who once ventured into the district in the company of a policeman marveled at its rankness, observing how the area was "literally swarming with the scum of creation." He elaborated further by writing:

> *Every land under the sun has contributed toward making up the crowd of loafers, thieves, low gamblers, jay-hawkers, dirty, filthy, degraded, hopeless bummers, and the unsophisticated greenhorns from the mines, or from the Eastern States, who, drawn here by curiosity, or lured on by specious falsehoods told them by pretended friends met on the ocean or river steamers, are looked upon as the legitimate prey of all the rest.*[14]

The Barbary Coast was not for the feint. Scarred and tattooed sailors, fresh from months at sea, frequented the district in search of a hard drink, a winning poker hand, and the company of a loose woman. The combination often led to trouble. A drunken dispute over cards or a prostitute — or both — could easily spark a round of violence. Only these disputes weren't merely settled with fists, but sometimes at the end of discharged pistol or point of a knife.

Fistfights were elevated to the realm of entertainment in the Barbary Coast district. Smoke-filled saloons and gambling dens routinely catered to underground fights, where the roughest and toughest men clashed for pride and money. Side bets were the norm. Spectators also wagered on these barbaric contests in which they would crowd the two gladiators with a ring of humanity and raucous enthusiasm.

From the shadows of these dimly lit dives emerged a teenage fighter of special distinction — a native San Franciscan.

Irishman James John Corbett searched the Barbary Coast for the roughest talent, exchanging punches with any and all comers. He was a strapping lad, even with the undeveloped physique of a teenager. He stood tall and erect at six-foot-one, with broad shoulders and a trunk that tapered dramatically at the waist.[15]

Corbett always stood out from the crowd due to his fluid, seemingly natural instincts as a fighter and his gentlemanly appearance. The latter made him an oddity on the mean streets of the Barbary Coast district. As a young bank teller, Corbett constantly took special pains to maintain a professional appearance. He was a natty dresser who groomed meticulously and often sported a flashy, pompadour hairdo.

Corbett, in short, looked out of place.

Those who frequented the haunts of the Barbary Coast were naturally shocked by his presence. Through the misty haze of smoke, first-time observers would have seen a strikingly handsome, well-dressed young man with brilliant blue eyes step to the floor to challenge any pug present to a fight.[16]

Rumors would later arise that a hustling, young Corbett promoted a number of these fights, coaxing larger opponents into a scrap with bets on the outcome.[17]

Either way, the district never ran out of rugged, willing brawlers.

A young James J. Corbett experienced his "first look at the good life" as a bank teller. *Author's Collection*

These were men borne from the cut-throat existence of local or distant waterfront dives, or wild, frontier saloons. They were generally bar-room brawlers who usually jeered Corbett as "a dude," a derogatory name that suggested he was too much of a dandy to be anything more than easy prey.[18]

Corbett's fists said otherwise.

"I found the road pretty tough going for a while, but stuck it out, never losing a single bout," Corbett recalled decades later in his autobiography. "All these were earned without any real boxing instructions . . . but here I feel I developed resourcefulness, generalship, and the ability to size up all kinds of men."[19]

The proving ground was nothing new to Corbett.

As Corbett gravitated toward pugilism, he surrounded himself with friends who shared his passion. One such chum was Lew Harding, who trained and sparred with Corbett twice a week in his father's cellar. In time, Harding saw a natural ability in his friend that Corbett himself didn't even see.[20]

Harding observed Corbett's darting eyes, slick footwork, and quick instincts.

"Jim wasn't a trouble-maker or a wise-guy," Harding later recalled. "Fighting just came natural to him."[21]

Soon, Harding coaxed Corbett into rougher circles to test his raw skills.

Corbett later mused how Harding began to take him to "various places" where he would "mix it" with "the toughest characters in town." On Wednesday nights, Harding pitted Corbett against the rough talent that congregated at a local engine house. Friday nights were likewise reserved for a neighborhood blacksmith shop, where Corbett remembered "the crowd was even worse."[22]

Corbett always held his own in these tussles. Eventually, he graduated to the seamy waterfront district in search of rough and tumble foes.

"I had a good many fights at each of these places — some of them pretty tough ones, as I said, the gangs were composed of noted scrappers of the town," Corbett remembered. "When I first came there they used to sneer at me and look upon me as a 'dude' . . . However, I fought myself into their estimation, and soon they forgot to call me this withering name and made no more remarks about my white collar or kid gloves . . ."[23]

Not everyone celebrated Corbett's fistic success on the street circuit.

Patrick Corbett, James John's father, disapproved of his son's after-hour activities. The elder Corbett — an immigrant from County Galway, Ireland, — didn't sail to America to see his children scuffling on the streets like animals. The truth is, he feared his son's fighting might jeopardize his position as an assistant teller at the Nevada State Bank.[24]

Patrick Corbett likely didn't have any control over his son.

James was a freethinking, albeit stubborn, Irishman whose blood flowed similarly to someone else he knew and loved — his father.

Born into poverty, Patrick Corbett was the third of four brothers raised on a farm in the village of Ballycusheen. By the age of eighteen, he had already survived a potato famine that killed more than 750,000 of his countrymen. That year — 1854 — he sailed for America, inspired by the glowing reports sent by his older brother, John, in New Orleans.

Patrick arrived safely with other siblings in New Orleans, then the fourth largest city in the United States with more than 100,000 residents. Thanks to John, Patrick avoided the grueling labor subjected to most immigrants on the docks and found employment at a hotel where John worked.[25]

A booming cotton market greeted the Corbetts. So too did a yellow fever epidemic.

By the start of 1856, yellow fever had claimed two of Patrick's sisters and two of his brothers, including John. Patrick lost his enthusiasm for New Orleans and soon turned his wanderlust toward San Francisco.[26]

Patrick sailed away from the port of New Orleans and never looked back.

Although no account of his journey is known to exist, it was undoubtedly an arduous one. He would have sailed one of two routes. One route would have carried him around "the horn" of South America, while the other required him to disembark at Colon, travel fifty miles overland to Panama City by either stagecoach or wagon, and then board another ship for the final leg of his trip on the Pacific Ocean.

The latter option offered the cheapest fare for passengers at between $50 and $75.

Regardless, Patrick landed at the San Francisco docks in 1856 and into a world he would soon embrace with great ambition. Patrick immediately found familiar work, being hired as a porter at a Market Street hotel where he also secured room and board. In 1858, he became a porter at the swank Hotel Nucleus.[27]

Patrick eventually opened his own business driving hacks. His timing couldn't have been better.

The discovery of the Comstock Lode in the silver mines of

Virginia City once again made San Francisco a boomtown for adventurers and speculators. During this historic time, Patrick often worked late into the night and early morning hours shuttling passengers about the sleepless city.

In November 1858, Patrick, now twenty-four, married Catherine McDonald, a twenty-one-year-old fellow Catholic whose family had taken the overland route from Philadelphia a few years earlier. A year later the young couple celebrated the first of their ten children — Frank.

The Corbett family would grow in symphony with San Francisco.

Nine more children would be born to Patrick and Catherine, prompting the Corbetts to move from one home to the next as their family grew. On September 1, 1866, the Corbetts gave birth to their fourth child and baptized him, James John.

Shortly after James John's birth, the family moved again into

The Corbett clan found permanent residence in a six-bedroom house at 520 Hayes Street. Downstairs, one could also find Patrick Corbett's funeral parlor and livery stable – the scene of his son's earliest sparring sessions. *Author's Collection*

a rental house south of "The Slot" — a name locals gave the cable car line which divided the city along Market Street. Finally, when James was six, his father purchased what would become the Corbett family's permanent home at 520 Hayes Street in the newly surveyed section of town known as Hayes Valley.

The home was grand.

Victorian gables and large, bay windows peered out the second story, which housed the family's main living quarters. A family room, complete with a piano, anchored the center of the upstairs with a parlor and dining room on each side. In the rear, the home offered six bedrooms and the latest in modern luxuries—two indoor bathrooms.[28]

Downstairs, one could find Corbett's new livery stable and funeral parlor. Two, large swinging gates sat in the middle of the first floor with office space on either side. Beyond the gates were the stables in the warmest section of the building with a storage area for carriages and wagons at the rear.[29]

In a few short years, Corbett's business would become a bit of a local landmark. The business would play a prominent role in the lives and deaths of local residents who rode Corbett's hacks for christenings, weddings, and funerals.[30]

Young James John Corbett wasn't so impressed at first.

James long harbored bitter memories of the move north of "The Slot." He led the procession at age six, being given the duty of guiding the family's milk cow across a busy Market Street. He felt so humiliated he wept as he walked.[31]

Crying never came easy to James, though. Fighting did.

"James J. Corbett is an exceptionally friendly boy," one old school record revealed. "However, he is too free with his fists and often involved himself in street fights."[32]

One such fight became the stuff of local legend while James was attending the Jesuit-run Saint Ignatius Academy. As James remembered, he was fourteen when he encountered a bully some six years his elder by the name of "Fatty" Carney after school.[33]

A playground tussle prompted Carney to inform young Corbett, "I'll get you after school."[34]

One classmate whispered to Corbett after school that Carney was waiting for him outside. Corbett wanted to run.

"There were two exits, and I was trying to decide which was safer when it suddenly occurred to me that if I ran away all the boys would laugh at me and I would be looked upon as a coward," Corbett later recalled. "I kept thinking it over while I was marching, but my pride was now aroused, and I said to myself, 'I will go out and get licked.' "[35]

Corbett determined he would be the aggressor despite shaking on the inside. Then as the fight began, Corbett found himself instinctively bobbing his head, sidestepping the much huskier Carney, and flicking jabs.

Shouting students encircled the two boys as Carney stalked the elusive Corbett.

Suddenly, the police sent the crowd scurrying in different directions. The boys continued the fight a short distance away at the "Circus Lot," where traveling circuses of the day would pitch their tents. Corbett continued to dazzle with his quick feet and fists until Carney tackled him and pummeled him with punches on the ground.

An old man bearing a cane broke up the fight, but not before Carney had blackened one of Corbett's eyes.[36]

The next day Corbett received both the praise of his peers at school, as well as an expulsion from Saint Ignatius.

Corbett didn't care. He had learned his first and most important lesson in fighting.

Size alone didn't mean anything. A smaller man could beat a larger man by using his brains and speed. Corbett would carry this lesson with him from that day forward.[37]

Patrick Corbett, meanwhile, enrolled his combative son into Sacred Heart College the following year as a last resort to keep him in school. Sacred Heart required tuition, and offered an educational environment framed by strict rules and regulations.[38]

The school was designed for wayward boys like James.

The experiment, however, ended poorly. Corbett was again expelled for fighting. Only this time Corbett's adversary turned out to be a portly priest whom the youngster rammed with his head while fleeing other pursuing schoolmasters.

Corbett, as it turned out, refused to allow a priest to swat him on the hand with a stick for disciplinary reasons.

Corbett's formal education thus ended at age fifteen.

An opportunity of a different kind soon landed in his lap. J.S. Angus, a customer at Patrick Corbett's livery stable, was a cashier at the Nevada State Bank. Angus secured James a job at the bank as a messenger, and within three years, the youngster had earned a promotion to assistant bank teller.[39]

Corbett now had a taste of the finer things life had to offer, not the least of which was respectability. People started to view him differently, and he fostered his newfound reputation with immaculate grooming and dress.

His strapping, athletic frame and handsome looks made him a crowd favorite.

"You could always tell where Jim's cage was," one bank worker recalled. "It was the one with all the girls crowded around in front."[40]

Corbett would later recall, "At the bank, I had my first look at the good life. I swore that someday those things would be mine, though at the time I had no idea of how I would get them."[41]

If Corbett were to fulfill his vow, he eventually realized he would do so with his fists. Corbett's revelation likely came during one of the numerous fights he engaged in on the streets of San Francisco.

Fighting soon became an addiction and passion.

At home, he often ventured into his father's stables to engage in sparring sessions with his older brothers, Frank and Harry. Occasionally, he would mix it up with his father's hack drivers. Patrick Corbett allowed his boys to keep boxing gloves in the stables for such sessions, although he constantly encouraged them to "be gentleman" and to "keep out of rows."[42]

James couldn't help himself. Eventually, he took his thirst for boxing into the seamy alleys and very waterfront saloons his father warned him against. The elder Corbett feared his son's street fighting would ultimately cost him his bank job.

On a February day in 1884, James thought his father's fear had become reality. John W. Mackay, owner of the Nevada State Bank, called James into his office. Rumors of Corbett's fights on the Barbary Coast had reached his desk.

"I hear you're interested in boxing," Mackay said to his young teller. Corbett respectfully nodded in the affirmative, nervous and uneasy about how his employer might react. What Corbett didn't know was that Mackay was a big sporting fan and an officer at the swank Olympic Club.

"Why waste your time brawling in the gutter for experience?" Mackay challenged. "I'll take you to the Olympic Club and introduce you to a professor who can teach you real boxing."[43]

Organized boxing appealed to Corbett who sought to feed his competitive appetite while continuing to climb the social ladder. Soon, Corbett could be frequently found at the Olympic Club trying to refine his raw abilities.

Corbett, however, entered the club with the cockiness of a street tough. His first lesson would be that of humility.

At the time the chesty Irishman waltzed into the Olympic Club, its members had taken refuge at the Turn Verein after a fire destroyed its original building June 20, 1883. The morning blaze ravaged everything accumulated in the club's first twenty-three years—furniture, paintings, apparatus, mementos, and documents. But the gatekeepers of the Turn Verein graciously opened its halls to the club's members, who were given full access to an open gymnasium, gallery, and running track.

Corbett scanned the temporary facility with a casual interest before locking in on the person he desired to meet most: the club's boxing instructor. Confidently, Corbett told him he wanted to box.

The instructor glanced at Corbett, inquiring if he had ever boxed.

"Oh, yes," Corbett beamed proudly, "hundreds of times!"[45]

"Box with me a while," the instructor beckoned. Nearby, a group of the boxing professor's friends perked up as if sensing what would happen next.[46]

The next few minutes were a blur.

Punches rained on Corbett in rapid succession, unlike anything he had ever experienced in the saloons or weekly scraps in the shadows of the blacksmith shop where he so often dominated. Blow after blow snapped his head, and with each jolt, roars of laughter could be heard at ringside. Corbett's competitiveness soon turned to anger — an emotion he had always been able to harness on the streets.

Corbett felt the instructor was "showing off" for his friends by making a "monkey" out of the new "kid." The action soon turned rough, Corbett scuffling blindly as if in a street fight with his Hayes Valley gang. Members viewed such behavior as ungentlemanly, and the professor threatened to report the youngster and have his club privileges stripped.[47]

Corbett left that day with his pride dented, but undeterred in his quest to box.

The next day Corbett returned with his pal Lew Harding in tow. Corbett spotted a large fellow with a long flowing black beard similar to those worn by the old 49ers who still milled around the city. The 215-pound man possessed a "magnificent torso," although Corbett wasn't overly impressed. He had seen plenty of muscular toughs on the Barbary Coast. Instead, his eyes were transfixed on the man's incredible beard.

"A fellow who would wear a beard like that cannot box," Corbett thought smugly to himself. He leaned over to Harding, suggesting he arrange a sparring session with the aged "Blackbeard." Harding made the request known to the boxing instructor, who was still sore at Corbett for his behavior a day earlier. The professor smiled.

Moments later, Corbett's hands were being laced with boxing gloves as he stared across the ring at the man with the unforgettable black whiskers. Corbett soon found one more reason to never forget the man.

The last thing he remembered was striding toward those whiskers. Suddenly, water dripped from Corbett's body as he sniffed on smelling salts while seated in a chair. His eyes peeled open to find Harding and the professor feverishly rubbing his legs, trying to circulate his blood.

Corbett had been knocked cold.

Groggy and in disbelief, Corbett pushed his way out of the chair and said, "Come on, let's box."

"No," the 'Blackbeard' replied mercifully, "you have had enough for today."

Determined to show he wasn't hurt, Corbett began to jog around the track. He lurched about three yards before groggily banging into the parallel bars and flying rings. Harding rescued his chum from further damage, leading him to the dressing room to recover.

Corbett later learned the hard-hitting "Blackbeard" was the club's heavyweight champion — a fact he would later find amusing. More importantly, as Harding led him to the dressing room, he experienced the sobering realization that he had been knocked out for the first time in his life. He recalled all his victorious moments in the saloons, and at the firehouse and the blacksmith shop. What had those matches meant? Everything? Nothing?

At that moment Corbett set aside his pride. He understood then that he needed formal boxing lessons.[48]

A year later those lessons would be taught by the Olympic Club's new boxing professor, Walter Watson. Club administrators imported Watson from England. He arrived in San Francisco noted for his skill and expertise, although his rather lumpy mid-section belied his resume. But his reputation left a young stable of prospects somewhat timid and reluctant to aggressively display their abilities.[49]

Watson grew impatient and testy.

"Have you ever boxed?" Watson asked Corbett.

"A good many times," Corbett replied.

"Open up," Watson commanded. "I want you to show me what you have."

"Do you really mean it?" asked Corbett, hesitant of being ungentlemanly or disrespectful.

"Of course," Watson snapped.

"Open up with all I have and hit you as hard as I want to?" Corbett asked.

Watson smiled, "That's what I want."

Corbett raised his gloves and flew into Watson like "a runaway horse," showering the burly professor with speedy blows in every direction. Finally, Watson held his hands up to halt the action.

"Is there any Irish blood in you, by any chance?" Watson asked playfully.

"Yes, sir, my father, and mother are Irish," Corbett replied.

A grin crossed Watson's face. He then proclaimed, "In three months you will lick any man in this club."[50]

The words struck Corbett like a bolt of lightning. Inside, he quietly swelled with pride — a sort of pride he had never before known. Corbett felt the adrenaline surge through his body. Watson had given him something he had longed for in the organized circles of pugilism — confidence.

Corbett suddenly found himself feinting and jabbing everywhere he went. He became determined to master the finer points of the Sweet Science.

The quest became an obsession.

During the day, the young Corbett's mind seldom strayed far from boxing. He began to study his physical limitations in search of ways to improve his fighting prowess. One day at work he noticed his left hand, which had rested on an account book all day, ached. Meanwhile, his right didn't. He quickly deduced that was because his right hand had been busy all day writing.[51]

Corbett became dogmatic in his pursuit to greatly strengthen his left. He began shooting his left hand in a powerful, jabbing thrust whenever the moment allowed. At work, he sparred whenever possible with fellow clerks on lunch breaks. He practiced guarding with his right and jabbing with his left. At home, he repeatedly threw left jabs into a cushion, always trying to hit the same mark.[52]

But there was no substitute for live sparring sessions.

James always welcomed newcomers to his stables, and once in the early days of 1884, he encountered a local tough who would profoundly change the course of his life. His name was Joe Choynski, a muscular Jewish lad who lived about a mile away on Golden Gate Avenue.

Choynski, then fifteen, refused to attend school and was working at the time at a blacksmith shop on the Barbary Coast where he developed great upper-body strength. On the streets, Choynski was renown in his neighborhood for fighting and tossing older men to the ground during frequent tussles.[53]

Choynski's brawling reputation eventually seeped into City Hall, where his older brother, Maurice, worked alongside Corbett's older brother, Frank. One day the two men became quite animated about the fighting prowess of their younger siblings. The bragging soon became confrontational, and by lunchtime, the two city employees nearly came to blows.[54]

Frank Corbett finally challenged Maurice Choynski to bring his little brother by the stables the next night for a set-to with his brother. Maurice gladly accepted on his brother's behalf.

The next evening Frank nonchalantly broke the news to his younger brother while sitting at the supper table.

"Say, Jim, there's a boy named Choynski coming over here to box with you, and I want you to box better than ever before in your life," Frank said. "Go out to win, Jim."[55]

James thought the request strange on such short notice but didn't ask any questions. His fondness and respect for Frank ran deep.

No questions were asked.

"All right, Frank," James said between bites. "I'll show the best I've got."[56]

Soon after supper, the doorbell rang.

Frank went to welcome their guests. He escorted the Choynski brothers — Maurice and Joe — into their father's dimly lit stables. Harnesses dangled from the walls, and a musky odor filled the nostrils even with the stable doors flung wide open for fresh air. James, then seventeen, finally strode into stables and stood beside Frank as he gazed upon Joe Choynski for the first time.

Corbett beheld "a magnificent looking fellow with a blonde head and great strength."[57]

On physical appearance alone, Choynski stood far and above any of the burly pugs Corbett had encountered on the streets or in the dingy Barbary Coast saloons. James soaked in every detail as he sized up his foe for the evening —"a wonderful looking youngster, blond haired, pink-cheeked, extremely intelligent, clean cut, and beautifully built."[58]

"He appeared to me then as a young Hercules," Corbett later recalled, "and he certainly was the finest looking kid that I'd ever had for a ring foe."[59]

James subtly leaned into Frank, whispering, "Who is this kid?"[60]

"Well, he's a champion — so his brothers say," Frank replied. "Joe is the best boxer in his neighborhood, and his brothers think he is a lot better than you, Jim. Now I want you to prove tonight that he isn't."[61]

Buggies were pushed from the middle of the stables to form a rough square from which the two youngsters could box. Frank and Maurice

This is the most famous photograph of Joe Choynski, who built a muscular physique wielding a sledgehammer at a blacksmith shop and carrying 300-pound barrels of sugar up a flight of stairs at a candy factory. *Author's Collection*

climbed into the buggy seats — a sort of grandstand—while the horses remain to mill in surrounding stalls.

The only light emanated from gas jets on a wall somewhat removed from the makeshift ring.

Within minutes, James and Joe peeled off their coats and stripped off their shirts. Both youngsters nodded and clenched their fists. Someone signaled the commencement of action by banging on a dishpan.[62]

What transpired next has forever been a matter of question.

No one disputed the beginning. Both boxers stood toe-to-toe. Fists pumped rapidly and from every direction. No quarter was asked or given. But in his 1925 autobiography, Corbett remembered, "We had only been fighting for a minute or two when I knocked him cold."[63]

In yet another account, written by Corbett eight years earlier in 1917 for a newspaper article, he recalled how one of the brothers hit the dishpan to signal the end of the first three minutes. "I don't know because I didn't hear it," Corbett confessed. "If Joe heard it, he ignored it."[64]

The two lads instead pounded away at each other for several more minutes. Corbett finally landed a right flush on Choynski's jaw. A stunned Choynski backed away, but Corbett ensued with wild rights and lefts. Alas, Corbett wrote, "my efforts were successful because the constant battering stopped Joe — and I was the winner of the bout."[65]

Choynski held a far different recollection of their initial scrap — an occurrence that would become a common theme decades later as the two legendary boxers looked back on their early days. In Choynski's account, there was no knockout.

Choynski instead remembered how Corbett's fists flew as fast and furious as the kicking hooves of Patrick Corbett's agitated horses in the first round of that first fight. The two combatants danced about a dirt floor strewn with straw in the strained light of a nearby gas lantern that dangled from a hook.

They moved like shadows.

"Corbett's speed dazzled me," Choynski recalled with a humble frankness. "He moved like a flash of lightning. The first round was fast as thought. Before the initial session was over, I realized I would have to pick up many pointers if I hoped to hold my own with Corbett. He danced around that stable like an apparition.

"He gave me a boxing lesson for two rounds. I was busier than a bird-dog. When I wasn't ducking Corbett, I was trying to dodge the flying heels of the excited horses. There was no referee and no decision. But I gave Corbett credit for out-boxing me."[66]

Corbett and Choynski ended the short session by politely shaking hands, although the tension failed to cease. Frank chose to stoke the fires of pride.

"Hey," he yelled as the Choynski brothers departed the stables, "do you think my brother is champ now?"[67]

"No," Maurice shot back. "Your kid's good alright, but Joe can beat him. And he'll do it some day — you just watch and see if he don't."[68]

Frank sneered and replied, "You'll find Jim Corbett ready any time Joe wants to meet him again."[69]

A competitive strain lingered thickly in the still dusty air.

"I knew there was going to be bad blood between us," Joe Choynski later recalled. "Trouble was brewing."[70]

Chapter Three
'Chrysanthemum' Joe

— —

San Francisco, California: 1884

Joseph Bartlett Choynski always stood out in a crowd. Even as a teenager, people were drawn to his brilliant mop of blonde hair and muscular upper body. Choynski's torso, shoulders, and arms, and back rippled with muscles from wielding a sledgehammer at the waterfront blacksmith shop where he worked in dripping sweat. He also developed great strength at his second place of employment — a candy factory where he hoisted 300-pound barrels of sugar on his shoulders and carried them up narrow flights of stairs.[71]

Yet people seemed most drawn to Choynski's shock of golden locks, which gave him a curiously wild appearance and spawned the nickname "Chrysanthemum" Joe.[72]

The nickname stuck for life, as did his charismatic allure.

To those who knew and loved him, he grew to be a "gentle man" with "compassionate blue eyes" and an intellectual mind that honored the literary environment of his youth. Both his parents were avid readers, and his father — Isador Nathan Choynski — was a renowned San Francisco newspaper publisher, columnist, and antiquarian bookstore owner. But beyond the serenity of Joe's engaging eyes and inquisitive mind grew a fiercely competitive soul with an insatiable appetite for fistic combat.[73]

Choynski recognized his destiny early.

"Some men are born to preach," Choynski once said. "Others are born to teach. Still others are born to dream. But I was born to fight."[74]

And San Francisco provided just the type of setting to foster his pugilistic urges.

Choynski remembered how he and other youngsters in the neighborhood "were always fighting."

"First, we battled for the championship of our block," he said. "Next we fought to see which kid would be the king-pin of his school. Ultimately, of course, we had gang fights.

"There was jealousy and keen competition. You fought well, or you didn't. And, if you didn't — well, that was just too bad."[75]

The young men of his generation were inspired by a living legend, World Heavyweight Champion, John. L. Sullivan. Of the great John L., Choynski once fondly remembered:

> *Sullivan was the idol of every boy in our city. I doubt that there was one section in San Francisco where boys congregated that didn't boast of at least one fistic aspirant. In the Mission Section, hairy-chested hard-boiled mugs each tried to emulate the Great Boston Strong Boy. Some succeeded in fighting their way to the front, but many failed.*
>
> *Sailors aplenty were among the scrappers. These tattooed, burly-shouldered fellows, full of fight, kept the local bullies busy and many scraps, often impromptu affairs, were replete with action.*
>
> *Finish fights were the rule . . . Two- or three-ounce gloves were used when the knuckles were upholstered at all and skin-tight gloves or bare knuckles were frequent. There was no padding on ring floors. When your bean hit the boards you felt it—if you remained awake.*[76]

Choynski learned from experience, usually giving better than he received in what generally amounted to crude street brawls. His aggressive nature shadowed him wherever he went. Fiercely rebellious, he refused to attend school, and by 1884, was working as a blacksmith — a job his mother deemed unworthy of "having a future." His rebel ways may have betrayed his affluent upbringing, but certainly not the independent spirit of his immigrant parents.[77]

* * *

The Choynski family embodied the American dream.

Isidor Nathan Choynski, who went by I.N., experienced the hardships and hopes of an immigrant. Evidence suggests he was born in Choyno, an estate west of Strasburg (Polish Brodnica) in West Poland around 1834. He was one of five children born to Rabbi Mordechai Nathan and Rosalie Choynski, and his childhood was likely filled with stories of Jewish lore, traditions, and religion.[78]

The Choynski roots were humble.

I.N. described his ancestors as starving rabbis with the noted exception of "my grandsire, who was *Rittergutsbesitzer* of Choyno — the original family name." Translated, that means lord of the manor of Choyno.[79]

As for I.N., Joe's rebellious behavior must have reminded him of someone he knew intimately. The elder Choynski once recalled how by age nine he had

I.N. Choynski, an immigrant from Poland, never missed a chance to brag on his son's fistic exploits writing for the *American Israelite*. *Courtesy of Christopher J. LaFrance*

already been punched in the back and scolded by a rabbi who told young Isidor, "*A Nillah werd warden aus dir*" — "You'll never amount to anything."[80]

A stubborn Choynski would prove the rabbi wrong.

By his own account, I.N. arrived in America in 1851 at age seventeen, landing in New Haven, Connecticut, where he found refuge with relatives in the Asher family. In his eulogy of Harriet (Lewis) Asher in 1890, Choynski would recall the love that nurtured his dreams.

> *I came to New Haven a poor friendless boy, trying to grasp the American idea as did Franklin the lightning, and was given a home and mother's encouragement by the late Mrs. Lewis Asher, and I owe much to her forbearance and cordial treatment while trying to raise myself in the scale of youths, as a fresh boy in a free country.*[82]

Choynski brought with him mementos of his childhood, and a strong sense of where he came from and who he would always be.

"I came to this country a mere lad," he once recalled. "I brought with me my knapsack, containing *Tephilin* (phylacteries worn during morning prayer), and extra *Arba Kanfolth* (a four-cornered garment with ritual fringes worn by men under their shirt), a *Chobath Halobath* (Ibn Pakuda's classic text), the likenesses of my parents, my *diarium meinen Kinderfreund* ("my childhood friendship book") and other mementos [sic] of my youthful and schoolboy days — which I treasure to this day very highly – but I brought with me, in my heart of hearts, Judaism, pure and undefiled . . . I have helped build up this State. I have contributed largely in clearing the forests wild and made portions of them blossom like a rose."[83]

Those contributions occurred only after a long, arduous journey in a foreign land.

Choynski's travels reportedly carried him to the Hudson

River Valley township of Monroe, New York, where after receiving a teacher's certificate from Yale University, he worked as a schoolmaster. He also labored for a time as an itinerant basket peddler in Poughkeepsie, New York, with his cousin, Israel Morris Goldreich, before making his way westward. Edwin Choynski, I.N.'s youngest son, said his father first journeyed for California in 1852, but the trip didn't go as planned. Edwin stated:[84]

> For the purpose of coming to California, he went to Philadelphia. There he took a ship to the Ishmus. In the Pacific, the Captain missed the port of San Francisco and passengers were landed in Oregon. There he lived for two years and in 1854 came to San Jose, California.[85]

By September 1859, I.N. had received his naturalization papers as a United States citizen and was residing in the burgeoning city of San Francisco. He quickly became entrenched in San Francisco's social and political circles, first as a reporter for Rabbi Julius Eckman's *Weekly Gleaner*, where one can find the first hints if his firebrand approach to journalism. In one column, Choynski publicly chastised his publisher and editor for shortening one of his articles on the grounds that "critiques of sermons" are not the proper subject for newspapers. Choynski lashed out at Eckman, contending that all pulpit sermons and stump speeches were "public property" and therefore subject to criticism and analysis. As a journalist he claimed the "right" to offer his own opinions on such public talks as an "enlightened Jewish community" could draw its own conclusions.[86]

So began the journalistic career of I.N. Choynski, whose acid pen would challenge pious rabbis, miserly millionaires, and corrupt public officials for the next forty years of his life.

Choynski wasted no time in also plunging into the political arena of his adopted country. By 1860, he was stumping on behalf of Republican candidate Abraham Lincoln during the hotly contested presidential race against Democrat nominee Stephen Douglas. Lincoln's supporters recruited I.N. to appeal directly to German-born voters — many of whom were Jewish — and he delivered with a number of eloquent speeches. Following Lincoln's victory that year, the newly elected president rewarded Choynski with the position as Customs Collector for the Port of San Francisco.

Lincoln's appointment would be one of many accomplishments to come for the ambitious immigrant.

Nothing, however, would prove more meaningful in his life than the day he met a teenage Kentucky girl of Jewish-English parentage named Harriet Ashim. Harriet's family migrated to San Francisco from Louisville in 1850 when she was eight, and her family's financial means allowed her the time and opportunity to be educated. In 1861, Harriet became a member of the first graduating class of the General High School of San Francisco. Her studies would later be credited for her destined meeting with I.N. Choynski — her future husband.[88]

Family oral tradition states the rabbi arranged the meeting after calling on the Ashim family one afternoon at their home. The rabbi — most assuredly Rabbi Eckman — found young Harriet lying on the floor on her home studying.[89]

"Harriet, what are

Harriet Ashim Choynski never approved of her son's desire to become a professional prizefighter. *Courtesy of Christopher J. LaForce*

you doing there?" the rabbi asked.

"I am writing a report for school on President (James) Polk," Harriet replied.

"Harriet, I will introduce you to a young man who can tell you more about President Polk than you can find in all those books you're reading," boasted the rabbi, referring to I.N. Choynski.

A whirlwind courtship ensued, and Harriet and I.N. were married by Rabbi Eckman March 20, 1862, after starting a romance that would last until I.N.'s death from throat cancer in 1899.[90]

Their relationship was almost immediately tested when I.N. parted for Nevada's gold and silver mines in November of 1862, leaving in his wake a pregnant wife. I.N., accompanied by his father-in-law Morris B. Ashim, journeyed to the mining boomtown of Aurora on the Nevada-California border in search of a "rich claim." Mainly what the two men discovered was the dirty, lonely life of a prospector in the chilly, windswept mountains some 7,400 feet above sea level.

Choynski made the most of his adventure, though. He wasted no time in staking a claim, dubbing it the "Hattie" — one of his pet names for Harriet. In a letter dated Dec. 14, 1862, he informed his wife, "Tomorrow I shall go into the stock business, and perchance, [sic] put my Hattie onto the market." I.N. told Harriet two months later, "I go daily to examine the quartz lode in the Hattie, it is a fine claim, and I love to examine the stratas in the shaft, because it bears your name."[91]

I.N. busied himself by also filing articles for newspapers under various pseudonyms regarding life in the mining district. When he wasn't writing as a paid correspondent, he was penning tender letters home to "My dear beloved little wife" and fawning over news of his firstborn.

Harriet gave birth to the couple's first child, Herbert, January 8, 1863, and I.N. beamed with pride some 256 miles away.

One month after Herbert was born, I.N. proudly wrote his wife, "He looks like me — so I have already heard . . ."[93]

Choynski's joy was tempered by his wife's prolonged illness. "Try and be well, Ducky," I.N. wrote Harriet in a February 8, 1863, letter. "You have no idea how miserable it makes me to hear of your sufferings." He closed the letter by writing, "Love, yours, till time shall be no more. Isidor."[94]

Days toppled into months in the drone of the mining camp as I.N. longed for the comforts of home and the embrace of his newlywed wife. By May, the rugged life was starting to wear on him when he wrote:

> *Ducky, I too have been sick, and only left my bed this afternoon; the chills stomach and headache have plaged [sic] the very deuce with me for the last three days, but I am now on a par with most men in this camp. It is rather unhealthy here this season on account of the drought and very many are suffering. Dad is doing very well but the sudden change from the high life in the city, to thanks to a wise Province and my strong frame I shall be all right again in day or two.[95]*

One week later I.N. again poured out his lonely heart to Harriet, writing, "I am at last settled again, for a time at least, the fever has left me and I am once more contended as I can well be without you. Would I not wish to have you near me!"[96]

The hopes of striking a "rich claim" had all but vanished a month later for the weary journalist-turned-prospector.

"I tell you the market looks very dull, and my assessments amount to far more than most of my stock would bring were I to throw it now to the market," I.N. wrote his wife in a June 1 letter. "But I hope it will all come right again for your sake, and for the sake of our boy!"[97]

Sometime after June, I.N. returned to San Francisco to reunite with his wife and newborn son. He returned broke, but not defeated.

I.N. thrived off a renewed zest for life and the promises that tomorrow might bring. With Harriet by his side, he believed they could conquer anything the world might toss their way. He immediately began clawing his way back, first by selling newspapers off the streets to earn a few bucks. By December he had scratched enough money together to open the Antiquarian Book Store at 146 Second Street — a business that would become Choynski's primary livelihood and a San Francisco landmark.

The Antiquarian Book Store reportedly attracted a number of the city's self-educated intellectuals — including political Irish exiles — who would gather there and debate the pressing issues of the day. In time, Choynski's bookstore would take on a folkloric status, attracting famous visitors like Bret Harte, Joaquin Miller, Bob Ingersoll, and Mark Twain. Author Henry George reportedly even wrote his classic *Progress and Poverty* (1879) in the back room.[98]

And Joe Choynski was privy to all of those colorful characters and scenes throughout his childhood.

"These men often visited our home," Joe recalled, "and I listened

In San Francisco, I.N. Choynski operated a popular antiquarian bookstore frequented by the likes of Mark Twain, Bret Harte, Joaquin Miller, Bob Ingersoll, and Henry George. *Courtesy of Christopher J. LaForce*

in on many of their conversations with my dad, embedding much of their philosophy." His mother, he would note with a touch of pride, "entertained them royally."[99]

No one commanded a more charismatic presence in San Francisco at the time than I.N. himself. One young customer from those days — Robert Ernest Cowan — remembered I.N. as "a large man," and a "picturesque character" who strode the city streets in a distinctive "huge stovepipe hat."[100]

I.N.'s fancy choice in headwear certainly matched his bold writing and wickedly biting editorials, which undoubtedly fostered his reputation as a "guff and uncompromising" man. But Cowan witnessed a gentler side of the elder Choynski in the winter of 1879 when he entered his bookstore in search of John Frost's *Indian Wars of the United States* — a book he fondly recalled reading at his grandmother's house in Canada.

With money burning a hole in his pocket, the young Cowan walked into I.N.'s popular bookstore before Christmas. "I am told that you have Frost's *Indian Wars of the United States* in stock, Mr. Choynski," Cowan said.[101]

"I have it, but it is upstairs among the second-hand books, and I haven't time, this Christmas trade is keeping me too busy, to go upstairs and hunt it out," Choynski replied. "Come back after the first of January."[102]

"What will the price be, Mr. Choynski?" Cowan asked.[103]

Choynski replied, "Three dollars."[104]

So Cowan waited until after New Year's Day to return.

"Yes, I remember you," Choynski said. "Come upstairs."[105]

Amid volumes of shelved and unshelved books, Choynski soon located Cowan's desired history text and handed it to the youngster. Cowan gladly paid Choynski three dollars in return, only to have the eccentric book dealer give him back a dollar.

"You remember, you said the price was three dollars, Mr. Choynski?" Cowan said.[106]

"Yes, I said three dollars, but you came back!" Choynski animatedly replied. "No one in this town ever comes back. The book will cost you two dollars."[107]

Choynski had made a friend for life. Such displays of kindness and generosity weren't uncommon for I.N., especially among those who earned his respect and trust. At home I.N. and Harriet worked hard to create a trusting and respectful environment for their children with a healthy balance of love and discipline.

In addition, they gave each child the freedom of individuality. The Choynski household therefore fostered culture, education, and love.

As a result they were a family of freethinkers.

No one possessed a stronger will to pursue his or her own passions than Harriet, who often indulged in literature and the arts. Harriet's interests, however, did have limits. For one thing, she hated to cook.[108]

Servants of her parents therefore delivered meals to the house each day. One day, shortly after her marriage, I.N. became distraught by the arrangement.

"Harriet, I did not marry to have my mother-in-law provide the meals in my home," he said in frustration before leaving the house. "I expect my wife to do it."[109]

"Very well," she replied, wanting to be the obedient wife society expected. Harriet lit a fire in the wood stove, and put a pot roast on the burner to cook. She then returned to her copy of Charles Dickens' classic, *Bleak House* — an enthralling novel that illustrated the evils of long, drawn-out suits in the English Courts of Chancery.[110]

Harriet became engrossed in the novel.

Time passed away, as did the stove's budding fire. I.N. eventually arrived home to find an uncooked dinner and a wife buried in a book.

Family oral tradition stated Harriet never again cooked another meal, and I.N. apparently never tried to force her to do any differently. After all, being a literary man himself, how could he not be smitten by such passion and independence?[111]

* * *

Joe flourished in this environment.

He too developed into an independent, freethinker who despite dropping out of school and working as a blacksmith, earned a reputation for being "soft-spoken and scholarly." Those who knew Joe intimately described him as "highly intelligent and well-read in the classics, and often in his correspondence referred to some quotation to make a point."[112]

Music provided another form of entertainment for the brawny youngster in those early days. One of his old friends humorously recalled "hearing battling Joe . . . play a waterlogged piano."[113]

Joe pursued any endeavor that intrigued him, and he did so thoughtfully and unabashedly. Ironically, Joe's independent and sometimes rebellious ways led him to the one thing his mother probably hated more than cooking — pugilism.[114]

Harriet Choynski despised fighting. Joe didn't.

In his fists, Joe realized he possessed a gift. He thrived off the adrenaline rush of a good bare-knuckle fight, and his pugilistic conquests on the streets gave him a sense of place and respect in his neighborhood. Friends admired his fistic abilities, while others learned to step aside.

At least one observer credited Joe's "prowess as a pugilist" to "Jew-baiting." The observer claimed:

> *He had been teased and snubbed by his non-Jewish schoolmates until his pride resented it with good, hard fistic impressions upon his tormentors' physiognomies . . . While, however, we may refer to these facts with undisguised satisfaction, we do not mean to propose pugilism as the most desirable means of subduing demonstration of homeopathy. But we do mean to imply that a little more se-*

rious consideration of . . . "Muscular Judaism," may often
be a most effective antidote.[115]

Joe certainly wasn't the only youngster to encounter racism in San Francisco, but was one of the few who could silence it through his talents. His father battled racism with his mouth and pen. Joe did so with his fists.

Yet the truth is Joe simply loved fighting — anti-Semitism or not.

Fighting gave him a sense of purpose, dignity, and pride. He loved the adventure of battle, craved competition, and chased the thrill of victory with an unbound enthusiasm. Older lads — even men — fell in the path of Joe's heavy punches, although even he realized his skills were unrefined.

Now, suddenly, Joe encountered something that intrigued him — a local rival whose speed and skill would either force him to improve as a fighter or leave him knocked out cold. A few minutes in a livery stable taught him that much.

Another fight with James Corbett was destined to happen. The only questions that remained were when and where.

Frankly, Joe didn't care. He just wanted to fight.

Chapter Four
Blood Feud

— —

Sand Hills North Of San Francisco: Circa 1884

Frank Corbett and Maurice Choynski couldn't keep their mouths shut. Such restraint wasn't in either one of them, especially when it came to family pride and honor. Corbett continued to brag on his boxing brother, James, and Choynski continued to brag on his brawling brother, Joe.

James Corbett or Joe Choynski? Who was the superior fighter? A few minutes of scrapping in a livery stable did nothing to settle the dispute. Nor did it do anything to quell the childish rants of two stubborn, older siblings. The spark of disagreement was about to be fanned into the flames of a full-fledged feud.

"Oh, well, it's no trick to win a bout with gloves," Maurice taunted Frank the week following their brothers' encounter in the stables. "But in a bare knuckle contest — a man's fight — Joe could give your brother Jim an artistic beating."[116]

Frank fumed, and then verbally punched back at his adversarial co-worker.

"Joe can have his chance — any time he wants it!" Frank retorted.[117]

Right then and there, without the principals present, a second match was arranged — a bare-knuckle "fight to the finish" scheduled for the next Sunday morning.[118] James Corbett and Joe Choynski would fight until one could no longer continue.

Word of the Corbett-Choynski scrap soon spread throughout the neighborhoods. By Sunday morning local lads were buzzing about the fight, eagerly inquiring about its location. A number of prospective onlookers even milled around Patrick Corbett's livery stable in hopes of learning of the fight's whereabouts firsthand.

"This must be the place," one youngster said outside the stable. "The fellow who runs it is the father of Jim Corbett who's going to fight Joe Choynski today."[119]

Patrick Corbett overheard the young man's comment from the shadow of the stable entrance. He immediately marched upstairs to his son's bedroom, catching him just as he was about to slip away.

Patrick's eyes locked on his son's.

"Is it true, Jim, that you are going to fight the Choynski boy today?" Patrick asked in his thick Irish accent.[120]

"Yes," James replied.[121]

Silence stifled the air momentarily before James took a jab at persuasion, adding, "Dad, I haven't a grudge against him, but he's been threatening me and you wouldn't have me back out, would you?"[122]

"Jim, I don't want you to fight him," Patrick pleaded. "They'll hear about it at the bank, and you'll lose your job. I wouldn't have you lose your job for anything in the world, Jim."[123]

James' position as bank teller served as a great source of pride to the Corbett family, especially for his parents. They even envisioned their son someday rising to the lofty status of bank president. How could the son of Irish immigrants throw away such an opportunity on a scandalous street fight?

Patrick stood firm in his conviction.

"But, father," James protested. "If I don't fight the fellows will think I'm yellow. And anyway, this will all be kept quiet and the bank people won't hear about it."[124]

"But they might, Jim, they might, and I wouldn't have you lose that job for the world," Patrick replied. "Jim, I want you to go over to that Choynski boy's home right away and tell him you can't fight him."[125]

James knew further debate would be futile.

"All right, Dad, if you feel that way about it I won't fight," said James, conceding defeat. "I'll go up to Choynski's home like a man and tell him I can't."[126]

"Fine, my boy," said Patrick, clearly pleased. "You know where they live?"[127]

"Up on Golden Gate Avenue," answered James, unable to disguise his frustration. The young Corbett harnessed his pride at that moment, and resigned himself to his father's wishes. Soon, he departed for Choynski's house with his brother, Frank; friend, Jack Gallagher; and several neighborhood chaps who perhaps tagged along in hopes there would be a change in plans.

* * *

Corbett stopped walking when he arrived at 1209 Golden Gate Avenue.[127]

By then, he had thoroughly rehearsed what he would say to Choynski, likely even uttering the words aloud to his brother and friends on the way for practice. The prideful Irishman still needed to convince himself he was doing the right thing — that his actions were those of a responsible young man. Finally, he determined he would be honest and humble, and hoped for the best.

He then rang the Choynski doorbell.

Maurice Choynski answered the door.

"Where's Joe?" Corbett asked.[129]

"Inside," Maurice replied sternly. "Why?"[130]

"I want to tell him I won't fight him," replied Corbett, insisting that he talk directly to Joe. Maurice cared nothing of Corbett's demand.[131]

"Hum," Maurice chirped. "I thought so. Afraid, eh?"[132]

"No, it isn't that," said Corbett, quickly losing his composure. "My father doesn't want me to fight him. He thinks the bank people might hear about it and fire me."[133]

Maurice taunted Corbett further, saying, "You wait until this afternoon, you'll see him then, all right. He'll knock you all over the lot."

Corbett had heard enough. Anger now consumed his thoughts.

"I'm not afraid of Joe and just to prove it I'll fight him right here and now!" Corbett shouted. "Bring him out!"

Maurice happily obliged. Seconds later Joe Choynski stepped into the doorway, pushing his way past his brother until he stood face to face with Corbett. But no fists would be thrown. There would be no fight on Golden Gate Avenue.

No one wanted the fight stopped.

Corbett and Choynski agreed instead to take their fight to the sand hills outside the city limits – a place fittingly known as the Dog Pound.

* * *

The group walked for three miles before coming to a small, secluded valley. Corbett scanned the horizon, and saw only a man sitting with a baby atop one of the surrounding hills.[135]

"This is all right for me," Corbett said.

Choynski calmly replied, "Suits me."

The two youngsters stripped off their shirts, and began to loosen up by punching the air. Gallagher agreed to keep time. Choynski offered no objection as Maurice and his pal, Frank Nichols, patted him on the back.

Corbett's gang — some "eight or ten" in total — gave their neighborhood favorite words of encouragement.[136]

Gallagher then called time.

Instantly, Choynski and Corbett rushed at one another like colliding bulls, furiously firing punches from all angles. Each fighter wanted an early knockout, or at the very least, blood.

Without boxing gloves, the punches stung much harder as tightly clenched fists crashed into flesh. Neither fighter gave an inch.

Corbett's speed and slick footwork again began to dazzle Choynski, who ate one lightening jab after another. The punches arrived in a blur.

"I stopped plenty," Choynski mused years later. "Bang! This is a left to my chin. Bam! That is a left to my nose! Smack! Another left to my eye! Corbett kept repeating the dose."[137]

Yet Choynski absorbed the punishment like an anvil, desperately cutting loose punches amid the onslaught. Suddenly, Choynski swung a "mighty heave" at Corbett's temple. The punch landed.

Corbett toppled to the ground.

The knockdown thrilled Choynski, who secretly stood in disbelief as a stunned Corbett shook his head and slowly climbed to his feet. A number of fighters — men even — had been toppled by Choynski's fists, but none as skilled or naturally gifted as Corbett.[138]

Choynski savored the moment.

Then, as quickly as Corbett hit the ground, Choynski was jolted back to reality by the shout of his friend.

"Run, Joe!" Nichols yelled. "You and Maurice — you've got no chance here now!"

Choynski knew instantly Nichols was referring to Corbett's Hayes Valley "gang." Outnumbered and sensing a melee, the Choynski brothers and Nichols began to retreat.

A furious Corbett ran after them. He jumped on Maurice.

"You're responsible for this!" yelled Corbett, who instantaneously hammered Maurice with a punch to the nose. Maurice fell back to the ground.[139]

Harsh words were exchanged before a truce. Tense moments ensued, matched only by the adrenaline of the young men as they crowded around like angry dogs. How a melee was diverted, no one ever said. But one thing was now clear: The two sides grudgingly went their separate ways, knowing this would not be the last time Choynski and Corbett would exchange punches with bad intentions.

Not by a long shot. For this feud was no longer about boxing, but rather blood.

* * *

Corbett returned to his house with a rather different version of the fight — one he intended to keep secret from his father for fear of being punished. He therefore entered the house, slipped past his folks, and retreated quietly to his room "to clean up the marks of the battle."[140]

The secret didn't last long.

Corbett's friends, still intoxicated by the thrilling fistic encounter, rushed into the stables and told Patrick Corbett how his son "whipped Choynski." The elder Corbett did not receive the news well. He immediately walked upstairs to his son's room.

"Jim, is it true that you had a fight with Choynski, after what you promised me?" Corbett's father said sadly.

James looked his father in the eyes.

"Yes, Dad, but I couldn't help it," he replied. "If you had only heard the names they called me you'd have fought, too. If I had backed out I would have been a coward. I licked him and his brother, too."[141]

Catherine Corbett, James' mother, then appeared in the doorway. Wringing her hands, she said, "Oh, Pat, the boy is disgraced now — he surely will lose his good job in the bank."[142]

"And so you fought him after I told you not to, eh?" Patrick Corbett said.

"Yes, sir — to prove I wasn't yellow," James answered. "I went over to the Choynski house and told Joe's brother that I wasn't going to fight Joe because you thought it might be found out and that I'd lose my job in the bank. And the Choynski boy said I was a coward."

"And is it true, Jim, that you whipped Joe Choynski?" Patrick continued.

"Yes."

"And those Choynskis called the son of Pat Corbett a coward, did they?"

"Yes."

"And you're sure you beat him good, Jim?"

"Yes, sir. I gave him a good licking."

Patrick Corbett scratched his head while looking at his worried wife. The hardened Irishman then turned toward his son, and slapped him on the back enthusiastically.[143]

"You licked the two of them — the two Choynski boys," Patrick bellowed. "Aah! To hell with the bank!"[144]

Chapter Five
Rising Star
— —

Olympic Club, San Francisco, California: 1885

Professor Walter Watson knew a prized boxing protégé when he saw one, and he had long determined he beheld one of special stature in James J. Corbett. The teenage phenom seemingly possessed all the right ingredients of a future champion with his size, speed, strength, athleticism, toughness, smarts, determination, and willingness to learn.

Corbett possessed one other key attribute — ego.

Watson realized a healthy dose of ego meant a healthy dose of confidence, just as long as his protégé's confidence didn't stray into the realm of overconfidence. The balancing act proved to be a delicate one for Corbett, who was already hailed as a local legend on the streets.

Colorful stories emerged whenever Corbett's name tumbled from the lips of sporting hacks. Men who had witnessed his savagery in the saloons of the Barbary Coast recalled his bouts with the same luster some might recall a great Civil War battle or countryside duel. Observers never forgot the time the teenage Corbett — then weighing all of 145 pounds — trashed a 215-pound blacksmith at a firehouse on Market Street. Another favorite story takes place in a Barbary Coast saloon when Corbett supposedly stripped to the waist, climbed atop the bar, and faced the bar's giant mirror in order to demonstrate his fancy footwork. A boxing fan, jarred by Corbett's showy behavior and his own fill of bourbon, quipped, "Five hundred says

Corbett's shadow will take him."

That night "shadow boxing" was born. Or so the legend is told.[145]

Beyond the hype stood a true boxing phenom, though. Corbett's mindset made him even more special. He became restless about honing his skills, and concluded soon after arriving at the Olympic Club that he had much to learn in the ring. Corbett owed his dose of humility to the club's heavyweight champion, who welcomed the newcomer by knocking him on his ass. All of which made Watson's job infinitely more enjoyable. Watson simply drilled Corbett on the fundamentals, only to watch his gifted prospect blossom and improvise with slippery moves on the balls of his feet or head-feints rarely seen at any level.

Watson, whether he realized it, was staring at the future of boxing.

By the time the calendar turned to 1885, Watson's meticulous instruction and Corbett's dogged training began to show rapid signs of progress. Still, Watson kept his young protégé under wraps to those who might still view Corbett as nothing more than a noted street fighter. They trained three nights a week at the club in the relative obscurity of outsiders.

Finally, Watson decided to unveil his prized pupil in an exhibition at his first Olympic Club "Fight Night." Watson matched Corbett with none other than the club's reigning middleweight champion Dave Eiseman, a slugger whom members generally thought possessed too much power and experience for the novice Irishman.

Little did Corbett realize the "exhibition" meant something much more to members, who whispered in corners of an ongoing grudge between Eiseman and Watson. Eiseman supposedly treated Watson "roughly" at their first meeting, and the two men were not on speaking terms. A number of members secretly came to believe that Watson had been grooming Corbett for his own personal revenge on Eiseman, although many doubted whether the untested fighter could succeed in an organized setting with gentlemen present.[146]

So there was a buzz in the crowd when Corbett and Eiseman entered the ring. Corbett expected nothing more than a friendly exhibition, but learned otherwise when Watson advised, "Boy, from the call of 'Time' you go for that fellow with all you've got!"[147]

"What?" Corbett replied in bewilderment. "You want me to try to knock him out? I thought this was just an exhibition."[148]

"Never mind the exhibition part," replied Watson hurriedly. "He is going to try to knock you out, and you'd better get him first."[149]

Young and inexperienced, Corbett didn't dare debate the wisdom of his respected mentor. After all, his mind was too busy trying to grasp the moment. This marked a big night for Corbett whose previous bouts amounted to glorified street fights in saloons, blacksmith shops and his father's stables. Wealthy Olympic Club members and their guests packed the main gymnasium on this night at the club's newly constructed venue, which had re-opened with great fanfare May 5, 1885 — a date that marked the club's 25th anniversary. More than 1,500 special guests showed up for the grand opening that night as rooms were adorned with tropical plants, flowers and bunting. Guests were then treated to a promenade concert and ball.[150]

A similar excitement greeted the boxers and their handlers. Corbett peeked into the crowd. Spectators appeared everywhere, overflowing from the temporary bleachers placed around the ring and standing all along the balcony that encircled the main floor. Corbett's nerves told him he wasn't in his father's stables anymore. So he tried to quell his fears by focusing on the task at hand — Eiseman.

Soon, Corbett stood in the opposite corner of the ring, staring at Eiseman after a few polite introductions. Watson's urgent instructions raced through his mind. The timekeeper finally yelled, "Time!" Eiseman and Corbett both rushed from their corners, and began slugging it out in the spot where they met. For three minutes neither boxer gave an inch. The crowd cheered wildly.

Corbett noticed Eiseman already appeared to be breathing hard as he lowered himself into his stool between rounds. Watson leaned into his game protégé.

"No matter how tired you feel," Watson said as he rubbed Corbett's shoulders and arms, "remember the other fellow is worse off than you are and that pace is killing him."[151]

The timekeeper again yelled, "Time!" Again, Corbett and Eiseman collided like two charging bulls. The cheers descended from the rafters as the two fighters whaled away at each other with bad intentions. Suddenly, as if out of nowhere, a straight right hand crashed into Eiseman's chin, sending the club champion through the ropes and into a spectator's lap.

Pandemonium instantly reigned. At some point in the ruckus Corbett picked up the referee's count, " . . . seven . . . eight . . . nine . . . ten!" A stunned Corbett stood in a euphoric daze; thrilled, speechless and victorious. A tidal wave of men suddenly rushed into the ring, swept him off his feet and hoisted him onto their shoulders. Bankers, lawyers, business owners . . . some so enthusiastic that they even showed their appreciation by planting a kiss on Corbett's cheek.[152]

The James J. Corbett era at the Olympic Club had officially arrived.

* * *

Corbett's reputation continued to grow in the months that followed. To Corbett's credit, the more praise he received, the more diligently he trained. He worked out three days a week with Watson, but often appeared at the club on his off days to spar or to simply watch visiting professionals train.

San Francisco's athletic clubs served as a magnet for some of

Jack Dempsey, "The Nonpareil" – the World Middleweight Champion – worked Choynski's corner during the barge fight, but lost Joe's confidence during the bout. *Author's Collection*

the world's top professionals in those days, and Corbett studied everyone he could. One of his favorites was fellow Irishman Jack Dempsey, "The Nonpareil" of New York. Dempsey stood 5-foot-8 and weighed only 144 pounds, but was muscular, agile and cleaver. Dempsey possessed blurring speed and a snapping left jab, and often frustrated his foes with his masterful head-feints. Corbett studied Dempsey's moves as if studying the fine details of a great painting. By the time Corbett first laid eyes on Dempsey, the New York transplant was also already an unbeaten, middleweight contender and a household name to any sporting hack.[153]

One afternoon Dempsey showed up at the club's boxing room downstairs, donning tights and looking for sparring. He approached heavyweight Mike Cleary, a noted slugger who occasionally mixed it up with the smaller and quicker Corbett for a workout. Dempsey asked Cleary if he wouldn't mind going a few rounds, but the heavy-hitter declined due to a sore mouth.

Cleary glanced back at Corbett and replied, "There's a young fellow over there, named Corbett. He'll box with you."[154]

"Hell," Dempsey snapped. "I want a sweat!"[155]

Corbett quietly dressed at the other end of the room, pretending not to hear the conversation.

"Oh," Cleary said with a grin, "he'll give you a sweat, all

right."[156]

Curious, Dempsey walked across the room and patted Corbett on the back, saying, "Young fellow, put on your gloves with me, will you?"[157]

Dempsey's request flattered Corbett. Fight fans always spoke of Dempsey in awe, and Corbett knew he was standing in the presence of greatness. He himself considered Dempsey a living legend and a wonder to behold in the ring — so much so he tried to mimic his signature head-feints.

Corbett watched on several occasions as Dempsey's sparring partners flinched or blinked or back peddled in the face of his jutting head-feints. That's how much opponents feared his speed. As usual, Corbett calculated his fight plan as he slipped into his gloves.

The club itself was fairly quiet. A few members worked out on the pulleys, while others were in adjoining rooms playing billiards or swapping stories. No one suspected they were about to be treated to something special, not even Corbett and especially not Dempsey.

At first the two boxers circled each other for several minutes without throwing a punch. Out of respect, Corbett didn't want to throw the first blow. So he circled and waited. Dempsey tried to lure Corbett into an opening with a few head-feints, but each time the youngster never flinched.

"Again and again he feinted, but each time I knew by distance between us that he couldn't touch me," Corbett later recalled. "He looked at me in surprise and I could read him enough to know that he was thinking, 'Is this boy really clever, or just plain dumb?'"[158]

Finally, Dempsey landed a smart, left hook flush on Corbett's face. Corbett, eager to give Dempsey "a sweat," countered moments later with a punch to the nose, sparking a lively exchange that lasted several minutes. The action escalated, and without a timekeeper, each fighter disregarded any notion of three-minute rounds. Even Cleary forgot to keep time as the punches flew fast and furious. The two boxers battered each other from one spot to the next, until word spread throughout the club that a serious scrap was underway.

Billiard cues clanked on the wooden floor. Cards were left scattered across gaming tables. And waiters abandoned their posts. Soon, spectators crowded around the two fighters. Neither man gave an inch in a "sparring session" that began at 6 p.m. and featured no breaks.

The clock now read 6:30 p.m.

Finally, in a clinch, Dempsey displayed one of the tricks he had picked up on the professional circuit. He bloodied Corbett's nose with a wicked elbow at close quarters. Angered and probably embarrassed, Corbett charged his idol only to have him hold up his glove.

"Boy," Dempsey said in a fatherly tone, "that's enough for today."[159]

Dempsey draped his arm around Corbett's shoulders, and defused the tension with some friendly banter. Spectators watched the two fighters disappear into the locker room in this fashion: The great Dempsey embracing the Olympic Club's young, rising star.

In the locker room, Dempsey inspected Corbett's bloody nose to ensure nothing was broken. He then escorted Corbett upstairs to the scales to check his weight. Dempsey watched with curiosity as the arrow stopped at 160 pounds.

"About 160 pounds," Dempsey mused. "And you're about six feet tall, eh?"[160]

"Yes, a trifle more," Corbett replied.[161]

Corbett asked how much Dempsey weighed. Dempsey instantly obliged, tipping the scales at 144 pounds. Both boxers were amazed — Corbett at how light Dempsey was; Dempsey at how heavy Corbett was. Dempsey felt Corbett's shoulders, and studied the youngster for a few seconds in quiet reflection.

"What did you say your name is?" Dempsey finally asked.[162]
"Jim Corbett."[163]

"If I were as big as you, I'd lick any man in the world!" said
Dempsey as he walked away. Glancing over his shoulder, he
added, "Boy, I'll see you again."[164]

The next night Corbett attended a minstrel show. As he
handed his ticket to the ticket-taker, Corbett began to walk
through the entrance when the attendant grabbed his shoulder.

"Are you Jim Corbett of the Olympic Club?" he asked excitedly.[165]

Corbett nodded. The ticket-taker yelled over his shoulder,
"Hey, Bill, this is the kid who boxed Dempsey yesterday!"

* * *

A few months later Corbett and Dempsey met again, this
time "in a friendly set-to" at another Olympic Club "Fight
Night" and at the urging of Watson. Dempsey kindly agreed
to the exhibition despite having already danced a few rounds
with Cleary. In the end, a gracious Dempsey cast a few kind
words toward the eighteen-year-old amateur, telling reporters
Corbett "had a lot of talent."[167]

The event gave Corbett his first taste of media exposure.
Sports writers were soon dropping Corbett's name in columns
about the local fight scene, extolling the virtues of this up-and-
coming, "scientific" boxer. Corbett earned his reputation. His
accomplishments — and the ensuing praise — mounted with
each new show. By November, he held both the Olympic Club's
middleweight and heavyweight titles. His resume also included a Golden Gloves title and seven Silver Cup Championships,
making him a household name on the Pacific Coast.

Corbett's rise occurred simultaneously with the rise of boxing in the city. San Francisco was already one of the only places
in the country where popular "fights to the finish" were legal.
Amateur boxing shows also attracted large crowds regularly

at the Olympic Club, as well as three other competing men's organizations — the California Athletic Club; the Golden Gate Athletic Club; and the Acme Athletic Club across the bay in Oakland.

Only the Olympic Club promoted solely amateurs, while the other three clubs offered purses, thus blurring the line between the status of amateurs and professionals. In time, these rival clubs aggressively pursued amateur and professional fighters alike by dangling money and by offering fans the unspoken allure of side betting. This business approach angered Olympic Club members who feared losing their own boxers such as Corbett to these financial temptations. Yet the power of the athletic clubs were so strong that the city council passed a law that required a $100 licensing fee for every boxing match held in the city, accept for those held in the "rooms" of an athletic club. Boxing matches outside athletic clubs therefore almost entirely vanished in the city.[168]

To Corbett's credit, he remained loyal to his club. Time after time he brushed off talk of professional matches, claiming he was completely content to work under Watson's expert tutelage as an amateur boxer. Still, sports writers often attached his name to prospective fights with various professionals.

The gossip didn't appear to get to Corbett. Success did.

Corbett coveted the limelight both in and out of the ring. Over time he began to feel invincible, which is often the downfall of promising, young athletes. Corbett's kryptonite proved to be alcohol. His desire to be viewed as "manly" or "a good fellow" prompted him to drink more frequently. Shots of whiskey became commonplace, especially at the urging of his "friends."

"I grew foolish enough to think it was smart to dissipate a little," Corbett wrote years later. At the time, his partying started to take a toll on his stellar conditioning — the foundation from which his natural abilities flourished.[169]

Sometimes Corbett's gang carried their party across the bay

to Billy Delaney's National Saloon on Eighth Street in Oakland. Delaney, who dabbled as a boxing trainer, and his partner, J.J. McCarthy, ran a rowdy establishment similar to those found along the waterfront in the Barbary Coast.[170]

Delaney himself presented an odd, yet interesting portrait of a saloon owner. He was in good standing with Oakland's elite class, yet was equally acquainted with the underworld characters who stirred in the shadows of the waterfront. Corbett remembered the first time he saw Delaney, noting his "womanish features," his keen "intelligence" and "cold, poker face."[171]

One night Corbett caught Delaney studying him coolly as he pounded down the whiskey. Finally, Delaney pulled Corbett aside.

Billy Delan

Billy Delaney owned and operated the National Saloon in Oakland when he first met Corbett. Delaney would later serve as Corbett's second in his famous barge fight. *Author's Collection*

"Jim," Delaney said, "it's against my interests to tell you so, for I can't make any money by this kind of advice; but I am interested in you and would like to see you make something out of yourself. I've watched you in bouts and you're a good boy. You can go a long ways, but lushing [sic] like this will ruin your constitution and never get you anywhere. Remember, you're not developed yet, you're only a kid."[172]

Corbett laughed. Inside, Delaney's words pissed him off. Then one afternoon Corbett found himself in a bout with a boxer he had always handled easily. Only this time Corbett labored to finish the fight. He concealed his weak condition the best he could, but now Delaney's uncomfortable words echoed in his head.[173]

Doubt crept into Corbett's mind. Were the late-night, drinking binges taking a toll on the toast of the Olympic Club? Deep down, Corbett knew the truth. He realized drinking and boxing didn't mix, but didn't know if he could stop. Suddenly, he was dodging the punches of temptation.

Corbett now stood alone at a crossroads. In every direction he foresaw the fight of his life.

Chapter Six
Prodigal Son

— —

Corbett stepped onto the Walker Opera House's parquet floor stage in Salt Lake City, Utah, already stripped to the waist and donning his fighting tights. He weighed a svelte 160 pounds and wielded a pair of five-and-a-half-ounce gloves, give or take some stuffing of hair. Across the stage Corbett stared at his opponent Duncan McDonald, an amiable, 178-pound professional who fancied himself as the "champion of Montana."[174]

The fact Corbett and McDonald stood on an opera house stage was ironic, if not entirely fitting given the pugilistic display they would provide. Two hundred paid spectators, many of them packing firearms, politely crowded the stage to witness the scheduled six-rounder, only to question at its conclusion whether what they had seen was truly real.

The bout may have been Corbett's darkest hour in the fight game.

Corbett, for his part, didn't use his real name. Referee J.G. McClellan announced Corbett as "Jim Dillon ... the champion of California." McClellan's declaration prompted one suspicious scribe to muse in the morning newspaper, "but exactly where he won that right to that title, is somewhat involved in mystery."[175]

"Dillon" certainly wasn't talking.

Corbett had apparently left any semblance of ethics or rational at a train station outside San Francisco weeks earlier. That's when he first decided to travel down a rebellious road. His journey began when he quit his bank job to elope with Marie Olive Lake, a local doll who was equally smitten with the dashing Corbett. Lake's biggest problem — or so Corbett's Catholic father thought — appeared to be her Protestant upbringing. So the two young lovers did what most young lovers do when told they can't be together — they ran away.

Lake and Corbett were married June 28, 1886, by a justice of the peace at the Utah House hotel in Salt Lake City. Utah law required couples to be at least twenty-one-years of age to marry. The nineteen-year-old Corbett solved the problem by changing his name to "Jim Dillon" and age to twenty-one on the marriage certificate. Within two weeks, Corbett and his newlywed were in dire need of rent money for their cottage.

Corbett therefore turned to the one skill he knew best — boxing.

He did so in desperation, which is probably why his conduct before, during and after the McDonald fight smacked of impropriety. One bad decision seemed to lead to another. In the end, paying customers left the Walker Opera House questioning whether they had been hustled. Corbett and McDonald were lucky they weren't shot, but a headline in the morning newspaper explained why they were probably spared: "The General Opinion is that it was a Hippodrome, but that it was a Good One."[176]

Eleven days earlier Corbett made his professional debut as "Jim Dillon" against Frank Smith in Salt Lake City. A referee declared Corbett the winner after four rounds when he disqualified Smith for excessive holding and wrestling.[177]

Were the rumors of Corbett hustling fighters and patrons in the saloons of San Francisco true? Maybe.[178]

In Utah, the circumstantial evidence didn't look good. Corbett's anonymity proved to be his best asset in Salt Lake City affairs beyond his dapper appearance and obvious boxing skills.

His use of the alias "Jim Dillon" is easy to understand. He desperately needed the money that a professional fight would bring, and by boxing under another name, he preserved his amateur status. Whether Smith or McDonald had any prearranged agreement with Corbett before their fights will probably never be known.

Either way Corbett and McDonald gave quite a show despite the hot night air that choked the opera house. After the colorful introductions, both boxers spent most of the first round cautiously circling one another. Corbett showed off for the crowd, prompting one reporter to note, "Dillon made a number of feints, and jumped around the arena nimbly and as spry as a cat." The round ended unceremoniously with a frustrated shout from the galleries: "Rats!"[179]

McDonald threw the first meaningful blows of the fight in the third round, spurring the crowd to cheer enthusiastically as the two exchanged punches in close quarters. By the fourth round, the sweltering heat began to take its toll. Sweat flowed freely from both fighters. Corbett slowed considerably, undoubtedly due to his drinking and lack of training.

Watson would have been appalled by his fighter's poor condition, unless of course Corbett was hamming it up for the audience. If so, Corbett made the most of his act. He cracked McDonald with a strong left early in the round. The punch again ignited the crowd, which now began to chant, "Dillon! Dillon!" Seconds later, both fighters exchanged some "stunners," and according to one spectator, the "cheers began to grow deafening." The round ended with the referee struggling to pull the two fighters apart as they pummeled each other about the head.[180]

Raucous cheers again filled the opera house in the fifth round. McDonald and Corbett exchanged another flurry of blows. At one point McDonald knocked Corbett down, partly from a punch but mostly from the slippery condition of the parquet floor. Both fighters hit the deck simultaneously later in the round, adding a wild flair of the scrap and luster to the cheers crowd.

The sixth and final round merely left the crowd wanting more. Corbett and McDonald peppered each other with punches for three minutes straight despite appearing weak and exhausted. Corbett struggled to raise his hands, while McDonald flailed away with seemingly every bit of energy he could muster. Yet the two fighters didn't stop throwing haymakers until the final call for "Time!" By then the spectators had worked themselves into frenzy.

"Give us another round!" one man cried. Another paying customer had a better idea when he hollered, "Go on to the finish!"[181]

Referee McClellan satisfied no one when he stepped to the front of the stage and declared, "I can't decide this match in favor of either of the parties and so will declare it a draw."[182]

Afterward, a reporter asked Corbett and McDonald pointedly whether the fight had been an act.

"Both Dillon and McDonald pooh-poohed the idea of the entertainment being a hippodrome, and each praised the other's qualities as sparrers," the reporter wrote later that night. "Ten minutes after the contest closed both men looked as fresh and neat as though they had been spectators instead of participants. Dillon at the end of the sixth round made some show of wanting to fight to the finish, but he forced off the stage in a very histrionic fashion by his second . . ."[183]

* * *

Decades later Corbett made light of his Utah adventures in his autobiography *The Roar of the Crowd*, although many of his details are factually inaccurate. Of Smith, Corbett recalled his opponent thinking he was the celebrated heavyweight contender Charley Mitchell. Corbett claimed he used this belief to his advantage, promising a frightened Smith he wouldn't harm him as long as he flopped in the second round. By Corbett's amusing account, Smith did as agreed.[184]

Corbett never wrote of his fight with McDonald, but rather another chap they christened "Danny Costigan." In Corbett's twisted version of events, McDonald helped promote him as none other than the great Jack Dempsey in Evanston, Wyoming, and the gun-toting fans at ringside were none the wiser even after the fight. Corbett never mentions who won the bout, only that he and McDonald "took the midnight train for Salt Lake."[185]

Corbett likely embellished his stories to put a finer polish on his image and legacy, which he guarded carefully throughout the years. He may have also been ashamed by his shenanigans in Utah, and yet he was often self-effacing in his remembrances about his own missteps. Perhaps the truth lies somewhere in the middle. If anything, Corbett can be credited as a survivor who never took a step back.

"Perhaps someone will question the ethics of all this, and doubtless it wasn't all according to Hoyle," Corbett later wrote. "But I have never laid down in a fight in my life or fixed one. These tricks were the worst I ever pulled. It was rather harmless showmanship, and the spectators got their money's worth."[186]

* * *

Shortly after the McDonald fight Corbett received a special guest at the hotel where he was living. A bellboy notified him that he had a visitor downstairs, "name's Corbett."[187]

"Corbett?" Jim said. "Well, show him up, he must be a relative."[188]

Moments later the door to Corbett's room swung open and there stood his father. Patrick Corbett threw his arms around his son and said, "Jim, don't you think you'd better come home?"[189]

Over the next few days Corbett and his father visited, probably exploring each other's feelings more than ever before. What they talked about is unknown, but the conversation was almost certainly about Jim's future. The elder Corbett pleaded for his son to return to San Francisco.

Finally, the son relented.

"Dad," Jim said, "I give you my word I'll be home in a little while, but I don't want to go with you now. I would look too much like a bad boy being yanked home by the collar."[190]

Eventually, Corbett fulfilled his promise. He returned to San Francisco with his new bride, although there was hardly a welcoming party to hail his arrival outside of the Corbett household. News of the McDonald fight had already been published in the *San Francisco Chronicle* in a blistering report that read:

> *Corbett, late "gentleman" heavy weight of the Olympic Club, has dropped to the lower plane of the professional "pug." He fought a draw with Duncan McDonald at Salt Lake last week under the name Jim Dillon. He at least is entitled to the credit of not having played the drop game . . . He stood up.*[191]

The Olympic Club's board of directors viewed Corbett's Utah adventures as scandalous. There was even talk of terminating his membership for a time, but the moralists failed to win the argument. In the end, Corbett was still just a young man who had never been in any prior trouble as a club member. In fact, he had served the club faithfully both in competition and character prior to his flight to Utah.

Still, the board demanded punishment, if for no other reason than to save face. Directors barred Corbett from competition for three months while they supposedly monitored his behavior. Then, in November, Corbett was allowed to spar with P.T. Goodlove during the club's annual Paper Carnival. The two boxers reportedly gave an entertaining show.

The board rewarded Corbett by giving him a few pupils to train. He embraced the challenge with great joy and humility.

Two months later Watson arranged for Corbett to tangle with slugger Tom Johnson in a three-rounder at the Acme Athletic Club in Oakland. Although no decision was declared, the *San Francisco Chronicle* reported: "Corbett's science asserted itself throughout the bout, and the Acme folks were enthusiastic in their appreciation of the fistic display."[192]

A day later the newspaper gushed about Corbett's growing maturity:

> *Jim has a few colts under his care and they are coming on wonderfully. With unmistaken capability, he combines good temper and patience, and does not indulge in any of the rough work so disheartening to those receiving initiatory lessons in the noble art.*[193]

But the city's sports writing scribes proved a fickle bunch where Corbett was concerned. While lauding his amateur endeavors, they wanted more. Much more. Soon, reporters prodded Corbett into matches by associating his name with a number of local fighters. By March of 1887, Corbett made it clear where he stood when he fired back with his own voice in a letter to the editor:

> *In the columns of a morning newspaper on Monday last, my name appeared as was used in connection with certain heavyweight boxers of the coast, Tom Johnson, Joe McAuliffe, Con Riordan and Mike Brennan. I wish it to be understood that I have made no arrangements to box any of the above named gentlemen, and I do not thank the sporting editor referred to for his unwarranted use of my name. I do not wish to box anyone, either amateur or professional, for monetary consideration, and no inducement can make me alter my intention.*[194]

Whether Corbett meant what he had written, or was merely reciting what he thought the Olympic Club brass wanted to hear, his position was now out there for public consumption. His words were clear, firm, and on the surface, seemingly thoughtful. They were also grossly premature.

Corbett made one mighty miscalculation. A familiar name was about to emerge from the streets; a charismatic brawler who would force Corbett to rethink his renewed ethical stance on professional prizefighting.

The brawlers name was Joe Choynski.

Chapter Seven
Coins

— —

Olympic Club, San Francisco, California: 1887

Joe Choynski might have never ventured into organized boxing had it not been for James Corbett.

No one will ever know for sure, but Choynski's departure from street fighting coincided with a special invitation extended by Corbett on March 23, 1887. At the time Corbett was scheduled to box a five-round exhibition at the Olympic Club with Joe McAuliffe, the celebrated "Mission Giant." Only McAuliffe backed out at a late hour.

Corbett, who never divulged his motivation, then reached out to his old rival. He even delivered his invitation in person, stopping by the candy shop while Choynski was at work. Corbett asked if he wouldn't mind standing in as a replacement for McAuliffe, or as Choynski later mused, "before the gents — in tights and everything."[195]

Choynski couldn't help but laugh. He had never fought in a real boxing ring before, let alone slipped into a pair of tights. Corbett tried to ease Choynksi's mind, assuring him that he would be provided a proper pair of boxing tights for the show. And Corbett did as he promised.

"But he got 'em so tight I was afraid to bend," Choynski recalled decades later in amusement. "They were three sizes too small . . ."[196]

Always on the lookout for an edge, Corbett made little concessions on this night. Professor Walter Watson and Billy Delaney were both standing in Corbett's corner when Choynski entered the ring for their introductions.

Choynski stood alone.

Naturally, bets were discreetly made at ringside on the outcome of the five-round exhibition, although it's doubtful there were many takers on the unknown Jewish lad with the bulging biceps. Choynski probably looked as out of place as he felt.

Corbett did little in the first two rounds to allow anyone to think Choynski stood a chance. Blurring jabs and left hooks peppered Choynski's face repeatedly with speed the candy-puller called, "indecent."

"I didn't know then," Choynski later said, "but I realized later that I was in there against the fastest thing in heavyweights that the ring has ever developed."[198]

Then, by the third round, Choynski began to realize Corbett couldn't knock him out.

"I forgot the swell club, ignored the clustered gentlemen and the influence of Corbett, and pegged away at him for all it was worth," Choynski recalled.[199]

Choynski brought the street fight to the Olympic Club, and for the first time, the finely dressed spectators began to take notice of the Jewish lad with the bulging biceps. They marveled at his grit, but mostly his power.[200]

Onlookers were pleasantly surprised by Choynski's raw display of strength as he hammered away at the elusive Corbett for the third, fourth and fifth rounds. The session became quite lively, and although the polished Corbett clearly outpointed Choynski and even knocked him down during one exchange, the gents were thoroughly entertained by the gameness of the match-up.

Frankly, they wanted more.

For Choynski's part, he gave Corbett credit for outpointing him even though no referee was present since it was an exhibition. Yet Choynski felt great satisfaction in his overall performance, especially considering the ring was a foreign place to him and he was used to fighting almost entirely with bare knuckles.

"I was strong, but untrained," Choynski said. "I guess I showed him (Corbett)."[201]

The exhibition ended with one other bit of drama, although its storyline wouldn't come into focus until months later. After the bout, Choynski sat in the dressing room, trying to catch his wind from the lively show. A man poked his head through the door, and tossed a pair of five-dollar gold pieces onto the floor at his feet.

Choynski didn't know the man, but wasn't about to turn down a bit of monetary appreciation.

Moments later, Corbett walked in and asked, "Did Brown give you some money?"

Corbett was referring to Billy Brown, who organized the fight cards at the Olympic Club.[202]

Choynski held out the palm of his hand with the two gold coins. Corbett snatched one of the coins, declaring, "Half of it is for me."

Nothing more was said. Choynski found the episode odd, but decided to let it go. Only later would Brown's generosity make sense.

* * *

By March of 1887, Choynski and Corbett were treating one another with respect on the streets, although their mutual civility belied the bad blood that brewed continuously behind the kind smile or gentlemanly handshake. They were both too proud to forgive and forget. In truth, they probably felt threatened by one another's existence, realizing one day they would clash in a bloody battle for everything they cherished — pride, reputation, and respect.

Secretly, both had planted seeds of doubt for the other to contemplate deep within his soul.

Choynski's knockdown blow in the sand hills a few years

earlier gnawed at Corbett's psyche, whether he admitted it or not. He took pride in slipping punches with his "panther-like" speed. Yet now he couldn't even dodge the memory of Choynski's raw power, or perhaps what really happened that day in front of his pals. His street fight with Choynski bothered him so much he began to tell a different version of the episode.

Choynski, in turn, struggled to comprehend Corbett's lightning speed. In all his street fights he had never seen anything like Corbett's combination of hand speed and dazzling footwork. Even in his mind they were a blur. Choynski prided himself as a street tough who could whack out any wisecracking Irishman with hands that tugged on taffy and wielded a blacksmith's hammer. But Corbett presented the ultimate challenge. Choynski knew how to fight. Corbett knew how to box. If Choynski were to compete with his neighborhood rival in the ring, he'd have to learn the science of boxing.

Ironically, Corbett unknowingly gave Choynski his first lesson.

"Corbett was, of course, in perfect condition," Choynski recalled. "He had been training every day — often spending hours on the development of one punch — while I knew nothing of gyms, and spent my time wielding a sledge-hammer and 300-pound sugar barrels. So I was pretty badly winded when we finished the five-round bout at the Olympic . . . For the first time, I began to see the real possibilities of scientific boxing."[204]

Boxing soon consumed Choynski's soul.

Timothy Michael McGrath — Choynski's chum at the candy shop — didn't help matters. McGrath fully supported Choynski's budding love affair with the pugilistic arts, and even liked to slip on the gloves himself for extracurricular activity.

In the coming months, the boxing ring at the Golden Gate Athletic Club beckoned the two youngsters next door from the candy shop.

"When things were quiet and the boss wasn't around we

jumped through the factory window into the club," McGrath confessed decades later. "That's how both of us became tied up with boxing."[205]

From the start, McGrath recognized his friend possessed something special: "Choynski could hit like a mule."[206]

McGrath saw Choynski's power firsthand many times. Back then, Choynski roamed the streets hatless "like a musician" with his wild mop of blonde hair bobbing freakishly in the wind.

The hair made him a magnet for ridicule.

"Well, he got a lot of fighting practice with the Irish lads," McGrath remembered. "Joe didn't exactly look for trouble, but he'd take a walk bareheaded, and get action most every time."[207]

Only now Choynski preferred his "action" in the gym. He became consumed with the science of boxing. He studied the footwork of seasoned boxers and the art of feinting and countering, while doing his homework on the anatomy of the body so he would know where his opponent was most vulnerable.[208]

As time went on he would learn other tricks of the trade, sometimes from the most unlikely sources. Once a friend who lived in Chinatown advised Choynski on how he might toughen his hands. The friend told him to stick his hands in a pickling vat, and Choynski did, often for hours at a time.[209]

The quiet, studious boy who grew up listening to thinkers like Mark Twain and Bret Harte in his father's antiquarian bookstore was now applying that same inquisitive nature in the gym. Every day he took mental notes, applying his brawn in a scientific manner.

Choynski, like Corbett, was instinctively evolving into pugilism's new breed of fighter. A street tough to be sure — and damn proud of it — Choynski was no longer satisfied with being an unthinking brawler. Instead of blindly firing off punches, he was now throwing punches with purpose . . . and bad intentions.

Four months after meeting Corbett at the Olympic Club Choynski climbed back into the ring for his first amateur bout, representing the Golden Gate Athletic Club. The fight was billed as a "contest to a finish" by the North Beach Athletic Club, although the sportswriter who covered the show for San Francisco's *Daily Alta California* mocked its legitimacy and Choynski's opponent — a stiff recorded only as "Moran."[210]

Some sixty spectators crowded into a dingy room on the corner of Green and Stockton streets to watch the affair.

"Upon what pretense the room is called an athletic club it is hard to tell, as only five or six rough pine benches and a patched up ring composed of the apparatus," the reporter wrote.[211]

The show went downhill from there. Choynski knocked Moran down with his first punch.

Organizers gave Moran twenty-two seconds to respond to the call of time, and then another six minutes to rest before the next round. Still, Moran wanted nothing to do with Choynski, prompting the reporter to declare, "Never has a more ridiculous exhibition been given in this city."[212]

Choynski's first victory thus passed with little fanfare.

Even so, his name started to appear in the local boxing columns. Only five days after knocking out Moran, directors at the Golden Gate Athletic Club were rumored to be offering a "large purse" for Choynski to fight Tom Berry.[213]

The fight never materialized, but plenty of other opportunities quickly emerged. In August, the Golden Gate Athletic Club formally announced a tournament for its diamond medal heavyweight title. Two Irish boxers — Joe Connelly and William "Forty" Keneally — and Choynski entered the tournament.

Connelly and Choynski were pitted in the first match-up, scheduled for September 7. Keneally, being trained by none other than Corbett and Watson, would then face the winner for the title.[214]

By then, the sporting community was already clamoring for a Choynski-Keneally bout. The two sparred in July, prompting Choynski's friends to supposedly brag about how Joe "played" with Keneally in the ring. Keneally's friends were offended by the comments, but the *San Francisco Chronicle* reported that "Corbett's pupil says nothing."

Corbett may have actually been the source of the discontentment, if not a prodding factor in the debate.

Privately, Keneally seethed over the disrespect.

Corbett, meanwhile, remained busy. He trained fighters two nights a week at the Golden Gate Athletic Club, and diligently went about his own training at the Olympic Club under the watchful eye of Watson.

A few weeks prior to the Golden Gate Athletic Club's tournament announcement, the Olympic Club made its own headlines by announcing that Chicago professional Jack Burke would engage in an eight-round exhibition with its prized amateur, Corbett, August 27 under Marquis of Queensberry Rules. The *San Francisco Chronicle* reported that the bout would be open to the general public, predicting "it is safe to assume that those who will be lucky enough to be present at the set-to will witness a magnificent exhibition of science."[215]

The newspaper also reported what most boxing enthusiast had believed all along: "There is no doubt that Corbett has been longing for years to stand before a professional of some repute in the pugilistic world, so as to gauge his own ability, and in Burke he will find an opponent who is a thoroughly adept in the manly art and who has gained a name on the fistic roll of fame less by brute strength than by cleaver and effective sparring."[216]

The publicity likely disappointed Corbett's father, who probably lectured his son once again about how prizefighting would ruin his reputation as a gentleman. By then, it's unlikely Corbett cared. His bank days ended after his adventures in

Utah, and he already knew boxing would be his life.

As for the elder Corbett, he still took solace in his son's amateur status. One of Corbett's close friends once heard the colorful old man say, "It's this way with me boy Jim. You can lead him, but begad he won't be driven. He's like myself in that. The Corbetts are all a bit pig-headed about havin' their own way, an' I ain't knocking either when I say it. Once he made up his mind to pass up the bank, there was no use in arguin' with him. An' I don't mind his lickin' all these chaps so long as he ain't making a living at it. A man can be a gentleman and a boxer, but I misdoubt if any chap was ever a prizefighter an' a gentleman. Thank God, me boy isn't a professional!"[217]

Patrick Corbett would eventually be forced to re-evaluate his opinion. Until that time, his son pursued his craft in typical Corbett fashion.

Onlookers at the Olympic Club saw Corbett doggedly preparing for his upcoming exhibition with Burke. His diligent work ethic and commitment was hard to miss, but Corbett always had a lot riding on the line whenever he stepped into the ring. There was his budding reputation to consider, as well as that of the prestigious Olympic Club and its prominent members. One newspaper report summed up the stakes when it declared, "Jim Corbett is in strict training for his eight-round bout with Jack Burke, and will do his level best to uphold the honor of the Olympic Club."[218]

The Corbett-Burke exhibition was expected to attract the largest crowd ever to the Olympic Club.[219]

Corbett was growing to understand pressure.

* * *

More than 500 spectators had crammed into the Olympic Club showroom to watch Corbett battle Burke. By the time the two boxers appeared in the ring that number had swelled to more than 800 people — a club record.[220]

Burke ducked through the ropes wearing flesh-colored tights with a green sash. Patsy Carroll, his trainer, stood in his corner.

Moments later, Corbett appeared to raucous cheers.

One sportswriter immediately noted how Corbett looked "a trifle pale, and had the appearance of being slightly over-trained," while Burke appeared "chubby, ruddy and unconcerned."[221]

None of which did anything to quell the excitement at ringside.

Billy Brown served as master of ceremonies, promising the crowd that despite the absence of a referee, he would ensure that both pugilists strictly adhered to the Marquess of Queensberry Rules in place. With that, the call for time commenced the action.

Burke quickly displayed his experience, adeptly blocking many of Corbett's punches. By the fourth round, Burke appeared to take control of the fight, continuously landing lefts to Corbett's chest.

The young Corbett certainly enjoyed his moments. He showed a growing confidence after the early rounds, and repeatedly carried the fight to his professional opponent. Throughout the bout Corbett also landed numerous punches, although most found their mark lightly or were simply glancing blows.

Burke proved to be "by far the more scientific boxer," according to one fight reporter who simultaneously lauded Corbett's progress.

"Taken as a whole the exhibition was, perhaps, the best, from a scientific point of view, that has taken place in San Francisco for years," the reporter wrote. "That Corbett is a cleaver boxer no one for a moment can doubt, and his display last evening both surprised Burke and drew him expressions of admiration . . . It is the general impression that if another exhibition were arranged Corbett would show a better advantage."

Fans once again wanted more.

* * *

The sharp-tongued I.N. Choynski never minced words, especially when it came to his boys. In 1884, while working as a San Francisco correspondent for the national leading Jewish newspaper — Cincinnati's *American Israelite* — Choynski gushed that his sons were "four great, big stalwarts, who are *Turn Verein* fellows, and who are, I think, able to knock Sullivan out . . . in a single round."[223]

Joe Choynski was sixteen at the time.

So it's without surprise that I.N.'s pride bubbled over when Joe dispatched Joe Connelly in three rounds during their Golden Gate Athletic Club's opening heavyweight tournament bout. I.N. celebrated the victory with lavish prose in the September 23, 1887 issue of the *American Israelite*:

> *We are coming, father Abraham! The boys of the Jewish persuasion are getting heavy on their muscles. Many of them are training to knock out J.L., and it may come to pass. It is almost an every-day occurrence to read in our papers that a disciple of Mendez . . . has knocked out the best sluggers, who point with pride to their ancestors, Yankee Sullivan, Mace and others. This week a youngster, who calls himself J.B. Choynski, nineteen years old, native of this city, weighing 160 pounds, fought for the championship and gold medal with one named [Joe] Connelly, and the lad with the Polish name knocked the well-knitted Irish lad of much experience out in three rounds, and carried off the medal and the applause triumphantly . . . I knew that boy's grandfather quite well — he is dead several years; but if the pious, learned grandfather could lift his head from the grave and gaze upon the arena where mostly the scum of society congregate, and behold his grandson slugging and sparring and dodging . . . he would hang his head and exclaim . . . what is this horrible show for?*[224]

Despite I.N.'s gushing, his son had yet to secure the club championship. One fighter still stood in his way — Corbett's pupil and pal, William "Forty" Keneally.

Choynski and Keneally were slated to tussle two months later in November to settle who would be crowned the club's heavyweight kingpin. The match-up intrigued the boxing faithful because both boxers were known for delivering heavy blows, despite the fact this would be Keneally's first official amateur bout.[225]

In addition, few were unaware of the heated bantering between the two camps behind the scenes. The feud — perhaps fanned by Corbett's distaste for Choynski — had become a public affair. Thus, the show of a lively brawl and wild crowd seemed promising.

Keneally and Corbett weren't always on friendly terms. In fact, like Choynski, the first time Corbett encountered Keneally was when they sparred at his father's dusty stables.

"I could hold my own with any of the bunch except a fellow named Keneally, and I wasn't quite sure about him," Corbett confessed in his biography. "He was several pounds heavier than I, had a dangerous right wallop, and I only sparred him once in the stable. That time I just stayed on the defensive and I fancy he thought I was afraid of him. At all events, he hinted as much to a mutual friend, and I let it go at that, not wanting to provoke any serious trouble."[226]

Corbett settled the score a short time later when the two were paired in a boxing show staged by an organization known as the Sullivan Cadets. At the time, Corbett hesitated at the scheduled four-round exhibition for fear of what his father might think, but was soon convinced otherwise when Keneally cracked that Corbett didn't like the idea of having "his pretty face spoiled."[227]

Corbett quickly donned the gloves.

For three rounds Keneally stormed after Corbett, intent on knocking him out with wild haymakers. Corbett determined he wouldn't exchange punches with his larger foe. He instead parried Keneally's punches and countered neatly with stinging jabs.

By the fourth round, Keneally became desperate and started launching punches from his hips. One wild right went whistling over Corbett as he ducked, and as Corbett rose, he caught Keneally square on the jaw with the back of his head.

Keneally dropped to canvas, nearly knocked unconscious by the accidental blow. But those at ringside thought Corbett delivered a stunning left, and declared him the winner.

Naturally, Corbett didn't volunteer the truth.[228]

As for Keneally, he became one of Corbett's biggest supporters, perhaps out of respect and admiration for the chap who knocked him out.

Boxing delivered a number of ironies in those days, none more humorous than the shenanigans that preceded the November 29 championship bout between Choynski and Keneally. Choynski arrived that night to face disgruntled club officials.

Billy Brown, the Olympic Club's boxing organizer, apparently thought so highly of Choynski he devised a plan to eliminate him from the amateur ranks. Brown filed a complaint with officials, claiming Choynski accepted money for fighting at the Olympic Club.

An official confronted Choynski about the allegation, asking, "Mr. Choynski, didn't a man named Brown give you money for boxing Corbett at the Olympic?"[229]

Quick to the punch, Choynski delivered a knockout blow without hesitation, answering, "A man I didn't know threw two five-dollar gold pieces into the shower-room, but Jim Corbett came in and took one of them."[230]

Brown withdrew his complaint.

In the ring later that evening, Choynski proved just as durable and powerful. He and Keneally waged a war from the opening call of time. Both met in the center of the ring and banged away at each other amid a hail of cheers.

Corbett cheered from Keneally's corner.

"It was a dog-fight; the rough-and-tumble," Choynski recalled. "Kenneally [sic] almost scoured the chrysanthemum from my dome before I got going good."[231]

The 180-pound Keneally, weighing twenty pounds heavier, pounded Choynski to the canvas for a knockdown. Choynski beat the count, and by his own admission, was "reeling like a merry-go-round."

Still, he weathered the barrage. Then he continued the brawl.

Keneally and Choynski hammered at each other throughout the second and third rounds much to the delight of those in attendance. Then, in the fourth and final round, Choynski connected with a chilling left "reminiscent of the blacksmith shop" that dropped the Irishman for good.

"Whereupon, Corbett's big sparring partner dropped out for the night," Choynski remembered with delight. "They didn't have to count over him. What they needed was smelling salts."[232]

One sportswriter declared the bout produced "four rounds of the fiercest fighting ever seen in the city."[233]

In the weeks and months that followed, Keneally doggedly pursued Choynski for a rematch. More than a year later, Keneally still fumed over his defeat, stating he would fight Choynski for either a medal or a purse.

Choynski never publicly responded, prompting the *Daily Alta California* to level a shot against the local champion.

"So evenly were the men matched that it was either man's fight at any time during the four rounds," the article stated in regard to the Choynski-Keneally match. "Since that time Keneally has made several attempts to arrange a match with the Golden Gate champion, who has always offered some sort of excuse, until it now looks as though he was afraid of Keneally."[254]

As usual, San Francisco's fight-crazed community wanted more.

Chapter Eight
'The Professor'

— —

Olympic Club, San Francisco, California: February 12, 1888

For those who might have doubted the popularity of "Pompadour" Jim Corbett, all doubt would vanish by the spring of 1888.

The year opened with the usual influx of newly initiated Olympic Club board members, who quickly sparked a controversy that would alter the future of boxing in San Francisco. Ironically, the debate itself centered on whether the club would continue to sponsor boxing exhibitions or eliminate the sport all together from its programming.

Professor Watson didn't like the rumors.

Watson, fearing he would lose his job, then made a surprise move in early February by resigning as the Olympic Club's boxing instructor. He also announced he would still maintain ties with Oakland's Acme Athletic Club, and would invest in a saloon.[235]

Olympic Club members were stunned by Watson's resignation.

Boxing, in truth, provided a booming business and great entertainment for San Franciscans. For the Olympic Club, boxing brought prestige. Board members soon came to their senses, and began the ever-important search for Watson's replacement. They didn't look far.

In an even greater surprise, Olympic Club officials named Corbett their new boxing instructor February 12. The position paid a monthly salary of $150, and officials believed Corbett's celebrity would translate into an infusion of new youngsters in all their amateur programs. Soon, some questioned the wisdom of handing such an important post over to a twenty-one-year-old pugilist.

The *San Francisco Chronicle* bluntly weighed in on the subject, stating, "Corbett is undoubtedly a clever young gentleman, but it is doubtful if he will prove the success as a teacher that Watson has."[236]

One can only speculate on how that article alone made Corbett feel. But whatever sting he might have felt initially quickly became a faded memory. By March, Corbett's boxing classes were brimming with young bucks who wanted to become the next "Pompadour" Jim.

The *San Francisco Chronicle* now back-peddled on its previous statement by lauding the new "Professor." The *Chronicle* gushed in an obvious attempt at a public apology:

> *Under the able instruction of Professor Jim Corbett, the popular boxing teacher at the Olympic Club, the boxing class has increased largely during the last few weeks. On each class night there is an average of 20 names on the boxing book, while 35 or 40 are frequently subscribed on several nights throughout the week.*[237]

Corbett was a star. A month later there was even talk of the Olympic Club hiring him an assistant to handle his mushrooming stable of pupils.

The boxing business continued to flourish in San Francisco. As usual, the local press produced copy that would both sell newspapers and entice some boxers into the ring against certain opponents. In most cases, these urgings were shameless attempts to stir controversy.

The promotion of the May 20 Joseph McAuliffe-Frank Glover fight to the finish proved a prime example of this tactic. The

California Athletic Club would sponsor the bout between the two well-known professionals with the winner receiving all gate receipts and the title of Pacific Coast Champion.[238]

The "finish fight" format was simple, and highly attractive to fight fans: Boxers fought until one either quit or was knocked out. As the McAuliffe-Glover bout approached, the *San Francisco Chronicle* couldn't help but meddle in Corbett's ring affairs. In a possible fabrication, the newspaper proclaimed:

> *A project is on foot among the members of the Olympic Club to put up a trophy to be contested for by Professor James Corbett, the club's boxing teacher, and the winner of the Glover-McAuliffe affair. Corbett says that he intends to challenge the victor to box ten rounds with small gloves. Corbett is a likely lad, who has increased wonderfully in science and who is quite heavy and clever enough to make it decidedly interesting for either Glover or McAuliffe.*[239]

The likelihood that either Corbett or the Olympic Club would be lobbying for a bout with the McAuliffe-Glover winner seemed suspicious at best, especially considering the club's holier-than-thou stance on professional prizefighting. This seemed clearly apparent less than four weeks later when McAuliffe delivered a vicious victory over Glover in forty-nine rounds. The fight lasted an unreal three hours and fifteen minutes, leaving Glover's face a bloody mess.

Newspapers, hypocritically, ripped the fight for its savagery in an attempt to encourage the "scientific" Corbett into a bout with McAuliffe, a fellow San Franciscan native. The Olympic Club responded as expected: "He (Corbett) is a clever boxer and a very gentlemanly fellow, and he has absolutely nothing to gain by becoming a professional pug. He need do nothing more than he does to maintain his name as a good teacher and good boxer."[240]

In June, Corbett met Glover in a friendly four-round exhibition. The bout did nothing but foster more talk of a Corbett-McAuliffe showdown.

By July, the press had moved on to another prospective foe for Corbett. This time Corbett's name was being freely tossed around with Peter Jackson, a brawny black boxer who held the title of Australia's heavyweight champion. One sportswriter claimed the two boxers were scheduled to spar in a benefit bout, but when Jackson learned that Corbett had spoken "disparagingly of him," he declined to appear in the exhibition.[241]

The writer threw out one more jab, reporting, "Jackson is willing, however, to meet Corbett in a set-to of four rounds, in which he guarantees to stop Corbett in that time."[242]

If Corbett declined the offer at that time, it likely had nothing to do with fear as history would later attest. At the time there was much to be gained by luring Corbett into the professional ranks, not the least of which was the business of selling newspapers. Yet Olympic Club officials appeared content to watch their popular "Professor" engage in controlled exhibitions under auspices of a club setting.

Corbett therefore spent 1888 sparring with the likes of Mike "The Port Costa Giant" Brennan, George Atkinson and Joe Bowers. None of those amateur bouts lasted longer than four rounds with Corbett getting the unofficial nod in each.

Even so, Corbett remained a popular figure at the club and about the city. Sportswriters penned his name regularly. Pupils aspired to follow in his footsteps. Olympic Club members lauded his gentlemanly persona and his scientific skills in the ring. In truth, his celebrity shined as bright as ever, with or without McAuliffe or Jackson or whomever.

Corbett seemed to stand alone in the spotlight.

Soon, that would change.

Chapter Nine
'Anyone In The House'

— —

Fight fans packed Stevenson Street on a breezy November evening, waiting to file into the Golden Gate Athletic Club. Hundreds of members and invited guests jostled for seating in the main showroom in eager anticipation of some fistic fury.

The main event of the night promised to be a fight to the finish between two heavyweights — the giant Bostonian, George Bush, and Ed Cuffe of Buffalo.

Anyone who was anybody in the San Francisco boxing scene was at ringside that night, including Joe Choynski. The up-and-coming amateur had just turned twenty six days earlier, and was prepared to enjoy a relaxing evening at a club where he was viewed as a budding celebrity.

Choynski had more than passing interest in the main event. In the weeks prior to that night, he had served as a sparring partner for Cuffe and was also the first San Francisco pugilist to lace up the gloves against Bush after his arrival to the city in August.

Bush, who moved from his native Boston to train in Los Angeles, arrived in San Francisco with the claim he had been traveling with the great John L. Sullivan's camp. San Franciscans were used to hearing boastful claims. Few took his claim seriously. The Board of Directors of the California Athletic Club wished to test Bush's credentials as a prizefighter, and asked Choynski if he would engage the professional in a three-round exhibition.

Choynski eagerly accepted.

On August 14, 1888, the five-foot-eleven Choynski stepped into the ring with Bush, who towered over him at six-foot-three. Fearlessly, Choynski carried the fight to his larger foe and paid the price. Bush landed a wild right hand that sent the local lad spinning to the floor.

An embarrassed Choynski rose and shook his head, adding, "That was a good one, for I saw stars."

Once the compliment had been issued, Choynski rushed Bush to resume the brawl until time was called.

Choynski opened the second round by crashing three consecutive rights to Bush's jaw. By the time the round had ended, Bush was nearly out on his feet.

The exhibition ended with a fairly even third round, prompting one sportswriter to conclude that "it was the general opinion that Bush was a good one and a hard hitter, but was out of condition."[244]

Bush passed the test.

Soon, Bush would lend his services to help fellow Bostonian George Godfrey prepare for an upcoming fight with Aussie Peter Jackson.[245]

By then, Choynski had been training under the tutelage of Australian Paddy Gorman and Eddie Graney, a featherweight scrapper who owned a blacksmith shop at Fourth and Howard streets. Graney staged many boxing matches behind his blacksmith shop over the years, most of which were of the rough-and-tumble variety. Like Choynski, Graney was only twenty in 1888 and although there are no known records, it's likely that Graney's blacksmith shop is where Choynski was employed for a time.[246]

The Bush-Cuffe fight card started with a dubious four-round scrap between a "pair of robust sea captains," and despite their lack of "poetry in motion," entertained the throng with a spirited fight nonetheless.[247]

Spectators were warming up for festive night of boxing.

By the time of the main event, the fans were highly charged and eager for the two big heavyweights to exchange mighty blows. Bush finally made his way to the ring with enthusiastic applause. Several minutes passed without a sign of Cuffe. The anticipation mounted. Then, without warning, the master of ceremonies stepped to the center of the ring to make an announcement.

Silence prevailed.

"I am sorry, but there has been a hitch in the arrangements," the man yelled. "Ed Cuffe has a poisoned hand, and the club physician will not allow him to go on with this fight."[248]

A chorus of hardy booing instantly filled the showroom. Bush paced the ring, angered the fight would be canceled. A cancellation meant no purse. The Bostonian shook his head in disgust.

Suddenly, Bush issued a challenge. He declared he would fight, "Anyone in the house."[249]

"A substitute!" one fan demanded. "Get a good man and give us a fight!"[250]

A few of Choynski's friends and associates nudged him to accept Bush's challenge. Flattered by their confidence, Choynski smiled politely and remained seated. Graney then turned to Choynski in bewilderment.

"But where'll they find a substitute?" Graney said. "There's nobody . . ."[251]

Choynski leapt to his feet, shouting, "Oh, yes, there is!"[252]

The booing suddenly turned to raucous cheers. Sportsmen slapped Choynski on the back and shook his shoulders in delight. They cheered him wildly as he marched toward the dressing room to slip into his black boxing tights. Choynski strode with purpose, determined to save the night from being a bust by making his professional debut.[253]

Yet the moment offered no time for Choynski to reflect on his spontaneous decision. His heart raced and adrenaline rushed, and he was thrilled. In a blur, Choynski found himself standing in his corner, staring across the ring at a fighter he described as "terribly big . . . hairy, and full of fight."[254]

Bush had reason to be in a foul mood.

Little did either fighter know at the time, the cancellation was a ruse to pit Choynski against Bush. Edwin Coe, Joe's younger brother, revealed the secret decades later. According to Coe, the gamblers who fronted the money for the purse watched Choynski batter Cuffe each day in sparring. Nervous they would lose money, they forced Cuffe to fake an injured hand in hopes Choynski could be coaxed into the ring in his place.[255]

Choynski swallowed the bait as planned.

Graney, likely in on the con, now shouted instructions and words of encouragement at his pal. Choynski, however, probably didn't hear a word. His mind suddenly drifted back to the wedding he had attended earlier that day. Choynski celebrated by gorging himself on cake, ice cream, and wine.[256]

A twinge of regret and fear crept into his thoughts.

"This fight has got to end quickly," Choynski told himself. "If that giant ever hits me in the lunch — goodbye wedding feast!"[257]

The opening bell then rang.

Bush, although taller by four inches and much heavier, appeared flat-chested and flabby as he moved toward Choynski, who according to one ringside reporter, displayed "muscles that stood out in bold relief."[258]

Choynski showed coolness from the start, his legs spread apart and his body leaning slightly backward. He delivered the first blow, tapping Bush lightly on the neck. Bush returned the favor with a right that struck Choynski's neck, but with an open hand.

Moments later Bush rushed Choynski with his hands down, and launched a wild right-hander in the general direction of Choynski's head. Choynski instinctively fired his own right. The punch crashed into Bush's nose with the sound of a popping balloon, sending the Boston behemoth reeling to the floor in a sitting position.

Bush wiped his nose with his glove and stared for a moment at his own droplets of blood. If Choynski's punch didn't dishearten him, the sight of his own blood did. His thirst for combat seemed to be vanishing with each tick of the clock.

Bush stood, only to find Choynski charging him. As Choynski hammered him against the ropes, Bush dropped again — this time, perhaps, to spare himself from further punishment. A blood-splattered Bush rose again, and survived the round by excessive clinching.

The action turned sloppy in the second as Choynski vied for the knockout and Bush hugged for preservation. At one point the two boxers tumbled to the floor in unison under the ropes. Both climbed to their feet, although Bush clearly looked like a beaten man.

Choynski ended the proceedings with two stinging lefts to the head and a thunderous right that again busted Bush in the face. This time Bush crashed to the floor on his hands and knees, settling below the lowest rope. There, he remained well after Choynski was declared the victor by knockout.[259]

Cheers erupted as Choynski's hand was held aloft.

Amid the celebration, Bush's handlers lifted their dazed fighter from the floor and carried him tenderly to his stool.[260]

Soon, someone in the crowd insisted on passing the hat in a show of appreciation for Choynski's unforgettable performance. Choynski received $900 for the purse, and another $760 from the hat — $1,660 total.[261]

Later that night Choynski, still dizzy from his memorable evening, returned to his family's home at 1209 Golden Gate Avenue. He found his mother, Harriet, still awake.[262]

Proudly, Choynski laid $1,250 on the table. His mother looked at the pile of money in shock.

"Where did you get that, Joe?" Harriet asked in a gentle voice.[263]

Knowing his mother disproved of his boxing endeavors, he tried to dull the sting. Clumsily, he replied, "The fellow I was training won, Ma, and I'm taking care of his money."[264]

By the next morning, Joe's foolish fib had been exposed. Headlines in the newspapers revealed the truth: "BUSH BAT-TERED — Joe Choynski Defeats Him Easily" . . . "Joe Choynski Knocks Out George Bush in Two Rounds."[265]

Harriet wanted to cry. She couldn't bear to see her son pursue a career as a prizefighter. Joe wrapped his muscular arms around his mother to console her, probably promising he wouldn't ever get hurt or allow boxing to sully his good name.[266]

Eventually, Harriet accepted her son's decision. The newspaper reports may have eased the pain. One glance said it all. Her son was San Francisco's latest pugilistic hero.[267]

Chapter Ten
Collision Course
— —

San Francisco, California: 1889

Prosperity shined on California at the dawn of 1889. Immigrants continued to pour into the state daily, land-seekers ventured beyond the great cities of San Francisco and Los Angeles in search of prime real estate, and the fertile soil promised a bountiful harvest. Excitement and opportunity abound.

If the United States Postal Service statistics were any indication of growth, California had opened a total of 186 new post offices in the previous two years. Something special was afoot.[268]

These were indeed boom times for the Golden State.

Every industry seemed to flourish, including the business of pugilism. Nowhere could that excitement be felt more than in the crowded athletic club rooms of San Francisco, where a boxing revival was taking place like never before. A new breed of boxer was starting to emerge — the scientific variety, where gloved combatants still dueled like modern-day gladiators, but under the Marquess of Queensberry Rules.

Bare-knuckled fights — like those preferred by World Heavyweight Champion John L. Sullivan — were steadily decreasing in number, and were outlawed by the state's legitimate clubs. The transition only seemed to excite the masses.

In San Francisco, a growing appetite for the manly arts could be witnessed in every corner of the city. While the great John L. inspired a whole generation of pugilists, these hopefuls flocked to neighborhood athletic clubs to receive organized training.

Athletic clubs thus teamed with youngsters who dreamt of becoming the next world heavyweight champion.

Boxing shows were also in high demand, driven by the city's lust for fistic entertainment and wealthy gamblers. The California Athletic Club, Golden Gate Athletic Club, and Olympic Club, as well as the Acme Athletic Club in Oakland, willingly satisfied the throng by staging regular events and local sportswriters sold lots of newspapers by printing the latest scuttlebutt. In time, the California Athletic Club earned an international reputation of dolling out large purses to worthy prizefighters.

San Francisco soon became a mecca for talented, ambitious boxers attracted by the lure of opportunity. The city's thriving boxing scene attracted the likes of Canadian-born George "The Marine" La Blanche, a heavy-fisted middleweight contender who knocked down World Middleweight Champion "The Nonpareil" Jack Dempsey, in August of 1889 with his infamous "pivot punch." The punch was ruled illegal, and both sides claimed victory.

By then, the Irish-born Dempsey had already become a fixture on the San Francisco fight scene.

Then there was Australia's heavyweight kingpin Peter Jackson, who trekked 9,000 miles by steamship to San Francisco in the spring of 1888. Jackson, one of the greatest fighters of his era, hoped to establish himself in San Francisco and eventually wrest the world heavyweight championship from Sullivan. In the end, the color of his skin proved his greatest barrier. Sullivan never gave him a title shot.

Yet no boxers seemed to excite San Franciscans more than their own native sons, Corbett and Choynski. Both were popular figures in and out of the ring.

The dashing Corbett always presented himself as a natty dresser about the city, and a budding superstar in the ring with his ever-improving ring generalship and lightning speed. An aura of charisma also shadowed Choynski wherever he went, while his rugged good looks matched his warring, relentless style in the ring.

Perhaps, in reality, San Franciscans saw a bit of themselves in these two up-and-coming fighters — first-generation Americans who had the courage to chase their dreams. Hope, ambition, and hard work were the bedrock of the city, and these two youngsters epitomized that lifestyle as well as anyone in San Francisco.

Corbett and Choynski dared to live.

Now, as if by destiny, they were thrown together in the same moment and time. A rivalry that began innocently enough in Patrick Corbett's livery stable had since mushroomed into a full-blown blood feud. The rivalry intensified with each new success in the ring.

Outside influences undoubtedly fanned the flames of their disdain for one another as many had something to gain by a Corbett-Choynski fight. Gamblers, newspaper editors, trainers, fans, Irishmen, Jews, friends and even family all had a stake in the outcome, whether through financial gain, prestige or pride.

The anticipation swirled around Corbett and Choynski like a gathering storm.

Eventually, if not inevitably, it appeared these two forces would have to collide. Decades later, Choynski reflected on his rivalry with Corbett and the whirlwind that surrounded them in those thrilling early days of 1889. Choynski conceded it was fate, simply saying, "We were born to clash."[269]

Until that time, the suspense would mount.

* * *

Choynski's first test of 1889 would not be an easy one.

The California Athletic Club, where Choynski was now being employed as an instructor, scheduled him to fight Frank Glover in a February 26 main event for a winning purse of between "$1,000-$1,250." The loser would receive $250.[270]

Glover, a 168-pounder, was hardly a pushover, having extended the larger and more powerful Joe McAuliffe to forty-nine rounds the previous year before being defeated. That bout alone earned him respect locally.[271]

Choynski spent eight weeks training for the fight under the tutelage of Australian Tom Meadows and Graney at the ranch of Joe Dieves on the San Leandro Road. By the time Choynski entered the ring, he displayed a rock-hard physique at 158 pounds.[272]

Despite his magnificent shape, the gamblers favored Glover's experience in the days leading up to the fight. Bets were still flying at ringside as the handlers were lacing Glover and Choynski's gloves moments before the call for time.[273]

Choynski then proceeded to add more converts to his growing bandwagon. By the third round, his strength began to take an effect on Glover. A left-right combination dropped Glover momentarily and when he arose, the Chicagoan became desperate.

Coolly, Choynski kept Glover at bay until the bell sounded.

Two rounds later Choynski struck again, smashing Glover with lefts and rights. During one wild exchange, the two combatants tumbled to the ground simultaneously. Both fighters climbed to their feet, but Glover appeared groggy. Choynski proceeded to batter Glover, who was saved only by the bell.

The mismatch continued until the fourteenth round. Choynski beat Glover to the floor early in the round. Gamely, Glover again climbed to his feet. Choynski rushed in like a bull as the two fighters again clumsily fell to the floor, where Glover desperately tried to hold Choynski down to catch a break.

Only Choynski wiggled free with the intervention of the referee, and continued his assault on the exhausted Glover. Finally, Choynski delivered a sledge-hammer right to Glover's jaw, sending him backward through the ropes face up. Glover's head struck an iron railing two feet from the ring, and that's where he remained unconscious before being carried to his dressing room.[274]

A later inspection of the defeated Glover revealed that he also lost a number of teeth in the process.[275]

Choynski's entourage — an ever-increasing crew — hailed their hero once again, enthusiastically declaring him the best heavyweight "on the West Coast."[276]

The praise was premature at best, but the prospects were real.

Somewhere in San Francisco that night — perhaps even at ringside — Corbett learned of his rival's rousing victory, as well as the boastful claims echoing from the Choynski camp. The words alone would have stoked his competitive fire. Corbett desired to be known as the best. He didn't like sharing the spotlight, let alone with a man he disliked.

Choynski became convinced Corbett seethed with jealously over his ring success, media coverage, and swelling ranks of admirers. Corbett heard the chiding banter. He remembered how "many were singing my praises, but there were those who scoffed at the idea that I was the best boxer on the Coast. It was claimed that Joe Choynski was an infinitely better man than I."[277]

Corbett, in turn, took solace in believing Choynski hated the fact he had suffered several early "beatings" at his hands.[278]

"Now the only blots on Choynski's record were several defeats by one Jim Corbett . . ." Corbett later wrote. "And all the credit he got for his hard work, seemed to be, 'Yes, yes, you whipped so and so, and so and so, but you can't whip Corbett!'
"That stuck in his craw!"[279]

The mind games toyed with each fighter. On the surface, they tried to maintain a level of civility with one another in public.

One day the two bumped into each other on the street. Corbett graciously forced out a compliment, saying, "Joe, you're getting on pretty well for a pro."[280]

"Yes, I've been working a great scheme," Corbett remembered Choynski saying. "When I clinch with some of these fellows, the first couple o' times I always say, 'Now come on and break away nice and gentlemanly,' and the fellow breaks away clean and drops his hands. I did this three or four times, but the fourth time or so, I set myself and as he breaks away clean I shoot over a right . . ."[281]

Corbett later admitted he "stowed this away" in his memory. By then, Corbett had already conceded he and Choynski were destined to fight.[282]

* * *

No one ever agreed on why Corbett and Choynski chose to illegally engage in a fight to the finish outside of a club setting in 1889.

Memories faded with time, recollections were likely altered to preserve legacies, and reputations of powerful men were probably spared by the exclusion of scandalous details. Of all those who witnessed the drama unfold firsthand, perhaps none were more truthful than Choynski's old pal, Tim McGrath.

"There was bad feelings between the youngsters," McGrath candidly recalled in 1931. He remembered the California Athletic Club offered an astonishing $10,000 purse for a legal finish fight between the two rivals in its showroom, but said "the boys preferred to fight for a fraction of that amount if they could murder each other."[283]

Corbett and Choynski ultimately agreed to a "finish fight" for a winner-take-all prize of $1,000.[284]

In doing so, they would risk felony charges if caught by police and their reputations within their respective clubs. The stakes were high, but nothing trumped pride.

Choynski and Corbett were both fiercely proud young men.

So when news of their prospective fight went public, it's not hard to imagine how they were swept into the swift currents that led them to dodge the law for a private battle.

The California Athletic Club board members may have fired the first volley that led to the Corbett-Choynski ring war of 1889. On April 22, the *Daily Alta California* reported that the club — likely driven by the prospect of a record-breaking draw — offered Corbett and Choynski a $3,000 purse for "a contest to the finish" in June.[285]

The newspaper also noted that the Olympic Club would never allow Corbett — the club's boxing instructor — to engage in a professional bout, predicting "the match is not likely to come off."[286]

In Corbett's version of events, by the spring of 1889, San Francisco's fight fans had worked themselves into a frenzy regarding a prospective bout with Choynski. Fans were routinely asking the same gnawing question: "What chance would Joe Choynski have against Jim Corbett now?"[287]

Soon, a California Athletic Club board member approached Corbett to inquire his interest in such a match.

"If you'll fight Choynski we'll put up a good purse," a club official asked.[288]

Corbett replied, "I don't care to fight professional."[289]

No one believed Corbett.

A new offer reached Corbett a short time later. This time a club official said, "Jim, if you'll agree to meet Choynski we will put up a $10,000 purse."[290]

Corbett again declined.

As news of his decision spread, fight fans were aghast. Few, if any, understood how he could pass up the chance to defeat Choynski for a small fortune of $10,000.

Choynski repeatedly claimed the offer even went as high as $20,000. Still, Corbett refused to fight in a club, regardless of the purse size.[291]

Corbett always contended the press lured him into the fight by printing inflammatory comments attributed to Choynski, but in truth that was never Choynski's style. Corbett undoubtedly wanted the fight as bad as Choynski. He simply wanted it on his terms.

Patrick Corbett supposedly also had a voice in the negotiations — a strong and stubborn voice, according to his son.

"The people over at the California Club, where Choynski is such a favorite, tell me there will be big money for a fight between us," Corbett recalled telling his father. "And money is no object. They're all rich men."[293]

"It's the money end of it that I don't like, son," Patrick Corbett responded. "Keep away from the club, and to hell with the money. If you must meet him, go out in the hills and fight him for nothing. I know you'll win, and I'll be proud of your licking him. But not if you scrap him as a professional. I just don't want one of my family to be a regular prize-fighter. That settles it, boy!"

At some point during this volatile period, Corbett and Choynski encountered one another on the street. Harsh words were exchanged, probably sparked by a debate over the California Athletic Club's hefty purse offer.

"Joe," Corbett said, "I'm a better boxer than you are, and I'm going to show you, too."[294]

"Yes," Choynski replied sharply, "wait until it's over and then you'll see."[295]

"I'll fight you for nothing — right here on the street," Corbett yelled. "I don't need a fat purse for fighting and beating you."[296]

Choynski walked away in disgust, if he wasn't dragged away by his friends. Corbett's repeated refusal to fight for $10,000 or $20,000 purse simply didn't make sense to Choynski or his backers.

Only later would Choynski suspect Corbett of dishonorable

motives.

"Damn fool says he," Choynski once told ring historian Nat Fleischer. "Corbett was afraid of me; and he didn't want to be whipped by me so in the open . . . With his mob he could wrangle the fight . . ."[297]

In those days, an old saying prevailed in San Francisco about how two boxers might "win, tie, or wrangle." If one boxer's friends and backers saw the fight going against their man, they would break it up with a free-for-all brawl.[298]

"Anything could happen under those circumstances," Choynski said. "But in a regular club, with supervision and everything, the 'win, tie, or wrangle' racket wasn't so good. And nobody knew this better than Corbett."[299]

In the end, perhaps fed up with the haggling or convinced by the sporting men who backed him, Choynski made the concession. He agreed to meet Corbett in a fight to the finish in private for a winner-take-all purse of $1,000.

At some point Choynski simply wanted to fight Corbett.

Details of the secret fight were hammered out April 23 in the office of *San Francisco Chronicle* sports editor Tom Flynn, whose very articles hyped a city over a Corbett-Choynski showdown. Backers from the rival camps agreed Flynn would be the stakeholder in charge of the money — a $1,000 a side.[300]

The clandestine meeting brought together a colorful cast of San Francisco personalities, starting with the two celebrated pugilists. Corbett's representatives included William P. Lawlor, later to become a Supreme Court Justice of California; horseman Tom Williams; and Porter Ashe, a notorious gambler who was once married to heiress Aimee Crocker. Aimee was the daughter of Judge Edwin B. Crocker, who served as chief counsel for the Central Pacific Railroad. The Crockers divorced in a highly publicized split in 1887, at which time Ashe's gambling habits and other illegal actions came to light.[301]

Apparently, where Ashe was concerned, some habits were

hard to break.

Choynski's entourage include his pal and trainer, Ed Grainey, and Moses A. Gunst, a renowned sporting gambler, tobacco pioneer, and one of San Francisco's wealthiest businessman.[302]

Gunst, known for his philanthropic endeavors in the Jewish community, lived a rags-to-riches life. He started with a small tobacco stand at a saloon entrance in 1877, and grew to become one of the city's largest tobacco import houses.

Now Gunst was helping choreograph one of San Francisco's most highly anticipated prizefights in memory. The diminutive, stalky Gunst did his part by posting Choynski's $1,000. Ashe and Williams each chipped in $500 to cover Corbett's part.[303]

The issue then turned to the size of gloves. Choynski preferred "skin-tight" gloves, while Corbett argued for two-ounce gloves — gloves likely padded with finely curled horse hair and sewed from the finest imported leathers. A heated debate ensued. Someone tossed a coin, and Corbett won the toss.

A secret battleground also needed to be chosen — one that would be hard for the police or public to find. Lawlor and Grainey were given the task of finding an appropriate location.[305]

Mose Gunst, San Francisco's cigar mogul, paid Jack Dempsey $1,000 to work Choynski's corner on the barge. Gunst wagered a large amount of money on a Choynski victory. *Author's Collection*

Lastly, Corbett and Choynski signed the articles, finalizing their commitment to engage in a private fight to the finish. With a few strokes of a pen, the grudge match was set to take place at a date sometime "within the next six weeks."[306]

Corbett summed up the mood of the two fighters in the *Daily Alta California*. A sportswriter quoted him as saying that he now expected Choynski to "put up or shut up."[307]

The time for words had ended.

Chapter Eleven
High Drama

— —

Marin County, California: May 1889

News of a private Corbett-Choynski fight to the finish triggered a tidal wave of excitement in the region's pugilistic circles.[308]

Bets flew fast and furious in every corner of San Francisco, heated debates cropped up over who would win, and the rumor mill spun frantically in an effort to locate the secret site of battle. Gamblers, fight fans, and newspaper hacks beat the clubrooms, saloons, and other haunts for that elusive tip.[309]

Officials at the Olympic Club and California Athletic Club received the news as expected. They were furious.

Corbett and Choynski's jobs as boxing instructors at their respective clubs were reportedly on the line. Some harbored hopes the boxers would come to their senses, and stage their fight legally inside a proper club like gentlemen. Choynski even continued to bitterly question why Corbett wouldn't accept his club's offer of a hefty, winner-take-all purse, but the Irishman's contract with the Olympic Club forbid him from boxing in other clubs.[310]

Insiders therefore predicted the fight would almost certainly take place in private, if at all.[311]

Tension shadowed Choynski, as well. An unnamed source — likely a disgruntled California Athletic Club board member upset about the prospect of losing a monster gate — told a reporter that club officials were "very sore over Joe's actions," and may prevent the bout from taking place. The article further stated that while the club was willing to supply a "heavy purse," it would not support "private matches, where both men lay themselves liable to be arrested for felony."[312]

Clearly, someone was trying to strong-arm Choynski into fighting Corbett at the California Athletic Club.

The irony is some of the most influential and wealthiest men from both clubs supported the two fighters in their pursuit of a "private" affair. Lawlor, Gunst and Ashe were a few prime examples, and none were discreet or modest about betting on prizefights. They probably didn't care where the two youngsters fought, as long as they did.

Gunst, for one, gained legendary status for his wagers on prizefights, horses, and even elections. Liberal with his money, he easily gained access to the sporting circles of New York, Chicago, and Denver. He became a ringside fixture at the nation's biggest fights, and often regaled his acquaintances with colorful lore of the ring.[313]

As for his gambling habits, one report noted in detail:

> *Men with a fancy for backing fighters commenced to entrust him with commissions on California club battles, and then he was entrusted with syndicate money at home. Frequently he announced himself as having $5,000, $10,000 or $20,000 to bet on a fight or an election. Nothing was ever said about the money belonging to somebody else, and consequently Gunst acquired a national reputation as being the heaviest betting man in the west.*[314]

In other words, Gunst operated quite a racket. No one would have been surprised to learn that he was one of the main orchestrators behind the Corbett-Choynski match.

Yet Gunst's involvement probably also meant something personal. In the muscular and hard-hitting Choynski, Gunst would have seen something special — a fellow Jew rising to notoriety in the ring. Joseph Bartlett Choynski shattered stereotypes. Timothy McGrath — a native San Franciscan and Choynski's close friend — later explained, in historic context, why many in the city's Jewish community rallied behind his pal: "Choynski was the first Jewish boxer to make a stir in fistiana."[315]

Therein was the magic.

So when I.N. Choynski publicly hailed his son in the aftermath of an amateur victory and zealously declared, "We are coming, father Abraham," his words reverberated in a growing number of Jewish neighborhoods nationwide. The outspoken Choynski elder summed up local sentiment a short time later after his son knocked out the Irish-slugging Keneally in November 1887. He wrote: "The Jews, who take little stock in slugging, are glad that there is one Maccabee among them, and that the Irish will no longer boast that there is not a Jew who can stand up to the racket and receive punishment according to the rules of Queensberry."[316]

I.N.'s article expressed what he believed to be a righteous anger.

Corbett undoubtedly enjoyed similar support in the Irish community, and without surprise, a Jew-versus-Gentile element existed throughout San Francisco. Corbett recognized the intensity of this ethnic feud in the days and weeks after the match was set. [317]

Choynski, for one, found the racial rumblings sad. Once, while addressing his feud with Corbett, he questioned why his ring antagonists "always" referred to him as "Jew-boy?" He spoke in a plural context.[318]

"If one is fighting," Choynski passionately stated, "one never should say a word of the religious beliefs of his opponent."[319]

Was Choynski including Corbett in this complaint? Although he never mentions his rival by name, one is left to wonder how deep the bad blood truly flowed.

One fact is without debate: Corbett and Choynski were immensely popular draws in the ring regardless of their ethnicity. They ignited an unfettered excitement in the ring — Corbett for his cleaver footwork and blinding punches, and Choynski for his raw power and relentless style. They were praised for their fine conditioning, idolized for their courage, and celebrated for their successes. They were also young, tough, and highly intelligent.

Above all they were damn entertaining.

Naturally, Corbett and Choynski attracted large crowds whenever they boxed. And with each new victory, their local fame — and fan base — grew.

Authorities were genuinely concerned a private fight might spark a riot, and they weren't alone in those fears.

San Francisco Chronicle sports editor Tom Flynn, now moonlighting as the fight's stakeholder, strangely seemed to be lobbying for a club setting only six days after the articles were signed. Flynn sensed danger when he wrote, "One thing is certain that if the men meet anywhere but under the auspices of some well organized club there is likely to be trouble."

Flynn viewed a private Corbett-Choynski showdown as an obvious powder keg. He too sensed the mounting tensions on the streets.

The drama would unfold in a very public way in morning newspapers across the city.

"It is well known that both Choynski and Corbett have a large following of young and ardent admirers, and where a ring is surrounded by two distinct factions composed of hot-blooded youths free from restraint the contest is not likely to be allowed to proceed with the peaceful hush which marks the progress of a lawn tennis tournament," he wrote. "Under such circumstances one fight begets many and nature's weapons moreover are not the ones used."[321]

Oddly, Flynn seemed to place the onus of the fight's location on Choynski. He did so while taking a jab at Corbett when he added: "As Choynski is very much in earnest as regards the coming mill and is anxious to obliterate the memory of one or two frock encounters which Corbett loves to recall, it is to be hoped that Joe's friends will advise him against risking his reputation under circumstances where outside interference may rob him of a victory or hasten his defeat."[322]

Despite the ominous warnings, training for the fight proceeded as scheduled.

Choynski trained across the bay in Sausalito, a small Marin County fishing village that could be seen six miles away in San Francisco. Sausalito provided Choynski with a quiet, rural setting to conduct his work because of its relative isolation. Despite its close proximity to the city, San Franciscans were required to take a half-hour tug boat ride or travel as much as 100 miles overland by carriage or wagon to reach its locale.[323]

Sausalito also offered mild and temperate climate for training. A mountain range that stretched southward to the Golden Gate shielded Sausalito from storms, providing protection for both anchored ships and residents. Visitors considered the township very salubrious, with the summer's heat being alleviated by the cool sea breezes and the winter's cold tempered by its proximity to vast bodies of water.[324]

Veteran George "The Marine" La Blanche trained alongside Choynski in preparation for a May 28 bout with New Yorker Mike Lucie — a fight billed as the "Middleweight Championship of America." La Blanche, thirty-two, surely proved to be a great asset to the twenty-year-old slugger, who always approached training like a Spartan.[325]

The loyal Ed Graney, meanwhile, capably oversaw Choynski's strict training regimen. He knew Choynski's strengths and weaknesses as well as anyone, likely having studied his protégé beyond the gym during informal sessions behind his blacksmith shop.[326]

Corbett set up training camp — his first — in the shadow of Mount Tamalpais, in the southern end of Ross Valley. Water flowed gently by his camp in a small creek, and the solitude of the countryside provided the necessary tonic for the task at hand. He was being trained by Fred Hansted, better known in San Francisco as "Professor Young Dutchy."[327]

Dutchy had a colorful and checkered past. Born in 1853 in London, he reportedly began boxing at age sixteen and claimed he rose to become lightweight champion of Australia before sailing for America. His journey was interrupted when a shipwreck left him stranded for a time in Tahiti, where he engaged willing islanders with his pugilistic skills.

Upon arriving in San Francisco Dutchy quickly embedded himself in the local boxing scene. In November of 1883, Dutchy and six other men were arrested and charged for staging an illegal prizefight. By Dutchy's own account, he acted as referee in the disputed bout. Charges were dropped three months later at the request of the district attorney, and Dutchy continued to pursue his pugilistic endeavors, earning a reputation as "a capable trainer."[328]

In Corbett, Dutchy found a true professional. Corbett, of course, needed no prodding when it came to conditioning. He diligently attacked his workouts, rising daily at 6 a.m. "to a cold sponge bath," his two-pound dumbbells, a rub-down, and a brisk mile walk.[329]

Breakfasts consisted of a thick, juicy porterhouse steak daily, dry toast, and a couple of soft-boiled eggs washed down with a cup of tea — minus milk and sugar.

After a short rest, Corbett ventured into the hills for a scenic, fifteen-mile jog. He returned to a shower and an alcohol rub-down that prepared him for a lunch of fowl, calf's foot jelly and ale. The jelly was made by boiling calves feet until the natural gelatin was extracted. The liquid was then strained, and generally mixed with wine, lemon juice, and spices and chilled until set.

A game of billiards or a good book generally allowed Corbett a short respite before his afternoon workout.

At 3 p.m., he swung clubs, lifted dumbbells, and punched the heavy bag for six, three-minute rounds. He finished his routine by jumping rope 300 to 400 times, burning his lungs with a rapid finish.

Dutchy then gave him another rub-down before supper, which featured another fat porterhouse steak. Corbett retired each evening at 9 p.m., but not before a few more minutes of lifting dumbbells.[330]

Corbett had just recovered from a bout with pneumonia when he signed the articles to fight Choynski in April. Now, nearly three weeks later, he showed no ill-effects of weakness and was instead gaining muscle.[331]

By May 11, a *Daily Alta California* sportswriter visited Corbett's rural camp to find the pride of the Olympic Club in great shape and expecting "to enter the ring at 185 pounds."[332]

Corbett also appeared to be in good cheer. When asked about his condition, Corbett paused from his billiards game and playfully replied, "Go ask the landlady about my appetite since coming here a little less than a week ago. She has twice raised the price of board on me, and says that if my appetite keeps increasing she will have to go into bankruptcy."[333]

Dutchy raved about his fighter, stressing that his punching power shouldn't be underestimated. The advice was likely intended to toy with Choynski's psyche.

"If he doesn't win it won't be because he hasn't confidence or lacks training, and mark my word, when the time comes those who think he lacks heart will be treated to a big surprise," Dutchy predicted. "He is a game 'un, as I have good reason to know by my feet, which are blistered and burnt in an endeavor to keep up with him in his walks."[334]

A short time after Corbett's arrival to Ross Valley an old

friend stopped to pay a visit.

Billy Delaney, the Oakland saloonkeeper with the "poker face," traveled to Corbett's Marin County retreat with a proposition.[335]

"Jim," Delaney said, "I'd like to train you."[336]

"But I'm not getting any money for it Billy, and I couldn't pay you," Corbett replied.[337]

"That's all right, Jim," Delaney said. "I don't want any money. I just want to be in your camp here to help you in every way I can to get into shape."[338]

"All right, Billy," Corbett concluded. "You're on."[339]

Delaney would render invaluable service in the weeks ahead as he inherited a prominent role in Corbett's training. The saloonkeeper displayed a knack for training fighters, and a way with handling the often stubborn Corbett — a pugilist he would guide for the next seven years.[340]

Updates, meanwhile, were reported daily by the press on Choynski and Corbett's "private" fight. Periodically, "troops of clubmen and other patrons of the manly art" embarked on excursions across the bay to visit each fighter's Marin County training camps.[341]

As expected, Corbett and Choynski were monitored like prized thoroughbreds. On May 12 — the day after an interview with the *Daily Alta California* — roughly "one-half of the Olympic Club" visited Ross Valley to find Corbett "confident and strong."[342]

Yet the big news that day came out of Sausalito, where onlookers noticed one of Choynski's wrists bandaged. No one, however, expected that injury to prevent the gritty Choynski from his appointed brawl with Corbett.[343]

In fact, the strain of anticipation appeared to intensify with each passing day.

"The contest between Jim Corbett and Joe Choynski is creating more interest, by reason of the principals being so well known and so evenly matched, than any previous encounter arranged here," one article proclaimed. "Everything points to a successful termination, as the principals intend to settle the question once and for all as to who is the better man."[344]

The reporter then optimistically predicted that those lucky few "favored with the tip" of the fight's secret location would witness "an encounter which they will remember for days to come as being the best" ever arranged in San Francisco.[345]

Corbett and Choynski's well-documented feud certainly fed the imagination of the city's press corps, as well as its hardy fight fans. Everyone associated with the city's boxing scene believed their disdain for one another to be genuine. If they didn't, they would soon read otherwise. As one report stated, "If the battle . . . is only half as savage as the verbal assaults the boxers are represented as making on each other . . . the encounter will be one of the most memorable in the ring."[346]

The suspense mounted.

Directors of the California Athletic Club, meanwhile, moved to publicly distance themselves from the looming illegal prizefight. They went so far as to pass a resolution to condemn the match and dissolve their club of any involvement:

> WHEREAS, Inasmuch as a great deal of feeling has been created in local circles regarding the proposed Choynski-Corbett prize fight, the Board of Directors deem it proper and right to inform the public of San Francisco and the public in general, that the club will not countenance or encourage prize-fighting; and, furthermore, owing to the bitterness of feeling that has been engendered thereby, this club will neither offer any inducements to have a meeting of the two men take place in the clubrooms, nor receive any advance from them toward such an end. The attention of the members of the club is called to section 12 of the constitution and by-laws: "Any member who shall conduct himself in a manner unbefitting a gentleman or calculated to

disturb the harmony or impair the prosperity of good name
of the club, either in the rooms of the club or elsewhere,
shall be liable to expulsion by the Board of Directors."
Furthermore, it having been asserted that Mr. Choynski
is a representative of this club, we beg state that he has
resigned his position as boxing instructor of this club.[347]

In truth, club officials ditched Choynski to save face. As for the proclamation, the document reeked of hypocrisy. A large number of California Athletic Club members — if not the very board of directors themselves — were undoubtedly on the hunt for the date, time, and whereabouts of the illegal fight.

The hunt for information grew desperate with each new day. Rumors came and went like the tide. No one wanted to miss what they anticipated would be the grudge match of the century. Rumors swirled over the secret place of combat — San Bruno . . . San Pablo . . . Ocean House Road . . .[348]

One report stated Corbett and Choynski were even "prepared to go to Mexico" if needed to fight, narrowing the search for the battleground somewhere between San Francisco and the Mexican border.[349]

The madness reached such a frenzy that the *San Francisco Chronicle* was forced to run an article one day with the headline: "THERE WAS NO FIGHT."[350]

Someone spotted Choynski and Joe McAuliffe "in a heated condition," and assumed there had been a fight in Sausalito. The report caused quite a stir in the city, especially with the fight's stakeholder Flynn, who was supposed to be kept abreast of every detail about the clandestine fight. Fans quickly jumped to the conclusion Choynski must have defeated Corbett by virtue of his otherwise calm disposition — and no sign of his rival. Upon further inspection a *Chronicle* reporter — likely Flynn himself – found Choynski fresh and relaxed, and skipping "down the pier and along the parade as lively as a kitten."[351]

Turns out Choynski and McAuliffe had simply gone for a

brisk, two-mile run.

And so went the drama.

The next day the *Daily Alta California* reported that "wiser counsels have prevailed," and the Corbett-Choynski fight had been canceled. The article chastised the handlers of both fighters, claiming, "These young men were hounded into the present match by certain parties who hoped to reap a little gain from it."[353]

Probably no truer statement had been uttered about the fight to that point, but the article didn't stop there. It further accused those same "parties" of now yelling "the loudest in calling upon the authorities to prevent" the fight from happening. In a parting shot, the article blasted the rival *Chronicle*, saying the newspaper was "as deeply in the mud as Corbett and Choynski are in the mire if any felony is being committed" by virtue of accepting the "onerous position of stakeholder."[354]

Flynn had been called out publicly.

Clearly, San Francisco appeared to be splitting down the middle. Everyone, or so it seemed, took sides. Corbett or Choynski?

Nowhere was this more evident than in local clubs, saloons, and underground gambling halls. Bets were "quietly" made in every imaginable place in the city, or as Corbett quipped, everywhere "but in the churches."[355]

Corbett opened as an early favorite, perhaps as a result of his reputation as a skilled and cleaver boxer, if not because of his advanced experience. Olympic Club members remained confident their man would prevail, especially after visiting his camp in late May and watching Corbett spar McAuliffe. They left confidently declaring Corbett "a sure winner."[356]

Choynski, meanwhile, had confined his training mostly to roadwork as a precautionary measure due to his hand injury. Still, onlookers reported him to be in great shape and tipping the scales at a solid 168 pounds — a weight that told the betting public he was unquestionably "hard as nails."[357]

By late May, betting had also become more evenly split.[358]

As the hour of combat drew closer, the suspense intensified. Larger wagers were boldly made, debates over the outcome became more heated, and the fighters themselves had grown noticeably restless and edgy. Reportedly, Choynski lashed out at Corbett only days before the fight, saying the only reason he studied boxing in the first place was so he could "thrash his rival."[359]

If Choynski truly made the comment, it was uncharacteristic of his quiet nature.

Regardless, the comment surely reached Corbett's camp in the foothills of Mount Tamalpais. By then, Corbett needed no further motivation to defeat his most hated foe. If anything, the comment only stoked his hatred.

The furor spilled into the streets. Heated debates turned into fistfights.

"Not a day passed that a half dozen street brawls didn't occur as a climax to arguments between the Choynski and Corbett partisans," Corbett recalled.[360]

San Francisco authorities were now more concerned about riots than the embarrassment of an illegal prizefight occurring under their noses. Police patrols were ordered on heightened surveillance.[361]

The prospect of violence and mayhem from a large crowd also began to concern the fighters and handlers who had agreed in advance to allow only ten witnesses per side for their "private" battle. Everyone pledged secrecy about the fight's ultimate date, time, and location, but the potential of leaked information only strained nerves.[362]

Marin County authorities were naturally on high alert by the mere fact the fighters were training openly in their jurisdiction. County Sheriff John E. Healy and his deputies didn't want the embarrassment of an illegal fight taking place on their watch, either.

So Healy ordered deputies to shadow both Corbett and Choynski. Some even showed up in plain clothes from time to time to watch the training sessions, hoping to glean a tip.[363]

Finally, on the eve of the battle, Lawlor and Graney revealed the secret fight location to their respective fighters. They had chosen a barn loft on Peter Austin's old and deserted farm two miles outside Fairfax, a remote Marin County community at the northern edge of Ross Valley. The farm sat some fourteen miles from Sausalito, and was thought to be secluded enough to prevent police interference.[364]

The handlers agreed to commence the fight at 8 a.m. sharp.[365]

"That's all right, but how am I going to get there without being followed," Corbett told Lawlor. Sheriff's deputies were camped in an open lot across the road from Corbett's cottage.

"Oh, leave that to me, Jim," chimed in Hall McAllister, Jr., the son of a prominent San Francisco attorney. The young McAllister had befriended Corbett, and had a plan.[366]

"Can you fix it?" Corbett asked dubiously.[367]

"Sure," McAllister said confidently. "Leave it to me to help you give those sheriffs the skip."[368]

All through the night — May 29 — Corbett slept soundly, while Lawler and Grainey stayed awake to watch the deputies. By daybreak, McAllister was quietly waiting behind the cottage with his mother's private carriage — an enclosed rig with two fine steeds; the finest money could buy.[369]

Corbett and his handlers slipped out the back door and into the awaiting carriage, and were out of sight without any apparent detection. They cackled as they rumbled down the dirt road toward Fairfax. Not only had they escaped, but they did so in high fashion.[370]

Soon, the mood would change. Thoughts turned to the coming battle. Blood would be spilled today.

Privately, Corbett likely fought his own demons on the

bumpy ride to Fairfax. Corbett realized he had gotten the best of Choynski in their previous encounters, but even he later admitted those fights "were close enough at times to leave doubt in my mind . . ."[371]

Shadowed by uncertainty, Corbett stared at the passing countryside, oblivious to the exact location of their final destination. He saw only what he wanted to see — blood.

Chapter Twelve
A Fairfax Barn

— —

Fairfax, California: May 30, 1889

Someone couldn't keep a secret. Whoever, or how many, divulged the location of the fight didn't seem to matter by 5 a.m. Thursday, May 30, when a large and spirited crowd of sporting men flocked to the San Francisco Ferry Building to board a tugboat to cross the bay to Sausalito. Of all the rumors swirling about the city, someone received the right tip on the eve of Decoration Day late Wednesday night — Marin County . . . two miles north of the town of Fairfax . . . in a barn at Pete Austin's old farm.[372]

News spread like a wildfire.

Excited, hyped, and impatient, the men debated at the pier whether to wait for the earliest ferryboat to Sausalito. No one wanted to wait. They instead chartered two tugs to carry them immediately across the chilly bay.[373]

By then, sporting hacks and others eager to witness the showdown started to trail the war party.

Another group — eleven in all — also arrived in Sausalito early after departing Meiggs Wharf, which now encompasses part of San Francisco's popular Fisherman's Wharf and Pier 39. As they pulled into the Sausalito wharf, they would have seen sailboats docked at two yacht club buildings and fishing vessels moored along the shoreline in the still of the morning. Together, the interlopers caught up with Choynski and his entourage and shadowed them north across Ross Valley toward Fairfax, but not after securing every available team and wagon in town.[374]

Yet another band of men in the northeastern section of the county made quite a stir as they passed through San Rafael, where they probably disembarked a train at the San Francisco and North Pacific Railroad depot. Soon, they whisked away toward Fairfax in horse-drawn carriages, wagons and buggies. The cavalcade even included a few bicycles.[375]

Tom Flynn, nervous about his role as stakeholder, watched the surreal scene with a touch of amusement. Flynn later recalled, "The size and unusual character of the demonstration caused the astonished residents of the fashionable suburb to stick their heads out of their windows, curious to know whether it was a political parade, a picnic or a popular politician's funeral that had struck town."[376]

Residents would discover the truth soon enough, although some surely followed to find out for themselves.

The procession eventually reached Fairfax, a stopping point along a railroad line that linked Sausalito to the dairy and timber country in the north to Cazadero, the furthest most terminus at the time. Fairfax really featured nothing more than a one-room school house for twenty-four children who lived at a loose collection of family farms.

Prior to 1889, Fairfax earned a dubious reputation as a destination for shady picnickers on railroad excursions. Once, in May of 1884, picnic goers were shuttled to Fairfax for a day of fun and relaxation. The *Marin Journal* reported, "Last Sunday there was a picnic in Fairfax. About 2,000 attended and fifty fights occurred."[377]

By 1888, the railroad bowed out of the excursion business with its president declaring, "These picnickers are really unmanageable."

Fairfax's early history may have been an ominous sign of events to come. In 1861, the site became known as the place of California's last political duel. State legislators Daniel Showalter and Charles W. Piercy decided to settle a dispute while at the home of a mutual friend, Lord Charles Fairfax. Despite Fairfax's urgings of peace, the two men marched into a grassy meadow, brandishing rifles and firing at forty paces.

Piercy dropped dead.

Some of San Francisco's rowdier fight fans probably desired a similar outcome from the Choynski-Corbett grudge as they reached Fairfax.

Choynski's party traveled north out of Fairfax, curving around a horseshoe mountain known as White's Hill. Along the road Choynski could see a pristine countryside where coastal oaks, Douglas firs, and giant redwoods canvased the mountainside to his left and valley to his right.

Finally, an hour and forty minutes after leaving Sausalito, Choynski crossed a small, wooden bridge and arrived at the gate of the old and deserted farm of Pete Austin, a Maine-born farmer who had moved to San Rafael. Austin's property — a narrow patch of land — sat wedged between the steep, circular walls of White's Hill in a box canyon. A narrow road led downhill to the farm site sheltered mostly by trees.[378]

Rays of sunlight beamed through the trees as they descended the worn road.

The farm consisted of a main house with a small shed, a cottage, and a large wooden barn, nestled next to a curve in a shallow, slow-flowing creek. A lone hen house stood across the creek from the barn.[379]

Choynski's handlers immediately escorted him into the abandoned cottage, and claimed one of the rooms for his dressing quarters. There, Choynski could rest and meditate on the coming battle. The twenty-year-old pugilist might have been distracted by one other issue.

A day earlier police arrested his father — publisher of the *Public Opinion* — and booked him on three counts of libel and one for attempted extortion involving a watch company that advertised in his newspaper. One article detailed the allegations that morning:

> *The charge of extortion alleges that Choynski published*
> *. . . articles for the purpose of obtaining money from the*
> *corporation . . . Choynski does not appear to take the mat-*
> *ter at all seriously. He admits to publishing the statements*
> *and says he called the company some pretty hard names, but*
> *claims they are all true.*[380]

Whether friends and associates tried to shield Joe from the news is unknown, but news of the arrest was surely well known by some spectators in attendance at the time. The timing of the arrest also seemed to be strange, but neither Joe Choynski nor anyone else ever made it an issue.

Corbett, meanwhile, arrived shortly thereafter with his own party of handlers and friends, although he was unfamiliar with the site of battle. He did express shock at seeing more than 100 spectators milling about the property, and his handlers quickly hustled him into a vacant room in the cottage to prepare for the match.[381]

Upon entering the room, Corbett saw no other amenities other than an old bed with no mattress or blanket. He soon learned Choynski waited in a neighboring room.[382]

Handlers for both fighters then slowly began to prepare their respective boxers for the coming mill, starting with deep-tissue, alcohol rubdowns.[383]

Outside, an excited throng anxiously awaited the main festivities. Discussions were animated, strategies were speculated, and betting became lively.[384]

One reporter looked around at the dense woods that enveloped the property, pondered the distant trek that morning, and concluded, "The place is so secluded that it would be impossible for anyone to find it unless shown the exact spot."[385]

Inside the barn final preparations were being made in the

loft. A twenty-four-foot ring had been pitched the day before with resin sprinkled liberally on the floor for better footing. Several boards were also removed from all four walls to allow plenty of fresh air to pass through.[386]

Downstairs in the cottage, Lawlor grew distressed about the boisterous crowd outside. He calmly approached Corbett about his uneasiness.

"Jim, there is a lot of feeling over this fight and I am afraid there will be trouble and someone may pull a gun," Lawlor said. "Don't you think we had better search them before they are allowed in the barn?"[387]

Corbett thought a search would be a good idea, and someone suggested consulting with Choynski on the matter. He too agreed, and Grainey, Gunst, and another San Franciscan — Johnny Hammersmith — were charged with the "delicate duty" of searching the pockets of each spectator for weapons.[388]

Hammersmith, who dabbled in photography, worked as a dealer of toys, fancy goods, and perfumes in the city. Guns were an entirely different matter.[389]

The search provided some pre-fight entertainment, yielding a stack of pistols and bowie knives. Some men didn't seem too eager to shed themselves of their revolvers.

One man — the rough-and-tumble gambler Ned Foster — approached with a scowl.

"Moses Gunst and I both started toward old Ned Foster, and we hadn't taken three steps before Ned whipped out a Gatling gun that looked big enough to sink every ship in the Navy," Grainey recalled. "For a moment I didn't know whether he was going to shoot Gunst or me, and I don't mind telling you I was scared."[390]

The grumpy Foster surrendered his hefty firearm peacefully, and made his way into the barn for some fistic entertainment.[391]

By the time the "search committee" had finished their preparatory work, piles of guns sat in both Corbett and Choynski's rooms — or, in the amusing words of Grainey, "enough revolvers to stock an army of Central American Revolutionists."[392]

Finally, the fighters were summoned from the cottage.

As they exited the dwelling, Corbett saw his friend and World Middleweight Champion Jack Dempsey with Choynski's entourage. Gunst offered to pay the world-class Dempsey $1,000 to second Choynski during the fight along with Grainey.[393]

Dempsey's presence infuriated Corbett since the two had often sparred together at the Olympic Club.

"Jim, I'm going to second this fellow, but I'm only doing it because I am getting $1,000," Dempsey said sheepishly. "I don't know him at all, and it's not because I want him to win."[394]

"That's all right, Jack," Corbett shot back confidently. "You can't make him whip me."[395]

Corbett coolly turned away and slowly started to jog toward the barn. Delaney and Keneally followed their fighter closely as they started to climb the narrow, rickety staircase to the loft.

The buzz of the crowd drowned the creaking boards.

Corbett beheld a fascinating sight at the top of the stairs — the makeshift ring . . . missing slats of boards from the walls . . . . and more than 125 people from notorious gamblers to respected bankers to millionaires.[396]

The buzz grew louder.

Nathaniel Carl Goodwin, a prominent actor, vaudevillian, and ardent Choynski booster was also in the crowd that morning. Goodwin starred at the Baldwin Theatre in San Francisco at the time, but refused to miss the highly anticipated fight. He paid a messenger $50 to hustle his telegram back to San Rafael, where it was to be sent with great urgency to the theatre:

> *Taken seriously ill. Cannot appear today. Dismiss the matinee audience.*[397]

Later, Goodwin amused close friends with how the theatre

manager had to break the bad news to a packed house that day before refunding wads of money. Nor did he regret his decision. [398]

Electricity surged through the crowd when Choynski first appeared in the loft. Donning black tights and a black sash, Choynski looked to be in brilliant shape as his chest and shoulders bulged with muscles. He tipped the scales at 162 pounds, and at five-foot-eleven, appeared to be as hard as iron.[399]

Corbett, his rival's senior by two years, also made a magnificent entrance. He entered the ring wearing flesh-colored tights, brown shoes, and a stunning apple-green silk sash interwoven with red. He stood six-one and weighed a solid 183 pounds.

Both fighters were wearing the previously agreed upon two-ounce gloves.

Moments before the instructions, Ashe — one of Corbett's backers — approached Jim in his corner and stuffed a wad of cash into the palm of one glove.

"Now, Jim, when you go up there bet Choynski this $500 that you will lick him," Ashe said enthusiastically. "If you win, keep it."[400]

Referee Patsy Hogan, himself a pugilist and sometimes wrestler, then addressed the crowd with firmness in his voice. A hush fell upon the ring.

Actor Nat Goodwin actually cancelled one of his shows at the Baldwin Theatre in San Francisco so he could attend the Corbett-Choynski fight in Marin County. *Author's Collection*

All eyes locked on Hogan.

"Gentleman, I have been selected to act as referee of this contest by both men, who are my personal friends," Hogan said. "I shall do my best to govern this contest, and shall follow out the Marquess of Queensberry rules. My decision shall be final and no power, intimidation or influence shall change it. I will ask that you keep quiet, and not give your approval or disproval to any acts of these men during the contest."[401]

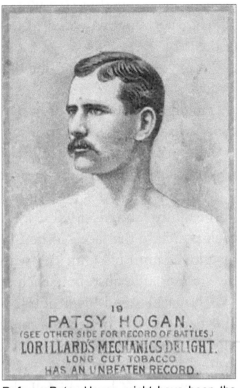

19
PATSY HOGAN.
(SEE OTHER SIDE FOR RECORD OF BATTLES.)
LORILLARD'S MECHANICS DELIGHT.
LONG CUT TOBACCO
HAS AN UNBEATEN RECORD.

Referee Patsy Hogan might have been the only man strong enough – or crazy enough – to officiate the clandestine fight between Choynski and Corbett. *Author's Collection*

Hogan looked into each corner: "Gentleman, shake hands."[402]

Choynski and Corbett moved to the center of the ring — Corbett with Ashe's wad of money. The two shook hands. Corbett grinned and said to Choynski, "I will bet you $500 on the fight."[403]

Choynski laughed, replying unabashedly, "I have no money."[404]

"I didn't have any either until Ashe gave it to me," continued Corbett, who turned to Dempsey.[405]

"Say, Jack, I'll bet you $500."[406]

Unamused, Dempsey replied, "I don't want to bet."[407]

Corbett returned to his corner, leaned over the ropes and extended the fistful of cash toward Ashe, playfully announcing,

"I can't find anybody to bet with so here's the money."[408]

The spectators crowded in toward the ring in anticipation of the fury.

"Are you ready boys?" the timekeeper asked. Both fighters nodded.

Finally, after months of hype, the timekeeper signaled the commencement of action by ringing a milkman's bell.[409]

Choynski and Corbett collided in the center of the ring like two roosters in a cockfight. Punches flew with bad intentions.

A jumbled mix of shouts and yells showered the fighters.

Instantly, Choynski felt Corbett's "hard, bony hands" with each punch to the face. Corbett had "kneaded" the stuffing in his gloves until his knuckles were almost bare, or so thought the slugger after absorbing each punch.[410]

Choynski stood his ground, whacking Corbett to the face and body, where he left his marks. Corbett, ever controlling, moved gracefully about the ring as Choynski closed in like a bull.

A left from Choynski fell short. Corbett dodged another left, only to watch his rival slip to the wooden floor. Choynski bounced up quickly, and continued to press the action, landing a solid left to Corbett's ribs.

Corbett responded with a fierce right to Choynski's nose, and repeated the punch only to whiff over a ducking Choynski. As Choynski bobbed up, Corbett uncorked another grazing right as time was called.[411]

An excitement filtered through the crowd, divided by partisans who were still yelling . . . shouting . . . fist-pumping. They clamored for blood.

Seconds before the call for time, another taunt emanated from Corbett's corner: Another offer for a $500 bet.[412]

The taunt went ignored.

The bell for round two rang, and Choynski and Corbett smiled at one another. After a few seconds of sparring, Corbett chirped, "Joe, give me a rush."[413]

Choynski obliged.

One ringside reporter noted how Choynski went "flying at him like an enraged tiger."[414]

For a moment, both men hammered away at close quarters as the crowd roared with pleasure. No one at the Olympic Club had ever seen Corbett hit so clearly or so hard. They must have been jarred at what they were seeing, but remained unwavering in their confidence as evidenced by their lusty cheers.

A moment later the two fighters clinched.

"Jim," Choynski said, "let's break away nice and gentlemanly."[415]

Flashing back to their conversation on the street, Corbett figured he wouldn't fall for any of Choynski's trickery. He would instead beat his advisory to the punch. On the break, Corbett unleashed a right uppercut that clipped Choynski on the chin and the pride of Golden Gate Avenue hit the boards in a roll.

Choynski immediately jumped to his feet.[416]

"Foul!" Choynski partisans yelled. "Foul!"[417]

Vehemently, Corbett's fans verbally lashed back. They clamored for justice; no, for blood.

Hogan ruled no foul. Again, the Choynski faithful protested with cries of, "Foul!"

The scene threatened to dissolve into a riot.

At that moment Goodwin's voice could be heard above the roar. The popular actor, one of the most recognized men in San Francisco, roundly chastised Choynski's rowdier partisans.

"Do you want the sheriff on us?" yelled Goodwin, his hair neatly parted and smartly dressed as usual. "Keep still, you idiots! Choynski will give him plenty!"[418]

Goodwin's demands brought quiet, and the action resumed as fierce as ever. The fighters again collided in a storm of punches, fighting desperately and at times grappling.

Hogan ordered the men to break. Neither boxer backed

away. He barked the order again to no avail.

Hogan, himself no weakling, struggled just as desperately to pry the two fighters apart. Finally, he succeeded and Choynski launched a vicious right that struck Corbett's neck, breaking his skin at the call of time.[419]

Clearly, this was anyone's fight.

Chapter Thirteen
Sheriff Healy

— —

San Rafael, California: May 30, 1889

Sheriff John E. Healy personally enjoyed a good boxing match. Frankly, the transplanted New Yorker didn't even mind those of the illegal variety.

He simply didn't like them in his legal jurisdiction.

For all that Healy was and wasn't, the thirty-nine-year-old sheriff was above all a lawman. An oath to uphold the law meant something to him, and those who knew him best believed him to be "eminently fair and square in his deals with men of all classes."[420]

So when Healy arose on the morning of May 30, it was with great reluctance that he heard the commotion around San Rafael. Whispers of the "private" Corbett-Choynski "fight to the finish" circulated town in rather loud tones thanks to the hubbub and excitement swirling in the air. The parade of people who swept through town at sunrise en route to the battleground certainly did nothing to preserve the secret.

Eager ring fans secured buggies and wagons for the trip to the Fairfax countryside in San Rafael. People surely talked. Friends told friends. Neighbors told neighbors.

Someone told Sheriff Healy.[421]

Less than six miles away, Corbett and Choynski were preparing for the ruthless business of a finish fight in Peter Austin's old barn. Little did they know, as they waged war on their hated ring rival, they would be racing against the clock.

125

Healy swore to uphold the law, and now here was a moment of truth. He realized weeks earlier this day might arrive with both fighters training in Marin County, and he did his best to shadow them with the help of some deputies and neighboring constables.

For a moment, he might have thought about ignoring the chatter. In the end, he chose duty and honor — qualities, ironically, dear to Choynski and Corbett.

The two boxers lived by an unspoken code of honor that ultimately pitted them against one another. They stepped into the ring for pride and respect, if not also for the scores of partisans who supported their fistic endeavors. Like it or not, they had become the pride of their neighborhoods, athletic clubs, and ethnic communities.

People idolized them for their skill, strength, and courage, qualities perhaps they wished they possessed. Such is the life of a pugilist who dares to bare it all before the world in the quest for even a small measure of respect.

Healy understood this existence, even if he didn't recognize it at the time. As an elected lawman, the people of his district looked to him to enforce the law and keep the peace. Sometimes, that might require him to bare it all before the world, to put his life on the line.

Healy didn't know what he might find that day when he ventured into the countryside: An angry mob? Gun-toting spectators bent on defying the law? Or both?

All he knew for sure was he had to ride.

Only Healy's undertaking wouldn't be easy. The first tip he received prompted him to catch a train toward the county's furthest southern township of Tiburon — some thirteen miles in the opposite direction of Fairfax. Healy started to rethink his direction as the train entered the town of Larkspur, where the train station passed by Claude Callot's popular vineyard, inn, and recreational resort.[422]

The sheriff spotted a large number of carriages at Callot's. So he grew suspicious.[423]

A short time later Healy listened to his instincts. He hailed the railroad engineer, and ordered the train stopped at once.[424]

Healy disembarked, and began to walk north. He appears to have ordered someone to ride ahead of him a couple miles into Tamalpais to secure him a horse, but when he arrived at that locale, found no steed in sight. Frustrated, he continued to travel north on foot along the country road.[425]

By then the carriages were out of sight, but he knew he was on the right trail.

Finally, after four more miles of walking, he reached Fairfax and found a horse to saddle. Most importantly, he learned from residents that the crowd traveled north toward White's Hill and the old farm of Peter Austin, now a neighbor of Healy's in San Rafael and a former Marin County sheriff (1867-1871). Healy knew the area well.[426]

Spurring his horse, Healy galloped northward at a brisk clip . . .

* * *

Inside the barn the third round passed uneventfully as the two fighters appeared to take a breather. Spectators looked for any signs of advantage; some pointing to discoloring on Choynski's left side. A two-and-a-half-inch mark branded his side, and onlookers speculated between rounds whether it was from a punch or his brief roll on the boards.

Choynski showed no sign of pain or discomfort.

In the fourth round, Corbett and Choynski resumed their furious pace to the joyous shouts of ringsiders. The exchanges were vicious. Then, Corbett unleashed a powerful right that caught the rushing Choynski on the top of the head.

The collision caused time to seemingly freeze.

In a blink, time sped up. Corbett heard the roar of the crowd and the pain searing in his right hand. The punch knocked his right thumb out of joint.[427]

From Choynski's corner, Dempsey instructed his fighter to back off and move. Choynski went into a defensive mode, clearly unaware Corbett had severely injured his right hand.

Corbett, meanwhile, cleverly worked Choynski around the ring with his stinging jab. At times he would feint with his right, but only as a decoy. He didn't want Choynski to realize he was maimed.[428]

Instead of bull-rushing Corbett, Choynski tried to lure him in. He led with his left shoulder, cast his eyes downward, and cocked his right "in a threatening manner."[429]

A tension hung in the air.

Suddenly, a voice rang out from the back of the loft: "Cops!"[430]

* * *

The lookout recognized the man riding down the road in a fast gallop — Sheriff John E. Healy. Panic spread throughout the crowd. Many bolted down the stairway to escape. A few dignitaries even leapt from two small barn windows and ran, looking of course, most undignified in the process.[431]

Hogan tried to restore calm.

"Boys, back to your corners," he loudly commanded. "This contest is postponed."[432]

Hogan then added with reassurance, "Gentleman, stay where you are. There is nothing to be afraid of."[433]

Moments passed before the six-foot-six-inch Healy shoved the lookout at the barn door aside. His authoritative voice boomed loudly: "I'm the sheriff of Marin County."[434]

Healy mumbled something as he climbed the narrow stairs. If he hadn't previously known the old Austin place, he might have rode past the front gate. Instead, he stopped and that's when he noticed some peculiar marks in the dirt — carriage tracks that had been obviously wiped away with brush. He then recognized several vehicles he had seen at Callot's vineyard.[435]

Reaching the loft, Healy stopped to absorb the scene. No one said a word.

Healy walked toward the ring and glancing at Corbett, said, "Young man, put on your coat."[436]

One of Corbett's friends — apparently an acquaintance of Healy's — stepped up and said, "Sheriff Healy, allow me to introduce you to Mr. Corbett."[437]

Healy extended his scarred right hand, which perhaps suggested his own rugged past. The two men shook hands.[438]

"Boys," Healy said apologetically, "I thought the fight would be over by this time. I'm sorry to stop it; and if you will go over to the next county I'll sit in; but I have to stop it now that I'm here."[439]

Slowly, a disappointed crowd and principals started to disperse. A few men began the task of dismantling the ring.

Healy supposedly considered arresting the participants, but didn't think there was enough evidence to prosecute. Or at least that's what was told to *Marin Journal* editor in his hometown of San Rafael. Healy most likely wanted the episode finished, and probably meant it when he said he would even "sit in" if they resumed their tussle in a neighboring county.[440]

Either way the mill in Marin County had ended.

No one could say the same about Corbett and Choynski's grudge. The parties traveled back to San Rafael, and while en route, agreed to take Healy's advice. They would move to the next county of Sonoma, transporting everyone — as well as the ring — by railroad.[441]

The parties reached the San Rafael train station to find an even larger crowd. Word of the fight had apparently traveled faster than a telegraph wire, and the station was overrun with folks in search of the battleground.

An hour passed as they weighed their options.

A couple of the backers — perhaps Ashe and Gunst – finally tried to procure an engine and car to carry the party north into Sonoma, but the railroad superintendent refused on the grounds he didn't want to be charged with "compounding a felony."[442]

Hogan then concluded the fight would be postponed for ten days. The decision was final.

At 3:25 p.m. — five hours after the two fighters stepped into the ring — Choynski and his team boarded a train for Sausalito, where they caught a ferry back to the city. Corbett and his handlers departed for his villa over the mountain in Tamalpais. Both were told to await the details for the next time and place of their battle.[443]

Corbett and Choynski were especially disappointed. For them, the bloodshed would have to wait.

Chapter Fourteen
Benicia

— —

The search for a new battleground was not done in haste, but rather methodic thought. Corbett and Choynski's financial backers and handlers were determined to avoid the same fiasco that unfolded in Fairfax.

This time, no sheriff or constable would be allowed to "spoil the fun."[444]

Associates were discreetly contacted, ideas discussed, and options weighed. Each detail had to be carefully considered to ensure Corbett and Choynski would finally be permitted to settle their grudge match once and for all. Too much was at stake — pride, honor, bragging rights, reputations, and above all, money. Lots of money rode on the outcome, most of which had been wagered by some of San Francisco's elite class.

Finally, on the night of June 4, a couple organizers visited Corbett's headquarters in Tamalpais. The instructions were simple: "Get ready to start."[445]

Few, if any words, were exchanged. Grainey and Corbett gathered a bundle of items, and stepped into an awaiting carriage outside the villa. The curtains were drawn.[446]

A long, bumpy ride ensued. They were eventually transferred to a ferry boat that carried them north across San Pablo Bay to Sonoma County, where they boarded a train as soon as they landed. No one bothered to give Corbett details about their final destination. Nor did he care to ask. He simply wanted to fight.

The long trip finally ended when the train came to a stop at a railroad station in neighboring Solano County. This, someone notified Corbett, was the end of the road — the site of battle. Weary from the journey, Corbett disembarked and read the first sign he saw, one hanging at the little depot: "Benicia, Cal."[447]

* * *

Fortunes and livelihoods flowed daily down the Carquinez Strait, a narrow tidal strait powered by the confluence of two great rivers — the Sacramento and San Joaquin. The two streams coarse through the mighty valleys that bear their name, drain into Suisun Bay and then down the Carquinez Strait. The waters of the strait then flow into San Pablo and San Francisco bays, passing through the "Golden Gate" and into the Pacific Ocean.[448]

The water route also carried the hopes and dreams of souls dependent on the shipments of grain, fruits, wines, fish, leather, wood, and every other imaginable good being produced in Northern California by 1889. In 1888 alone, more than 6.6 million pounds of salmon were packed and shipped along the Carquinez Strait to local and distant markets.[449]

The strait served as the lifeblood of countless Californians.

So perhaps it was with a touch of irony that the Carquinez Strait played a vital role in the Corbett-Choynski saga. Organizers determined the two fighters would clash on the north side of the strait in Benicia's Southampton Bay, some thirty miles from San Francisco.

Only this showdown would take place on a grain barge anchored in the bay, just out of the path of the powerful flowing strait. Organizers hoped by staging the fight on the water they would confuse authorities over the issue of legal jurisdiction, and if needed, pull up anchor for another locale.[450]

The plan sounded ingenious, but wasn't without precedents.

World Heavyweight Champion John L. Sullivan fought on a barge eight years earlier against John Flood, "The Bullshead Terror." Promoters towed the barge a few miles up the Hudson River, just out of the jurisdiction of the New York City Police. From the deck of the moonlit barge, Sullivan needed only twenty minutes to pummel Flood for the $1,000 purse in front of 400 spectators.[451]

Choynski and Corbett's camps desired a similar outcome.

A lot of factors came together to make the final battle site a reality, and Lawlor essentially devised the plan. For starters, Tom Williams — the horseman and Corbett's wealthy backer — offered the use of his barge, the *Excell*.[452]

Benicia served as a major port for the delivery of grain coming from California's rich inland valleys. Three of the largest grain warehouses on the Pacific Coast called Benicia home. Vast amounts of the grain exports ended up in Europe, as well as Australia and South America. The great depth of water in the strait and the railroad lines were so close in proximity, that mammoth loads of grain could be discharged from the cars on one side, while being loaded onto ships from doors on the other side.[453]

Williams in all likelihood knew the Benicia port and its people intimately.

Hall McAllister, Jr., Corbett's newfound friend from Tamalpais, might have also played an important role in the selection of Benicia as the chosen site for the private mill. McAllister's family wielded great influence in San Francisco and Marin County, and his uncle, Col. Julian McAllister, served as commander of Benicia's U.S. Army Arsenal from 1860 to 1886.

In short, the McAllisters enjoyed the company of equally influential friends.

Regardless, Benicia appeared to be the unlikeliest of choices for an illegal prizefight, which might have been the attraction.

Unlike Peter Austin's abandoned farm outside Fairfax, Benicia didn't exactly fit the bill as a secluded outpost in a densely wooded countryside.

While home to only 3,000 souls, Benicia sat perched in a highly visible locale along the Carquinez Strait — a sort of miniature San Francisco. The township, founded in 1847, actually served as California's state capital for a short time (1853-1854) and featured a thirty-four-acre arsenal with sixteen large stone and brick buildings; four celebrated tanneries; and several hotels, including the elegant Bishop House, which commanded a view of the water and distant Mount Diablo from a lofty hilltop. The two-story Bishop House offered sixty well-furnished rooms with running water, two dining rooms, a bar, barber shop, bathroom, laundry, and stable.[454]

A number of industrial buildings were also clustered on the west end of town on the shoreline of Southampton Bay. Passengers along the strait could see the Pacific Cement Works, a 400-foot flour mill, and the Turner Shipyard, where majestic ships were built on ways blasted from bedrock and extended some 200 feet into the water. Rocks and cement blocks were used to support the wooden superstructures during construction. A two-story, wood-frame sawmill and mold loft was the principal building on the shipyard, where 154 vessels were built between 1885 and 1908. During that time, the shipyard launched brigantines, schooners, stern-wheelers, tugs, and yachts.[455]

At times the shipyard employed as many as fifty workers, many of whom stayed at the Erickson Hotel outside the yard's front gate.[456]

Corbett spent his only night in Benicia at the home of its founder, Lansing B. Mizner, an attorney and former president of the California State Senate. Mizner and his wife raised seven children in the home, but he was presently serving as President Benjamin Harrison's Envoy Extraordinary and Minister Plenipotentiary to the Central American states at the time of Cor-

The Mizner home — Benicia's most prominent residence — is where Corbett stayed the night before his famous showdown with Choynski. *Courtesy Benicia Historical Museum*

bett's arrival.[457]

A carriage driver escorted Corbett and his party from the train station to the Mizner home, a dwelling originally shipped around the Cape Horn decades earlier. Upon his arrival, Corbett found a sturdy two-story house with a charming porch and a few quirky additions. A picket fence framed the corner residence, and several of the Mizner children warmly welcomed the pugilist to Benicia.[458]

Corbett was then shown to an adjoining cottage on the property.[459]

"Turn in now, Jim," a friend said, "and get a good night's rest."[460]

Corbett finally inquired, "What's the whole idea?"[461]

Someone pointed in the general direction of the water, explaining how he would fight Choynski the next morning on a barge presently anchored in the bay. Corbett's swollen right hand still throbbed with pain from whacking Choynski's skull during their brief skirmish in Fairfax. Convinced he had a break, Corbett turned to Grainey and said, "I hope Choynski and his trainers don't discover this broken hand."[462]

"Jack Dempsey has already found out about it and told Choynski," Grainey replied. "Do you want me to call off the fight?"[463]

"No," Corbett answered. "I can whip Choynski with one hand."[464]

Somewhere in Benicia that night — perhaps at one of the town's luxurious hotels — Choynski and his handlers arrived after nightfall. Choynski immediately removed to his room to sleep.

"I went to bed early, but not to sleep, for I kept thinking of the fight," Choynski recalled. "I was working out a plan to beat Corbett."[465]

Corbett also spent a restless night.

Nervously, he tossed and turned in a strange bed, thinking of the upcoming battle and his injured right hand. The gravity of the moment weighed on his mind; the eve of "the most important event" of his young life.

Members of his entourage milled around the porch outside his open window, "whispering in undertones" about Corbett's chances against the slugging Choynski. The chatter continued into the night, and Corbett struggled to fall asleep.[466]

In the distance, on the bay, carpenters like W.J. Fitzpatrick — one of Benicia's pioneer hotel keepers — hammered away by lantern to construct the ring flooring and posts on the deck of the barge. They worked through the night, probably curious about what might transpire at sunrise.[467]

Corbett and Choynski undoubtedly harbored similar thoughts, but unlike the carpenters, they understood the grim reality of what awaited them.

"The grudge had not been satisfied," Choynski said. "Not enough blood had been spilled."[468]

Chapter Fifteen
Dawn Of Battle

— —

A blood feud makes good theatre.

Even San Francisco's elite, endowed by a sense of privilege and self-righteousness, enjoyed an occasional peek into the darker realm of civilization. Nowhere could society's cream indulge in that forbidden zone more than in the shadowy world of prizefighting, where a boxing match sometime ventured beyond the doors of a respectable athletic club.

On those scandalous occasions, socialites and urban dandies were often lured by the adventure. Illegal fights to the finish provided that rare opportunity to witness a felony in progress, while discreetly dodging police. If the combatants were bitter rivals, the attraction sounded even greater.

The Corbett-Choynski grudge match offered all the enticing elements of just such a moral drama.

So when an exclusive group of invited guests reached the San Francisco wharf at 1:30 a.m. on June 5 to board the tugboat *Sea Queen* for Benicia, no one should have been surprised by what they found. Ardent fight fans emerged from all corners of the wharf, determined to join the excursion and witness the ballyhooed fight without an invite.[469]

Word leaked a day earlier that Hogan had ordered the two fighters to be ready Wednesday, June 5, to resume their battle. Based on the rumor, many hoped to latch on to the invited party for a free ride.

Some tried to take matters into their own hands by attempting to stow away on the tug. Numerous interlopers were identified to the captain, who ordered them off the boat. The safe removal of the unwanted guests caused some delay due to the fear some might try to jump back ashore and instead end up drowning at the pier.[470]

Drifters and pedestrians also soon appeared on the scene to gaze at the early-morning spectacle. The neighborhood suddenly sprang to life.

Amid the commotion, Jack Dempsey calmly strode onto the *Sea Queen.* He was the last passenger to board.

The captain of the *Sea Queen* finally pulled away from the dock at 2 a.m., but not after a half dozen persistent ring-goers jumped safely aboard in the cover of darkness. There were some 100 passengers.[471]

Nearby, another thirty-five sports chartered the tugboat *Joseph H. Redmond,* but were uncertain as to the exact location of

The tugboat *Sea Queen*, which carried Choynski to Benicia June 5, 1889, was still in operation thirty-six years after the legendary fight. *Courtesy San Francisco Maritime National Historical Park, W.A. Scott Collection*

the battle site. For the next several hours, the *Redmond* chased the *Sea Queen* across the San Francisco and San Pablo bays. State Senator Phil J. Crimmins, R-San Francisco; and Jimmy Kenney, clerk of San Francisco's Police Court No. 1, were among those on board.[472]

The *Sea Queen* also carried a number of notable figures, not the least of which was the world champion Dempsey. In that morning's *San Francisco Morning Call* — an edition no one on board had seen — Dempsey was quoted as saying Choynski had over trained for the mill in Fairfax, and noted how he had "gone stale" by fight time.

Passengers surely couldn't resist asking Dempsey about his thoughts on Choynski's chances this time around.

Another passenger of note was Marin County Sheriff John E. Healy, a man already well acquainted with the two fighters. Healy told them he would "sit in" on their fight if they moved to a neighboring county, and he was apparently a man of his word.[473]

Men probably asked Healy to recount how he stopped the last fight at Austin's barn.

A biting, cold wind hit the passengers as the tugboat plowed steadily through the choppy waters. Flynn remembered the weather being "cheerless, and the damp sea breeze was unusually penetrating." A number of men passed the time visiting while enjoying their hot coffee and ham and egg sandwiches. Others, meanwhile, spent the trip in misery, nauseous from sea sickness and puking overboard.[474]

These were signs of events to come.

* * *

The sun lifted on the eastern horizon when Corbett's friends entered his room at the Mizner cottage in Benicia.

"Get up, Jim, we've just got time to get breakfast before the journey to the battlefield begins," one friend said.[475]

Still groggy from a sleepless night, Corbett rose and dressed. A few minutes passed, and the friend informed Corbett he had bad news: "Doesn't look as if we're going to have breakfast, Jim."[476]

"Why not?" Corbett asked.[477]

"There's no stove in this place."[478]

"Did the fellows bring anything to eat?" Corbett inquired.[479]

"Yes, one of the fellows has a steak in his pocket and another one has some bread and crackers," the friend replied.[480]

"We're all right then," Corbett concluded. "We'll build a bonfire and cook the steak."[481]

William "Forty" Keneally did the honors, cooking the steak over an open fire in an adjacent field. Keneally earned his nickname because he was a fast sprinter, and horses were considered fast then if they could run a race in two minutes and forty seconds.[482]

Keneally grew up with Corbett, and probably wanted to witness his friend thrash Choynski as much as any of his supporters. Keneally harbored great bitterness toward Choynski, who knocked him out nineteen months earlier and had yet to give him a rematch. Making matters worse, local fight fans loved to recall the fight because it was such a thrilling slugfest.[483]

Keneally figured revenge was now in Corbett's hands.

Corbett clearly understood Keneally's feelings about Choynski, and thought he would have a little fun with his pal. At the moment of departure, Corbett stood before his friends and said solemnly, "Someone must stay here and watch the house until we get back — someone that I can trust."[484]

He then looked squarely at Keneally.

"'Forty,' you're the man," Corbett said firmly. "You stay here and watch this house until the fight is over."[485]

Keneally's eyes bulged from disappointment and panic. He became excited, and whenever that happened, he stuttered. Still chewing on mouth full of bread, Keneally begged his friend to reconsider, exclaiming, "J-J-J–Jim, I-I–I'm a f-f–friend of yours, b-b-b–but I'd c-c–cut my r-r–right arm off b-b-b–before I'd m-m–miss this f-f-f–fight!"[486]

Everyone shared in a hardy laugh before Corbett told Keneally he was only kidding. Relieved, Keneally couldn't stop grinning. The gang soon boarded buggies and buckboard wagon for the shoreline.

Silence replaced the laughter.

* * *

The *Sea Queen* chugged into the Carquinez Strait, where passengers first caught a glimpse of two long grain barges anchored in Southampton Bay. On one barge they could already see the silhouettes of men moving about the deck — carpenters who had worked through the night to erect the ring.[487]

The *Joseph H. Redmond* followed close behind.

By 2:40 a.m. — some two hours and forty minutes after leaving San Francisco — the *Sea Queen* turned into the bay at a headland known as Dillon's Point. Several stern-wheel river steamers were also anchored in the cove where the Turner Shipyard stood prominently to the east. Looking west of the shipyard, around a bend in the cove, one could see a sprawling marsh.[488]

Dillon's Point extended along the western rim of the cove with its rocky terrain distinctively jutting into the strait like the head of a mammoth sperm whale. The tidal flat was named after its owner Patrick W. Dillon, an Irish immigrant who first leased the property in 1851 to operate a sandstone quarry. Later, he built a kiln and began producing clay bricks. His three-story ranch house sat perched atop the peninsula, overlooking the bay.[489]

A short distance away, in the middle of the bay, floated the gently teetering barge where the showdown would take place. Captains for the *Sea Queen* and *Joseph H. Redmond* tried to nestle alongside the barge, but instead became mired in the mud. Passengers were then transported to the barge in small boats.[490]

The process proved hazardous.

Men carelessly leapt from the decks of the tug into the frail vessels below. The first craft held seven men, of whom insurance man Harry Kelley became the first to climb aboard the barge safely.[491]

A few moments later the *Joseph H. Redmond* started the same process. Eleven men crowded into a boat and despite a steady leak, reached the side of the barge. That's when disaster struck. All eleven men stood up simultaneously, causing the small boat to capsize. Each man plunged into the chilly water.[492]

Senator Crimmins and Officer Kenney were among those flailing in the water. Kenney didn't know how to swim.[493]

For a brief moment, someone actually stood on Crimmins shoulders as he struggled to reach the surface. He resurfaced and, along with Austin Fitzgerald, saved Kenney from drowning.[494]

One by one all eleven of the soaked spectators were safely plucked from the icy waters. They were immediately taken into the barge's pilot house so they could strip their wet clothes and begin drying off. Despite shaking from the cold, their spirits remained high.

Kenney even joked how he was glad no one had access to a telephone, or otherwise his family might receive the false report that he had drowned.[495]

A number of salmon vessels and smaller skiffs now began appearing on the bay to watch the coming mill. John Carty, a seventeen-year-old apprentice at the Turner Shipyard, skipped work to see the fight with his pal, Tom Connelly. He joined others — perhaps fifty in all — who sat drifting on skiffs in the bay to await the commencement of action.[496]

Several local residents tried to mount the deck of the barge, including a teenage Wilson Mizner — the son of Colonel Lansing Mizner. He instead received a badly bruised hand after being discouraged from boarding the overcrowded barge by a wielded boathook.

Clearly, the crowd was growing restless.

Someone then spotted a hack and buggies hurrying down the road along the shoreline, and the crowd of 234 feared the Solano County sheriff might be in town to halt the match. All fears quickly dissipated when it was learned that the hack and buggies carried Corbett and his handlers.[498]

Corbett and his entourage loaded into rowboats. The group represented Corbett's inner-circle, including Billy Delaney; Jim Carr, a local boxer; Frank and Harry Corbett, his brothers; Sol Bloom, an up-and-coming entertainment entrepreneur; Eugene Van Court, the Olympic Club member who introduced him to Delaney; Ashe; Lawlor; and the anxious Keneally.[499]

Bloom, nineteen, wanted to see the fight so badly he postponed a trip to New York and the World's Fair in Paris a few days. He later mused, "Officially the site . . . was unknown, but every man within a hundred miles of San Francisco, including the police, could have given detailed instructions about getting to the place."[500]

Now they rowed toward a barge anchored in plain view.

As they rowed, one member of the party took notice of the unusual weather: "Though early in the morning, it already gave promise of being a blistering hot day."[501]

Van Court, one of Corbett's closest friends, bluntly addressed the business at hand. He asked, "Jim, do you think you can stand a licking. You only have one hand, you know, and you're certainly going to take a lacing, even if you win."[502]

In a rare moment, in the comfort of friends, Corbett reflected on his thoughts aloud. He spoke from his heart, abandoning the usual confident or boastful armor he usually displayed.

"Gene," Corbett said calmly, "I don't know myself whether I can take a licking or not; I never got a really good licking and don't know how I'll act under fire, but I hope to find that out today."[503]

Corbett turned his eyes toward the barge. He noticed several hundred spectators crowded around the newly constructed ring, but was especially struck by the image of the pilot house. The two-level, box structure sat atop stilt-like beams in the middle of the long, flat deck. A comparison instantly popped into his mind; one he couldn't shake.

The pilot house reminded him of a hangman's gallows.[504]

Chapter Sixteen

Controversy

— —

Everyone told a different version of what happened next. Depending on where one's loyalties rested, themes ranged from apologetic and dismissive to cynical and accusatory.

A fully clothed Choynski reached the barge first at 6 a.m. sharp, along with Australian middleweight Paddy Gorman, Grainey, Hogan, and two gentlemen from Benicia, William Mizner and Ed Hoyt. Dempsey joined the others as they immediately ascended the wheelhouse, where Choynski started to dress into his boxing attire.[505]

Choynski's presence alone caused a stir on deck.

Feeling strong, Choynski envisioned the fight in his mind, convinced he had devised a solid plan. He would later say, "I thought I knew exactly what I was going to do."[506]

This time there would be no mystery for either fighter. By now they had already met twice in the ring, and had experienced each other's speed and habits firsthand, dating back to those stormy days as young teens brawling in the Corbett livery stable and then in the sand hills.

Corbett climbed aboard the deck of the barge ten minutes later with his large crew.

The buzz in the crowd grew louder as Corbett made his way to the newly constructed ring. A few offered words of encouragement, although they did so in orderly fashion. The tension began to mount with the anticipation punches would soon be exchanged.

Corbett, who rested for several minutes on an adjacent steamer 100 yards away, now stood relaxed in the ring, chatting with Hogan and his brothers. Carpenters built the ring aft of the wheelhouse, nailing new pine boards over the rough deck of the barge. Padded ring stakes from "a San Francisco club" were then mounted into place, and generous portions of rosin were strewn across the pine floor for better footing.[507]

Lastly, workers hoisted an old sail from the wheelhouse to shelter the fighters from the morning breeze, which one sporting hack described as "unusually raw and disagreeable." Sol Bloom also recalled how that early morning air hinted at weather to come. Even at fight time Bloom remembered being already "uncomfortably hot on board."[508]

The scene became more uncomfortable moments later.

Choynski climbed down from the lofty wheelhouse, donning his usual black. A sportswriter from the *San Francisco Morning Call* — one of four city newspapers to cover the fight — noted how Choynski appeared to "have grown heavier" since the termination of Fairfax fight when he ducked into the ring. He reportedly weighed 172 pounds, his muscular shoulders, arms and chest standing in stark difference to his "spidery" legs.[509]

Corbett immediately removed his street clothes, revealing a pair of pink tights, low running shoes and white socks. He weighed a reported 180 pounds, and as usual, appeared in top-notch condition with "shapely and sturdy lower limbs." A bandage of white linen could be seen covering his right wrist, while he also donned a pair of two-ounce gloves as required by the articles of agreement.[510]

The two fighters exchanged curt greetings.[511]

Instinctively, the crowd closed in tightly around the ring, anticipating the opening bell. Just then Hogan discovered a problem — Choynski had no gloves.

A heated argument ensued.

Hogan had ordered both the fighters to care for their own gloves after the postponement in Marin County a week earlier. Now only one pair of gloves was on board. The referee looked perplexed.

Corbett strode across the ring to confront Choynski, asking tersely, "What's this? Where's your gloves?"[512]

"Left behind by mistake," Choynski answered matter-of-factly. One writer reported that Choynski "put the gloves in charge of a friend, who failed to reach the place of battle" — a plausible explanation. But years later McGrath would claim Choynski's gloves were stolen by a "souvenir hunter."[513]

Partisans of Corbett weren't buying any of the stories.

One Corbett supporter cried, "Aw, Jim, they threw the gloves in the bay!"[514]

Naturally, Corbett's damaged right hand led his handlers to believe this was nothing more than a ploy to entice their man into fighting with bare knuckles. They blamed the crafty Grainey for devising the sinister plan. San Francisco's ardent ring fans generally believed this style of bare-knuckle fighting — or London Prize Ring Rules — would favor the bullish, heavy-hitting Choynski.

Or at least that was the general consensus.

Corbett's representatives vehemently protested. Lawlor, for one, declared that he would claim the fight and stakes for Corbett. He argued on the basis of the signed articles.[515]

An animated Dempsey now interceded on Choynski's behalf. He had heard enough hypocrisy and hot air from the Corbett camp. Dempsey argued that if they wanted to stick to technicalities, then the bout should be postponed on the basis that the articles also only allowed ten men to a side to witness the fight.[516]

Dempsey poignantly motioned at the more than 230 fans engulfing the ring.

Lawlor shut up.

Shouts then arose for a bare-knuckle fight from some of the more blood-thirsty fans in the crowd. Dempsey shook his head in disgust, adding, "We don't want to go to prison, do we?"[517]

"Jim," Hogan said to Corbett, "you don't want this fight without fighting for it, do you?"[518]

"That's right, I don't," Corbett snapped. "I'll keep these gloves on and let him fight with his bare knuckles."[519]

In reality Corbett wasn't about to remove his gloves, knowing they offered at least some protection for the broken knuckles on his right hand.

Dempsey then asked if anyone in the crowd could lend Choynski a pair of ordinary driving gloves. One man offered his, a pair of heavy, red "dog-skin driving gloves." Dempsey cut the holes from the tips of the fingers, and handed the gloves to Hogan.[520]

By then Corbett started to become agitated with the whole debate.

"I'm getting cold," he snapped. "I will waive the claim."[521]

Hogan handed the skin-tight gloves to Choynski, stating, "Corbett waives all claims to money and fight, and you must take these gloves to fight with." The referee announced one stipulation: If, at any point during the fight, Corbett wants to switch to skin-tight gloves, he may do so freely.[522]

Hogan's voice turned commanding.

"It was claimed that the last time the men met I showed favor to one man," he said sternly. "This I deny, and I have come here to see fair play, and I will now make the following rule, in addition to the Marquess of Queensberry, which I will strictly follow, and that is, in case of a clinch, I will order the men to break away, which they must do and step back one pace and clear."[523]

Corbett chimed in, "If men hit in clinch, how about that?!"[524]

"After a caution and upon repetition," Hogan answered, "I will call it a foul."[525]

Satisfied, Corbett firmly stated, "All right."[526]

Finally, 6:48 a.m., the fighters were ordered to shake hands and get ready for the opening bell. Again, the fans closed in tightly around the ring with their primal senses heightened. The fighters were now completely hemmed in by four walls of humanity, eager to see a war.[527]

Choynski and Corbett gave them something more.

Chapter Seventeen
A Grim Business
—— ——

Southampton Bay, Benicia, California: June 5, 1889

No one could speak as Corbett and Choynski toed the scratch in the middle of the makeshift ring.

Referee Patsy Hogan appeared commanding, yet tense as he awaited the opening bell. Fans nudged closer, hanging on the ring in breathless anticipation. Hearts pounded. Palms sweated. All eyes were fixed on the two combatants.

For all the heated debates, derogatory comments, boastful bets, and in some cases even fistfights, no one said a word. Only the sound of the waves sloshing against the side of the barge broke the silence.

Strangely, two of the calmest men on board were the fighters themselves.

Choynski, with his brooding eyes stalking Corbett, stepped confidently to the scratch. Bent to one side, he stood with his fists held high and his weight leaning heavily on his right leg.[528]

Corbett stood erect, balanced, calm, and cool as usual. He stared downward at his crouching rival.[529]

The hunters stood poised for battle. Then the timekeeper rang a bell.

Both fighters instinctively began to circle. Choynski fired the first shot — a right that glanced off the left side of Corbett's ribcage. Corbett responded by flicking two jabs; one striking the chest and the other the shoulder with no effect.

Cautiously, they studied one another while moving lively

about the pine flooring. Corbett showed his advanced rhythmic agility, dancing on his toes and floating around the ring. Moments later, he shot two more jabs and Choynski parried both neatly before the call for time.

"It's not right!" cried Tom Williams, a Corbett supporter and the barge's owner. "They ought to get out and go it with bare knuckles!"[530]

Dempsey lashed out, "Oh, no . . ."[531]

Williams didn't realize a bare-knuckle brawl was the last thing Corbett wanted, as well. Corbett planned to protect his damaged right hand as much as possible, and he didn't need one of his own wealthy boosters inciting the crowd.

Fortunately, no one listened.[532]

Round two opened with Choynski aggressively forcing the fight. He pumped a left jab that caught Corbett on the face, and followed with a right that fell short. Corbett countered with his own jab, only to have Choynski duck clear of the punch. In that moment, however, Choynski left himself open to a right uppercut.

Corbett froze.

"Oh, oh!" yelled Corbett partisans, winching from the missed opportunity.[533]

Corbett clearly appeared hesitant to throw his right, but didn't have time to dwell on his slip. The two fighters were soon embraced in a clinch.

Hogan yelled, "Break!"[534]

Corbett, ever suspicious of Choynski's trickery, repeated the command with his own stern voice: "Break!"[535]

Choynski and Corbett broke away cleanly, prompting the first outburst of cheers from the crowded barge.

Choynski dug another solid right into Corbett's ribs, taking a small piece of skin in the process. Each of Choynski's skintight gloves featured three heavy seams that extended across the back of the hand, and folded over the knuckles. Behind

Choynski's power, the gloves left red welts with nearly every punch.

Corbett answered Choynski with two snapping jabs to the face at the call of time.

The two fighters were clearly ready to open up.

Choynski again opened the round as the aggressor. He fired off a shot at Corbett, who quickly jumped back a safe distance, grinned and countered with a left. Like Corbett, Choynski swiftly backed up to avoid the blow, planting himself against the ropes.

Corbett instantly pursued and launched a smashing left to Choynski's midsection, dropping him to the pine boards. The knockdown triggered a wild outburst of cheers from Corbett's contingent, but Choynski jumped to his feet in an instant smiling.[536]

Overanxious, Corbett rushed in and fell short with a left as Choynski kept his distance. Corbett followed closely, and finally Choynski responded with a left-right combination that hit nothing but air. Corbett continued to press forward until the two boxers stood their ground in unison and let fly a savage flurry of punches.

"The crowd was deathly still," Choynski recalled later. "There wasn't much sound — only the sloshing of the water and the terrific impact of gloves. It was grim business."[537]

During the exchange Choynski absorbed a left-right combination on the jaw. He stepped back, grimacing and bleeding from the mouth. His lips already showed signs of swelling.

Corbett, who sported a slight abrasion on the left cheek, had drawn first blood in a round he dominated. Yet, secretly, Corbett was screaming inside with pain. During the exchange, Corbett shot a left toward Choynski's chin. Choynski shifted slightly at the last second, and the punch ricocheted off his forehead.

A sharp pain rushed from Corbett's left hand — one he would later learn suffered broken knuckles on his third and little fingers.[538]

Corbett walked to his corner with the sobering realization that he now had broken knuckles in both hands. As he sat on his chair he stared across the ring at a lion-hearted foe who would never give an inch. He stared grimly at adversity.

The sun began to burn down on the deck of the barge. For Corbett, it surely felt like Hell.

Chapter Eighteen
Slaughterhouse

— —

A sense of urgency now weighed heavily on Corbett. He had no idea how long he could continue to use his left hand with any effectiveness, only that he would throw it until he could no longer raise his hands.

The psychological war would soon become as important as the physical one.

Neither fighter wanted to show a chink in their armor. So both men answered the fourth round with a cocksure smile. Corbett did so while trying to camouflage the throbbing pain in his left hand; Choynski with fresh blood staining his puffy lips.

Corbett immediately opened on the attack by pumping his newly damaged left. The punch missed its mark, and Choynski countered with a pounding right to the ribs and a left that whizzed dangerously close to Corbett's jaw.

Corbett tagged Choynski a moment later with a left to the stomach and doubled with a straight left to the mouth — a punch that again brought blood streaming down his rival's chin. Each time Corbett landed his left, he tried not to wince. The act became more difficult with each passing minute.

At one point Corbett caught Choynski with a right, further damaging his already maimed thumb. Despite the handicaps, Corbett's fast and deadly accurate left had his ringside supporters clamoring for more bets between rounds. But there were few takers.[539]

Round five opened with a game Choynski "rollicking" about the ring, working Corbett's body with some punishing rights. The gloves — Corbett would painfully recall — "cut like razors."[540]

Corbett responded with the one weapon that had never failed him in previous fights, especially those rough-and-tumble matches in the seedy saloons of the Barbary Coast. He leaned on his superior speed.

Ringside observers — and the fighters themselves, for that matter — generally agreed on two points: Choynski punched harder and Corbett possessed the quicker hands. Secretly, Corbett conceded Choynski was "physically stronger" and "hit harder," but also realized he had his rival "buffaloed on speed." Corbett's assessment was both honest and accurate.[541]

Corbett depended greatly on his quickness, flicking his left with blinding speed. He spent most of the fifth round dodging Choynski's mighty right, while countering his stinging lefts to the nose and jaw. The punch landed repeatedly. The first solid left thrown by Corbett caught Choynski flush on the nose, starting another deluge of blood down his neck and chest.[542]

The punches seemed to hurt Corbett as much as Choynski. Winching with each blow, Corbett painfully concluded the broken knuckles in his left hand could no longer absorb the force of a straight punch. Intentionally, if not instinctively, Corbett tried to put the brunt of each left on his forefinger, and began hooking his punches with great success.

Corbett, unknowingly, had created boxing's left hook.[543]

* * *

The sixth round turned vicious.

Both boxers landed punches "savagely," according to one ringside reporter. The work was hot and heavy. Corbett connected on a counter punch that again drew blood from Choynski's swelling mouth. Choynski retaliated with a left-hander that clipped Corbett's right ear.[544]

By now, both men began bantering at one another as if alone on the teetering barge.

Choynski pushed a left toward Corbett's head, raking it across his face, perhaps out of desperation or frustration.

"That was pretty light," Corbett replied sarcastically. He then fired his own left, tagging Choynski on the jaw.[545]

Choynski never gave an inch. He instead returned the sarcasm, saying, "both together now." On cue, both fighters shot out a left with no effect.[546]

The showmanship continued.

With flasks of whiskey being flashed freely at ringside, Corbett chirped, "Joe, you have got your eye on that bottle."[547]

Choynski responded with a ferocious right to Corbett's ribs, adding in a playful taunt, "Don't get rattled, Jim."[548]

The call of "Time!" momentarily halted their conversation.

Between rounds Choynski leaned back in his corner, puffing hard and bleeding from the nose and mouth. He struggled to breath. Corbett's steady diet of left jabs and hooks had started to take its toll. Graney doused Choynski generously with buckets of salt water drawn by a bystander over the side of the barge.[549]

Dempsey, meanwhile, urged Choynski to fight cautiously against his faster foe. He had been drumming that advice into Choynski since the end of the first round, but the slugging candy-puller wasn't completely sold on the game plan.[550]

By the seventh round, red marks checkered Corbett's ribs and shoulders from Choynski's powerful blows. Yet Corbett clearly looked like the stronger of the two fighters as he stepped to the scratch, and according to one reporter, even "an undoubted winner."[551]

The two fighters opened the round where they had stopped.

"They passed a few pleasantries, as they had done before," one reporter noted, "but someone in the crowd objected."[552]

"Quit yer chinnin'," one spectator demanded.[553]

"Let 'em talk," a friend of Corbett's replied. "They haven't seen each other for a long time."[554]

The wisecracks soon gave way to a bloodbath.

Choynski launched a wild left well over the head of a ducking Corbett, spinning out of control as a consequence. Before Choynski could catch his balance, Corbett tagged him twice with lefts. He finished the round with a parting left uppercut to Choynski's nose, bringing forth another stream of blood.

Perhaps even more importantly, Choynski failed to land a single punch in three minutes of fighting.[555]

Now, realizing Choynski was being diced up by Corbett's lefts, Graney began urging his fighter to press the action. Choynski charged out of his corner for the eighth round, determined to punish Corbett. But Corbett proved elusive, bobbing and weaving clear of any damaging blows. He displayed the ring generalship that had earned him a reputation at the swank Olympic Club, where youngsters flocked in great numbers to learn scientific boxing skills from "Professor" Corbett.

The harder Choynski charged, the harder Corbett planted his right foot and drove another jab into his face. One such jab busted Choynski in the nose, prompting clots of blood to drop freely. This time the blood began to splatter the freshly laid pine boards.

Choynski ignored the sight of his own blood.

But when Choynski tried to answer with his own left, Corbett slipped the punch and connected with a left to the gut, sending his bloody opponent to the floor. Choynski, who may have actually slipped on his own blood, again bounced to his feet almost instantaneously.

Corbett effectively crowded Choynski for the remainder of the round, and wore the blood of his foe as proof.[556]

The ring looked like a slaughterhouse by the start of the ninth round.

Blood had completely soaked up the resin scattered on the ring floor prior to the opening bell. The fighters themselves were equally covered in crimson. Corbett's pink tights were now unrecognizable, and his gloves looked as if they had been dipped in blood.

Choynski's rugged good looks had vanished. His clean, narrow cheekbones and chiseled jawline were buried beneath bruises, cuts, and swelling. His thin lips were ballooned, cut, and bloody. If that weren't enough, Choynski had also endured the stinging pain from the ill-advised buckets of salt water being doused on his open wounds.

Corbett was hardly free of punishment. Cuts and red welts covered his face, shoulders and chest, and while he wasn't a bleeder like Choynski, he was being "busted up" internally by Choynski's strong rights. Corbett's cheekbone started to show signs of swelling around the left eye.[557]

Delaney watched in awe as the two fighters toed the scratch for the ninth round.

"With murderous little gloves they cut one another into ribbons," Delaney recalled decades later, "but instead of slowing up the loss of blood seemed to only spur them on and make them more vicious."[558]

Clots of blood made the ring floor extremely slippery by the time the two fighters squared off in the ninth round. Corbett, who had almost exclusively used his left hand, again hit his target with a left to Choynski's stomach and a hook to his ear. The punch sent Choynski reeling backward, and down to one knee.

Corbett fans again cheered wildly.

Covered in a mask of blood, Choynski once again climbed to his feet. Now, for the first time in the fight, he avoided Corbett for the remainder of the round. One reporter noted how Choynski appeared "very wary of his opponent after this, and seldom got to within hitting distance."[559]

The pride of San Francisco's Jewish community was clearly hurt.

* * *

Hard-core fight fans were repulsed by the blood.

Choynski looked dreadful as he climbed from his corner for the tenth round. Salt water dripped from his face, exposing excessively swollen cheeks and a blackened right eye that was rapidly closing.[560]

Spectators who so lustily wanted to witness a bloody, epic battle were now turning away in disgust. W.J. Fitzpatrick — the carpenter and local hotel owner — for one boarded a skiff and left the barge.

"Few, if any, watched the fight all the way through, because there is a limit even to the brutality of human beings," Fitzpatrick said. "The fight was so absolutely brutal that few men could watch it through. Many turned their faces away from the ring and gazed out over the peaceful water. I left in disgust . . ."[561]

The fighters, meanwhile, also dealt with the unseen brutality of their ring war. During the tenth round, Corbett first began to realize he had chosen to wear the wrong type of shoe for the occasion. He selected a rubber-soled pair used often on gymnasium floors, thinking it would be the perfect fit for the deck of a barge.

Corbett was now paying for his mistake. The extreme heat pounding down on the hard deck and the slick footing from the blood caused him to slide around in his shoes, leaving two painful blisters on each foot.[562]

Despite the hellish conditions, neither fighter showed any signs of quit.

Choynski opened the eleventh round with his nose already bleeding, and gamely took the fight to Corbett. He landed a vicious right to the ribs and another under the left eye, causing Corbett to throw his head back in an effort to cushion the blow.

By the end of the eleventh, Choynski's was choking on his own blood. He stalked the slick Corbett relentlessly while spitting mouthfuls of blood.[563]

Overhead, seagulls swooped down on the water, picking up discarded cigar butts and bloody cotton balls tossed overboard.[564]

For the next two rounds streams of blood poured down the bodies of both fighters, most of which emanated from Choynski's butchered nose and lips. They slipped often on the bloody pine boards, and even tumbled to the floor together in the twelfth and thirteenth rounds.[565]

Bloody and weak, Choynski continued to press forward despite eating Corbett's jabs and hooks from his now-numbed left hand. Choynski would take two, three or sometimes four punches to land one of his own, pausing only long enough to spit blood clots from his mouth.

He squinted from his one good eye.

Choynski miraculously forced the fight, and in the words of one ringside reporter, fought as "game as a lion."[566]

Unfortunately for Choynski, so did Corbett. Those who could still bear to watch were witnessing a prolific display of gameness and courage. Only years later could Corbett offer the proper perspective for what was taking place that day under a blistering California sun, saying, "We battled on with all the unrelenting do-or-die savagery of vigorous animal youth . . ."

Defeat was simply incomprehensible.

Chapter Nineteen
Shifting Tide
— —

Southampton Bay, Benicia, California: June 5, 1889

Referee Patsy Hogan searched his soul. By now, his conscience started to take hold, tugging at his heart and sanity. The gory sight of the two fighters, as well as the blood that stained his clothes, undoubtedly began to take its toll on the tough New Orleans native.

Hogan approached Corbett's corner with a proposition — one, he hoped, all parties would find reasonable and acceptable. He asked Corbett if he would be willing to have the fight declared a draw.

Squinting from a left eye nearly closed, Corbett wiped the blood from his mouth and firmly replied, "Not on your life."[568]

The fight would continue.

Choynski rushed from his corner at the bell, firing punches in a desperate fury about Corbett's face and momentarily dazed him. Corbett responded with stinging jabs, and for the first time since the opening bell, both fighters were bleeding profusely.

Sickened by the onrush of blood, some forty spectators turned away, and walked to the stern of the barge. They could endure no more.[569]

In the ring, Corbett gallantly continued to press the attack with two broken hands. He pummeled Choynski against the ropes, almost exclusively with an amazing array of left jabs and hooks.

Choynski appeared groggy and on the verge of being

knocked out as Corbett pelted him with punches. Still, as if subconsciously and blinded partially by blood, Choynski managed to return punches.[570]

Both men were painted in blood.

Then, Corbett landed a left and a severe pain shot up his arm. His body went limp, and his arms fell to his sides, dangling weakly. He nearly toppled over. Everything suddenly turned black.

For a second, Choynski hesitated. He must have thought Corbett was playing possum, but Corbett was clearly out on his feet.

Choynski pounced with renewed energy. For the first time, he sensed a knockout. He swarmed Corbett with a flurry of wild lefts and rights. Unable to see anything but blackness, Corbett instinctively rolled his head from side to side amid the torrent of punches, trying to "ride the blows."[571]

The world went silent.

Suddenly, the silence gave way to Delaney's desperate yell — a warning. The next thing Corbett remembered was a mighty blow — "the most terrific" of his career — smashing into his mouth. Fate then interceded in a strange way. Instead of putting Corbett to sleep, it jolted him back to a clearer state of mind.[572]

A second later the bell rang.

Corbett miraculously stood teetering and confused in the middle of the ring. Delaney quickly jumped through the ropes, grabbed his dazed fighter and led him back to his corner.[573]

Frantically, Delaney tried to revive Corbett for the next minute. Seconds before the next bell, Delaney asked, "Are you all right?"[574]

"Yes," Corbett replied, "I'll pull through."[575]

Not everyone was convinced.

Harry Corbett, Jim's older brother, abruptly left his brother's corner during the round as Choynski gamely pursued a knockout. Frank Corbett — the oldest of the ten Corbett children — noticed his brother's absence and frantically searched for him in the crowd.

Frank found Harry at the stern with his eyes staring down at the water, weeping. Grabbing his shoulder, a bewildered Frank asked what was wrong.

"I can't bear to see Jim lose!" Harry sobbed.[576]

"You're a hell of a fine sport," Frank responded furiously. "Now's the time when you ought to be on deck encouraging him."[577]

Enraged by shame, Frank walloped Harry in disgust. Suddenly, Harry and Frank were exchanging punches in a rough-and-tumble mix, but the cheering lured them back to their senses and to Jim's corner before the start of the fifteenth round.[578]

* * *

The buckets of salt water were ineffective by the start of the fifteenth round. No sooner were Corbett and Choynski rinsed in their corners, they were covered again by their own blood.

In the center of the ring they slowly circled the slick pine boards, looking for an opening, if not a miracle. Choynski continued to bleed heavily, and his spiny legs shook with each step.[579]

Corbett tried one of his nifty sidesteps, only to stumble and fall. His brain was clearly responding better than his battered and exhausted body. At this juncture, he struggled to merely hold his crimsoned gloves up.[580]

Then, out of the crowd, he heard the Lord's Prayer being recited in a Celtic accent:

Our Father in heaven,
Hallowed be Your name.
Your kingdom come.
Your will be done
On earth as it is in heaven.

Give us this day our daily bread.
And forgive us our debts,
As we forget our debtors.
And do not lead us into temptation,
But deliver us from the evil one.
For Yours is the kingdom
And the power and the glory forever.
Amen.

Corbett glanced out of the corner of one eye and noticed the voice belonged to a family friend and neighbor, a little Irishman named Tom Riley. The sight of Riley praying with all his might amused Corbett, who wondered how he even found his way onto the barge.

Riley continued to repeat the prayer over and over.[581]

Choynski then sprang at Corbett, flailing wildly at the pale Irishman. Corbett answered with his own bull rush, pushing Choynski to the ropes, where he arched his back far into the crowd. Corbett kept him pinned in that position by firing one punch after another only inches from the crowding spectators.

Again, Choynski responded with desperate punches. He refused to go down.

An exhausted Corbett then landed a straight left that stood Choynski upright at the bell. In unison, the two fighters staggered to their respective corners, weak and breathless.[582]

* * *

Graney shoved Dempsey away from Choynski.

"To blazes with this cautious stuff, Joe!" Graney bawled. "Corbett's cutting you to pieces at long range. Now, you go in there and fight him. Fight him! That's your game. The man's making mince-meat of you!"[583]

Inspired by Graney's words, Choynski drew on some unknown reservoir of strength for yet another rally.

"I plowed into Corbett and started throwing rights and lefts from every conceivable angle," Choynski recalled. "I think this amazed Jim. He thought I was all set for the killing . . . In the face of a terrific lacing, I was able to put a lot of steam into those punches."[584]

Corbett looked "terribly distressed" as a seemingly re-invigorated Choynski tried to out-muscle his foe. Corbett reeled about the ring, and then launched a counter-attack by crowding Choynski, but his punches were mostly weak and ineffective. Both men were greatly winded.

Choynski escaped Corbett's smothering tactics, only to slip on the clots of blood in his corner. Instead of bouncing to his feet, Choynski took a moment to catch his breath and rose at Hogan's count of six.[585]

Fans cheered hoarsely.

Amazingly, the two bloodied fighters again collided with a desperate exchange of haymakers. Choynski definitely levied the stronger blows, but Corbett continued to search for an edge. He found one by accident.

By now, the blazing sun hung high in the clear-blue sky, canvasing the deck of the barge with blinding rays. Those rays were especially unbearable for the two fighters whose eyes were nearly shut from severe swelling. Their facial cuts were also blistering from the sun's extreme morning heat, causing them to painfully squint for what little vision they could obtain.

Then Corbett noticed a shady spot — just enough for one man — caused by the shadow of the stilted wheelhouse, where men cheered from above. He backed into that tiny "oasis" as he called it, and like a good gunfighter, forced his adversary to face the glare of the sun.[586]

Corbett determined he would fight the remainder of the fight from that spot.

Wisely, Choynski recognized Corbett's new tactic. When the bell rang for the seventeenth round, Choynski bypassed the center of the ring for that one patch of shade. The two fighters would spend the remainder of the fight waging a war over that prized piece of ring real estate.

Choynski did so while gurgling from blood with every breath. Despite the flow of blood, Choynski still looked like the stronger fighter, and at the end of the seventeenth round, tagged Corbett with a left under his now-closed left eye.

One Choynski fan hoarsely yelled, "Good boy, Joe."[588]

Little Tom Riley continued to pray with all his might.

Chapter Twenty

Iron Man

— —

The last three rounds left both fighters dreadfully spent. Each time they answered the bell, they seemed to overcome great odds.

Delaney, for one, watched in wonderment.

"In the eighteenth Joe was bleeding like a stuck pig," he recalled. "His nose, mouth and eyes were pouring forth blood. Corbett himself was bleeding from the mouth and nose. Choynski was fading fast, but as Corbett's hands were broken at this time, he couldn't do much more than bull his way along."[589]

Corbett caught a second wind early in the round, and then caught Choynski on the nose with a smashing left — a blow that summoned a river of blood to the floor. This time the blood splattered ringside observers as Choynski moved about the ring, catching an occasional left from Corbett.

Gamely, Choynski spit out more mouthfuls of blood and stood his ground. Only now the powerful Choynski appeared as weak as ever, surely from the excessive loss of blood. He had been bleeding steadily since the third round.[590]

By the end of the nineteenth round, Dempsey concluded Choynski was finished. He leaned into Graney with a blood-soaked sponge in one hand and whispered.

Choynski couldn't hear what Dempsey was saying, but deduced the middleweight champion wanted him to quit.

Dempsey stood poised to throw in the sponge — a boxing gesture that would concede defeat.

Graney looked across the ring at a bloody and puffing Corbett. And then down at his own battered fighter. Both youngsters looked terribly tired. He wondered to himself, "Who is worst off?"[591]

Just then Choynski raised a blood-stained hand and pulled Graney's head down close to his. Cracking his bloodied and blistered lips, he spoke into Graney's ear, "Don't throw in the sponge, Ed! I'm not licked yet. I'm fighting my own fight now. Please don't stop it. Let him kill me, but don't say I quit!"[592]

The words jolted Graney, who swelled with pride. He realized he was in the presence of "an iron man of the ring."[593]

Graney told Dempsey that Choynski would go down fighting.

In doing so, he turned back toward Choynski, whose lips were bloated, cut, and throbbing in pain. Small pieces of his lips were even dangling loose.

Graney ordered Dempsey to hand him his knife. The bewildered Dempsey obliged, only to watch Graney trim the dangling flesh from Choynski's lips.[594]

Choynski never flinched.

Chapter Twenty-One
Desperate Courage

——

At some point that morning, beneath the searing sun and amid the pools of blood, Corbett and Choynski became living legends for those who beheld their bravery.

For each spectator, that magical moment probably varies in a fight filled with hundreds of defining moments. The ensuing rounds were as memorable as any, if for no other reason as the desperate courage displayed by each fighter.

Choynski could scarcely see Corbett or the fans crouching at ringside. His lips were split and hanging. Corbett's left eye was all but closed, and if not for his Spartan-like training habits, would have collapsed from exhaustion rounds earlier. They were oddly enough the portrait of winners — men not defined by how hard they were punched, but rather how hard they continued to punch back in the face of overwhelming adversity.

Neither man surrendered an inch, but instead fought with a warrior's heart.

In Corbett's own words, "We were both fighting to keep from getting killed."[595]

The flow of blood choked Choynski in the twentieth round as Corbett repeatedly flicked a left hand numb with pain. Still, Choynski doggedly went about his work and even finished the round with a hard punch to Corbett's neck.[596]

Choynski became increasingly desperate and savage with each round, clearly sensing he was on borrowed time. During the twenty-first round he again slipped on the bloody floor and took a few seconds to catch his breath.[597]

Corbett fought with equal desperation and courage, leaning almost exclusively on his amazing left hand. Later, Corbett would claim to have devised a plan with Delaney to camouflage the fact his broken right hand was useless. He advised Delaney to yell from time to time, "Jim, it's time you used your right now."[598]

Corbett would then telegraph the right hand and let the punch fly clear of its target. He never intended to land the right-hand, just dupe Choynski into thinking it wasn't as damaged as he might have thought.[599]

Or so went the theory.

Whether this bit of trickery fooled anyone, let alone his savvy rival, is doubtful. But it might have given Corbett a small degree of comfort nonetheless.

The twenty-fourth round offered additional drama. While Choynski and Corbett resumed a fast and furious pace in the ring, outside the ring two spectators started their own brawl over the merits of the combatants. The weaker of the two disputants was soon found clinging desperately to the side of the barge after an attempt by the other man to fling him into the water.[600]

Meanwhile, Choynski and Corbett waged their own epic brawl.

A savage and wild rush by Choynski resulted in flurry of lefts and rights that momentarily stunned Corbett, who clinched. Corbett then pushed away with his fist pressing on Choynski's nose, prompting cries of foul from Graney and Dempsey.

The street brawl resumed moments later as both fighters splashed through their own blood. Choynski gave Corbett a backhanded slap, and Corbett answered with a left hook that left Choynski staggering and bent, as if on the verge of dropping one last time. Corbett moved in for the kill only to see

Choynski stand upright and declare, "Oh, no, you don't."[601]

Choynski amazingly ended the round with a smashing punch to Corbett's chin.[602]

In the twenty-fifth round, Corbett returned the favor. He endured another hail of lefts and rights from Choynski before repulsing his attack with his own wild rush. As Choynski rolled away from the barrage with his face down, Corbett unleashed three successive uppercuts before Choynski could lift his weary and battered head.[603]

Choynski returned to his corner groggy and bleeding frightfully.[604]

Peering blurrily through the slits in his eyes, Choynski failed to block a repeated onslaught of left jabs and hooks from Corbett in the twenty-sixth round. Adding to the misery, Choynski's right leg began to cramp badly. Still, he spiritedly rushed Corbett in search of a miracle.[605]

By the end of the round, Corbett noticed Choynski dragging his legs back to the corner. He wasn't alone.[606]

Graney, desperate to keep his man revived, grabbed a flask of brandy between rounds. He tilted the flask into Choynski's bloody and deformed mouth, and told him to take a few swigs. [607]

Graney was out of options.

Chapter Twenty-Two
The Last Stand

— —

Southampton Bay, Benicia, California: June 5, 1889

Choynski could no longer see.[608] Wobbling from his corner, with both eyes blackened and swollen shut, Choynski stood like a statue with his hands dangling helplessly by his side. Blood poured freely from his nose and he struggled to breath, gurgling from his own blood with each laborious breath.

Corbett limped to the shady spot near the wheelhouse, equally too weak to raise his hands above his hips and unable to make a fist with his right hand. He stared at Choynski solely out of his blackened right eye. His left eye had closed, and the severe swelling of his cheekbones threatened to close his last portal of vision.

They now stood facing one another like two wounded gunslingers.

Only heat waves from the sun-baked deck separated them at the bell.

Choynski blindly rushed Corbett, forcing him into the ropes and connecting with a wild right to the head. Corbett reeled away, staggering. Choynski rushed again. This time Corbett fired a right-hander to the neck, knocking Choynski down to the blood-splattered floor.[609]

Corbett's weary faithful began to celebrate. Wild cheers erupted across the deck. Fists were thrust into the air.

Then, to the astonishment of all, Choynski again summoned

the strength to stand.

Choynski swayed for a moment, and launched another desperate rush. Corbett flailed with a right, causing Choynski to duck forward. At that fateful moment, Corbett instinctively shot a scissoring left from his hip, tagging Choynski squarely on the jaw with his wrist.[610]

Choynski teetered and dropped like a mallet. He rolled onto his back in the shade of the wheelhouse.[611]

Hogan began the count: "One . . . two . . . three . . . four . . . five . . . six . . ."

A delirious Corbett watched as if in a dream, counting along silently to himself: "Seven . . . eight . . . nine . . ."[612]

Choynski heroically rose to one knee, but could muster no further strength.[613]

Finally, Hogan yelled, "Ten!" The relieved referee slapped Corbett on the back, and would have toppled him had Delaney and Keneally not dove through the ropes to catch him. For a moment, Corbett looked at Delaney in confusion.[614]

"You knocked him out, Jim!" Delaney said exultantly.[615]

Corbett's brothers bolted into the ring, one planting a kiss on his bloody cheek. Olympic Club members, backers and other sports crowded the ring, excitedly shaking their hero's swollen and damaged hands.

Cheers spiraled upward in appreciation for the two fighters who had just delivered one hour and forty-five minutes of fearless savagery.[616]

Amid the celebratory chaos, Choynski gathered enough strength to stand on his own. He shuffled dejectedly to his corner, blood coursing down his face and body. Graney proudly wrapped his arms around his crimson-masked, ring warrior.[617]

Porter Ashe — Corbett's wealthy backer — called for a collection for Choynski. Ashe started the collection with $100, and fellow Corbett financier Tom Williams chipped in another $100. [618]

Hogan then passed the hat for Choynski.[619]

The two fighters were immediately rushed to the awaiting tugboat, *Sea Queen*. Both fighters were so weak they were lowered like infants onto a rowboat and then lifted onto the deck of the tug, which had anchored as close as possible in the nearby Carquinez Strait. Handlers promptly carried Choynski to the captain's cabin, where a surgeon tended to his wounds.[620]

Over the next fifty-five minutes other principals and invited guests boarded the tug for the return trip to San Francisco. For the first time, fans now began to hear the details of how Corbett entered the fight with a dislocated right thumb, and how he broke his left hand early in the fight.[621]

Passengers ducked into the captain's cabin to praise Choynski.

"Everybody who saw him sympathized with him and praised his courage as highly as they extolled Corbett's cleverness," recalled Tom Flynn, the *San Francisco Chronicle* sports editor and the fight's stakeholder.[622]

Nearby, atop Dillon's Point, rancher Patrick Dillon looked down at the anchored barge and two tugboats from a lofty sandstone ledge. The Solano County sheriff approached Dillon to inquire whether there had been a prizefight on the barge. Dillon pointed to the two tugboats cruising away from Southampton Bay, informing the sheriff he had just missed the show.[623]

Aboard the *Sea Queen* Choynski buried his battered face deeply between his knees, and quietly sobbed.[624]

Chapter Twenty-Three
Final Act

— —

The legend grew instantly.

By the time the *Sea Queen* and *Joseph H. Redmond* pulled into San Francisco's Vallejo Street wharf, a large crowd had already gathered to greet the valiant fighters. Word of Corbett's victory — and his epic twenty-seven-round battle with Choynski on the barge — reached the city shortly after the successful conclusion of the illegal prizefight, likely via telegraph from Benicia.[625]

The magnitude of the struggle became abundantly evident to those who mobbed the fighters as they pushed their way to awaiting hacks. Corbett and Choynski's blackened eyes; blistered and swollen faces; and noticeable limps left little to the imagination.

Clearly, there had been a war.

Patrick Corbett couldn't wait for his son to disembark. The proud father was the first man to board the *Sea Queen*. He embraced his battle-wearied son with a hug and an affectionate kiss.

The elder Corbett's booming voice — as well as his excessive praise — caused his son to cast him a few stern looks.[626]

A buzz of excited conversation filled the tugs on the return trip to San Francisco. Memorable rounds were recounted, strategies debated, and thousands of dollars changed hands. More than $50,000 was reportedly wagered on the outcome.[627]

175

Moses A. Gunst — Choynski's wealthiest backer — alone lost $10,000 on the fight.[628]

Passengers also praised their own civility during the mill, give or take a few heated exchanges or a thrown fist or two.[629]

Corbett held court with a few members of the press during the trip home. He genuinely praised Choynski as a "good" boxer, and with emotions still raw, declared he would never again step into the ring as a prizefighter.[630]

One reporter asked how he survived. Humbly, Corbett replied, "Joe had me dazed at one time, and at another I had cramps in my thighs, and if I had not been cool and used the good judgment of my seconds, I would have been whipped."[631]

In San Francisco, the fighters were driven immediately from the wharf to the New Hamman baths on Post Street to soak their wounds. New Hamman was open twenty-four hours a day, and was generally regarded as the best Turkish, Russian, Roman, and medicated baths in the city.[632]

Choynski quietly retreated to the inner-sanctum of the New Hamman to soak, sweat, and meditate. Paddy Gorman, the Australian middleweight who stood in his corner, loyally tended to his every need. The two became fast friends after Gorman's arrival from Australia in the spring of 1888 with heavyweight Peter Jackson, and he would scarcely leave Choynski's side over the next several days at the baths.[633]

Fans, meanwhile, fanned out into the city to spread the word about the greatness they had witnessed on the barge. They would become some of the most loyal messengers concerning the historic bout over the next few decades.

Eventually, their voices would die, leaving only second-hand whispers of the once-legendary battle that took place on a barge near Benicia.

By the next day, sporting circles would already be batting around speculation as to the fight's outcome under different circumstances. The gloves controversy drove a wedge into nearly every conversation, and according to the *San Francisco Chronicle*, several professional fighters argued that it was Choynski who actually faced a disadvantage by using skin-tight gloves.[634]

Two-ounce gloves, these professionals claimed, only provided Corbett's hands additional protection to administer greater punishment.[635]

Corbett's admirers countered by stating the fact their man won despite two damaged hands.[636]

If nothing else, the debate provided additional entertainment.

In reality, both lightweight gloves levied their own degree of damage. One boxing gloves manufacturer in Hoboken, New Jersey, probably explained it best, commenting, somewhat prophetically, a month before the June 5 Corbett-Choynski fight.

"What do I think about the lightweight gloves that fighters use?" the manufacturer said in a May 1889 article. "Well, I can tell you that a kid (sheepskin) glove soaked in water is the wickedest thing to strike a blow with there is. Such a glove does not bruise; it cuts like a razor and you will find that prize fighters prefer to battle with bare fists every time rather than use the apparently harmless kid."[637]

Choynski and Corbett's gloves were sufficiently soaked in enough salt water and blood to render them wicked.

Yet the night of June 5, 1889, belonged solely to Corbett. He returned to his home at the Florence House hotel on Ellis Street, and for the first time was able to celebrate his hard-fought victory with his wife, Olive. Since her presence at the fight would have been scandalous, she dutifully waited at home, undoubtedly in a state of anxiety over the safety of her husband.[638]

Rest would not come to Corbett on this night. No less than 300 Olympic Club members showed up outside his residence to serenade their conquering hero and escort him back to the club for a gala celebration.[639]

Clouds of cigar smoke hung the air, and brandy and whiskey flowed as freely as the details of the twenty-seven-round masterpiece. Toasts were repeatedly made in Corbett's honor, and his two broken hands were war trophies of great admiration.[640]

Corbett basked in the glory of the moment, although something was amiss.

No one present — not even the loyal and cleaver Delaney — understood what Corbett had truly experienced in the ring that morning. The pressure . . . pain . . . exhaustion . . . desperation . . . all took its physical and emotional toll on him. He was battle-fatigued, and in a club filled with hundreds of admirers, still felt somewhat alone.

Corbett therefore set out to find the one man who truly would understand.

Unannounced, Corbett returned to the New Hamman baths and asked an attendant at the registration desk to kindly escort him to patron Joe Choynski. The attendant obliged, guiding Corbett past bronze fountains, marble baths, ornate wood-carvings, and colorful walls that were magnificently frescoed.

Corbett hobbled on a cane.[641]

Finally, Corbett beheld Choynski, soaking solemnly in a steam-filled room where the temperature hovered between 120 to 130 degrees Fahrenheit. Sweat dripped from Choynski's blackened and scarred face. Corbett's broken hands were wrapped in white linen.

The two boxers looked at each other for a moment, but this time not as hated rivals. They no longer saw an Irishman and a Jew, a professional and an amateur, or an enemy from a neighboring gang. They had come too far together to see something so inconsequential. They had literally spilled each other's blood in a titanic battle that would bind them together forever.

Now, for the first time, they saw a fellow young man with similar traits — honor, courage, and heart.

Steam filled the room, void of cheering fans and vocal financial backers.

Corbett and Choynski stood alone as two young ring warriors on common ground. They spoke with mutual respect, exploring their shared experience.

Then, with the firmness of a mighty blow, the two men embraced with a handshake.[642]

Epilogue

— —

Former undefeated World Heavyweight Champion James J. Jeffries should be credited with bringing James J. Corbett and Joe Choynski together for a reunion bout twenty-one years after the June 5, 1889, barge battle.

If it weren't for Jeffries, the reunion might have never taken place.

Corbett and Choynski were summoned to Jeffries' training camp at Moana Springs, Nevada, in the summer of 1910 to help prepare the native Ohioan for his July 4 world championship fight with then-kingpin, Jack Johnson. Jeffries, who had not fought in six years, was badgered into returning to the ring to reclaim the heavyweight crown from the black Johnson for the "white race."

The comeback didn't end so well for Jeffries, who before more than 20,000 fans in Reno, Nevada, was knocked down twice in the fifteenth round when the referee mercifully halted the bout. Corbett and Choynski — two of Jeffries' favorite contemporaries — fared far better that memorable summer. The two boxing icons were requested to appear at Louis Blot's Arena in San Francisco June 11 for a friendly, three-round exhibition to commemorate their legendary barge fight, and both graciously accepted the invitation.

Choynski and Corbett made the 223-mile journey from Moana Springs to their hometown for the special occasion. By then, both men had surpassed the age of forty and were retired from boxing, although each remained in top condition.

Boxing remained a great part of their lives until the day they died.

At age forty-three, Corbett still dressed in a "natty street costume," as reporter Tom Flynn would observe that summer day as a guest sportswriter for the *San Francisco Chronicle*. Flynn, who served as the stakeholder in the barge battle decades earlier, reveled in the pageantry of the reunion.[643]

In describing the forty-one-year-old Choynski, Flynn wrote: "Increasing years and an active life have given his face and figure an appearance of leanness, which, combined with his profuse crop of brown hair, would make him pass easily for a music professor who had found the task of creating Beethovens and Mozarts out of common, everyday material a discouraging and melancholy vocation."[644]

Flynn marveled at their physiques, noting, "Neither man showed the slightest disposition toward that rotundity of waist and the heaviness of step which is characteristic of many healthy business men who have passed the forty-year mark . . ."[645]

Scarcely 500 fans showed up for the Corbett-Choynski exhibition in an arena that seated a capacity of 15,000 spectators. But those who attended were driven by that sentimental urge to relive the past as most claimed to have witnessed the classic barge bout.[646]

Choynski and Corbett entertained the old-timers in an arena office as they dressed prior to the exhibition.

The lively banter went as one might expect:

"Do you remember when Joe . . ."[647]

"No, you're wrong, it was Jim in that round . . ."[648]

And so went the test of memories, harkening back to that blistering and bloody morning on the barge when whiskey flasks and revolvers outnumbered spectators.

Finally, Corbett and Choynski exited the dressing room to walk toward the ring. They walked together.

"We didn't use the same dressing room the last time we boxed, Joe," Corbett said in amusement.[649]

Choynski grinned and replied, "No, indeed."[650]

The two heroes ducked into the ring to enthusiastic whistles and cheers. Corbett, as usual, sported colorful attire — a skin-tight and sleeveless pink shirt, white knee breeches, and peacock-blue stockings.[651] The blue-collar Choynski chose a modest white outfit with black stockings.

The ring veterans smiled at their admirers.

"I introduce to you a native son," bellowed ring announcer Billy Jordan, "one of the cleverest boxers that ever wore gloves, and the ex-champion of the world, famous Jim Corbett."

Jordan then presented Choynski as "another native son and the gamest man who ever stepped into a prize-ring — honest Joe Choynski."[653]

The cheers grew louder. For three "short" rounds, the two ex-boxers showed flashes of their greatness in a friendly display of pugilistic skills with large, pillow gloves. Fans kept the two men laughing throughout with playful references to the barge battle of long ago, and in the end there were only warm smiles, no blood.

At the final bell Corbett and Choynski hugged.[654]

"As a financial venture, the afternoon show of the Eagles was a frost," noted *Oakland Tribune* sports columnist W.W. Naughton, who witnessed the barge fight twenty-one years earlier. "But as a revival of old memories and the renewal of old associations, it was one grand success."[655]

*   *   *

Corbett and Choynski returned to San Francisco as living legends.

In the aftermath of the 1889 barge battle, Corbett would go on to international prominence by wresting the world heavyweight championship from the beloved John L. Sullivan in 1892 at the Olympic Club in New Orleans. Corbett outclassed the brawling and aging Sullivan with a masterful display of ring generalship, footwork, and elusiveness to score a twenty-first round knockout. In doing so, he re-defined boxing as a more "scientific" sport.

Future champions and contenders would sing his praises as a boxing pioneer.

James J. Corbett as he appeared circa 1894.
Author's Collection

"There were just prizefighters before Corbett," said Jess Willard, who knocked out Jack Johnson for the heavyweight title in Havana, Cuba, in 1915. "He put the game on a different basis — put science into box-fighting."[656]

Johnson also paid tribute to Corbett by recognizing him as "the first man to use scientific boxing" — a gracious admission considering Corbett would have never broken the color barrier to give a talented African American fighter a title shot during his four-and-a-half-year reign as champion.[657]

In London, following Corbett's death at his Bayside, New York, home February 18, 1933, from cancer, one commentator eulogized: " 'Gentleman Jim' is remembered here as the man who lifted boxing from the hands of thugs and brawlers to a great sport which now features bills at the great Albert Hall."[658]

The great Jack Dempsey — the world heavyweight champion, not the "Nonpareil" — bemoaned the passing of the sixty-six-year-old Corbett in eloquent prose.

"The fight game will probably never see another man like 'Gentleman Jim,' " said Dempsey, visibly shaken. "As a champion he was all by himself. As a gentleman, there was none finer."[659]

Three years earlier, Choynski praised his old rival in a 1930 issue of *Fight Stories* magazine when he said, "Jim Corbett was one of the greatest and trickiest men the ring has developed." Choynski would publicly and privately say much more about Corbett before his own death January 25, 1943, at his home in Cincinnati, Ohio, but it was his heart-breaking loss on the barge that fatefully catapulted Corbett onto the national scene.[660]

The first edition of the *California Sporting and Dramatic News* was issued in June 1889, featuring portraits of Choynski and Corbett and a report on their twenty-seven-round scrap in Southampton Bay. The publisher — a businessman who attended the fight — sent complimentary copies throughout the United States.[661]

Eventually, an issue caught the attention of heavyweight contender Jake Kilrain and his handlers. The New York native was regarded as one of the best heavyweights in the world then, having lost a seventy-round world championship bout to Sullivan in Hattiesburg, Mississippi, July 8, 1889 — one month after the Corbett-Choynski mill.

The Sullivan-Kilrain marathon would go down in history as the last bare-knuckle heavyweight championship of the world.

Kilrain's camp was looking for a "soft" opponent after the Sullivan war, and thought the unknown Corbett from the sporting publication would fit the bill. Corbett soon received a telegram:

> *Will offer a purse of twenty-five hundred dollars, two thousand to the winner and five hundred to the loser. Your railroad fare to New Orleans and return if you will box Jake Kilrain six rounds Mardi Gras week.*[662]

Corbett, who formally announced his retirement from the ring only four days after defeating Choynski, had already reconsidered his hasty and emotional decision. He accepted Kilrain's challenge, and boarded a train for New Orleans.[663]

Upon Corbett's arrival, Kilrain's handlers were amused to be in the presence of the "kid" from San Francisco. Kilrain himself supposedly took one look at the young, well-groomed Corbett and chuckled, "That dude? Why, I'll lick him in a punch."[664]

In the end, Corbett enjoyed the last laugh. He pelted the bullish Kilrain with a blur of jabs and hooks and walked away with a decisive six-round decision, setting him on the path to a showdown with Sullivan two years later.[665]

* * *

News of Choynski's death in January 1943 sent a ripple of sorrow across the nation. In San Francisco, his old friend Timothy Michael McGrath received the death notice with a heavy heart.

Choynski was seventy-four.

McGrath and Choynski forged a lifelong friendship shortly after he arrived in San Francisco from his native Limerick, Ireland. The two youngsters worked together at a candy factory, where on slow days they would crawl through an upstairs window and into the gym next door to indulge in boxing.

"Choynski was already the hero of the Hayes Valley Jewish colony and the despair of the Irish," recalled McGrath, who later became a noted trainer and manager based out of San Francisco and Los Angeles.[666]

McGrath, who died in 1950, earned national prominence as the long-time manager of the fighting sailor, Tom Sharkey. His managerial career essentially ended in 1930 when officials strongly suspected his fighter, Leon Chevalier, of taking a dive against Primo Carnera. The debacle earned McGrath a one-year suspension from the California Athletic Commission.[667]

California Governor James Rolph, Jr. named McGrath boxing inspector for that same state athletic commission four years later.[668]

In 1943, upon hearing of Choynski's death, McGrath did the only thing he thought appropriate. He raised a glass in his honor of his old chum.

"Ah, lad, there was a man," McGrath sighed at a local bar. "I knew him for fifty years and no finer fighter and gentleman ever came out of San Francisco . . . There have been and will be better men in the ring than Joe Choynski, but none could ever say they had a stouter heart."[669]

Choynski enjoyed a Hall of Fame career after his devastating defeat on the barge. He compiled a 50-14-6 record with twenty-five knockouts in a career that spanned sixteen years, and carried him to as far away as London and Sydney.

Choynski, who generally tipped the scales around 169 pounds, routinely fought much heavier boxers. In those days, there were no divisions between the middleweights (158 pounds) and heavyweights. So Choynski made the most of his situation.

Despite his relatively light weight, Choynski earned a reputation as one of the hardest hitting heavyweights of his era.

In 1897, Choynski battled Jeffries at a twenty-round draw at the National Athletic Club in San Francisco. The 219-pound Jeffries said he received the hardest punch of his career in that fight, a monstrous right to the mouth in the tenth round. The punch drove his upper lip between his two front teeth. His seconds had to cut a piece of the lip to release it from his teeth.[670]

Choynski weighed 167 pounds.[671]

Less than two years later Jeffries won the world heavyweight championship from Bob Fitzsimmons.

In 1901, Choynski rolled into Galveston, Texas, on a barnstorming tour. He saw a chance to pick up a quick $250 by fighting a local African American heavyweight Jack Johnson, then an unknown who was challenging all comers.

Choynski landed a smashing left to the temple in the third round, knocking Johnson unconscious. A Texas Ranger then stepped into the ring, and tossed both fighters into jail for engaging in an illegal prizefight.[672]

Choynski befriended Johnson, and for the next thirty days, imparted much ring wisdom on the young slugger. By the time Johnson emerged from jail, it was said he was a more "scientific fighter."

Johnson, like Jeffries, also moved on to win the world heavyweight title.

As for Choynski, he never received a title shot despite fighting — and defeating — many of the top heavyweights of his era. Choynski bitterly loathed the fact he never received a title shot, and always harbored a degree of resentment toward Corbett for never giving him a rematch.

"Corbett would never meet me again," Choynski said in 1930. "Why not? I don't know. But I do know this: I challenged him repeatedly. But he would have no part of me."[673]

Choynski even claimed in a 1933 interview that he and Corbett were offered $20,000 for a return match, but Corbett declined.[674]

Corbett's reluctance is easy to understand. As he would tell boxing historian Nat Fleischer shortly before his death, "I never dreamed as I waited for Referee Hogan to send us into action, that I would receive more punishment than I would absorb in any subsequent battle, and that the punishment to be inflicted would be more than ordinarily seen in a round of a dozen of present-day heavyweight contests."[675]

By Corbett's own account, he sat in a "steamer chair" at the New Hamman bathhouse for seven hours after the fight with his "blistered feet in two pails of hot water," both hands soaking in buckets of hot water and his "zebra-striped face" wrapped in hot towels.[676]

Why would he want a rematch?

Speculation of Corbett and Choynski's relationship always shadowed the two fighters.

In May of 1910, prior to reporting to Jeffries' training camp, one reporter asked Corbett if he had any concerns about working alongside his old rival. Corbett laughed.

"No, I don't suppose we could be called friends, for we've been enemies practically since we were boys, but it should prove no obstacle to our mutual efforts to help Jeffries," Corbett said. "I've forgotten any hard feelings I ever had, and I hope Joe has. This is too big a thing for petty bickering to enter into the plans. I don't suppose Choynski and I will room together, but so far as I'm concerned, I will greet Joe as cordially as I would if we never had any differences."[677]

Rumors of the Choynski-Corbett grudge persisted even after Choynski's death in 1943, but as was the case in 1889, how much can be attributed to the fighters themselves or prodding outsiders? For instance, one report filed in the aftermath of Choynski's passing claimed he and Corbett never even glanced at one another while working together at the Jeffries' training camp. If they needed to talk, they allegedly did so through "a third party."[678]

Yet a month later Corbett and Choynski appeared together at the reunion exhibition in San Francisco, where they openly displayed kindness toward one another. Long-time sports columnist W.W. Naughton, who knew both men, even noted at that the final bell "they hugged each other in a good-natured way to prove that the bitter fight in the late 80s had mellowed into memory."[679]

Twenty years later Choynski tried to set the record straight, although emotions can sometimes be as hard to corral as a world-class pugilist with a lightening jab and blurring footwork.

"My feud with Corbett is over," Choynski said. "We have long been friends. Time has a softening influence over most of us. Only the irreconcilables hate forever. I'm not one of those."[680]

Corbett always appeared complimentary where Choynski was concerned. He once told Fleischer, "Choynski was truly one of the 'salt of the earth,' an all-around good fellow, gentleman, who was always on the level, and certainly no gamer man ever answered the sound of the gong!"[681]

In days following the 1889 barge battle, Corbett and Choynski were seen sitting together during a boxing show at the Golden Gate Athletic Club. According to one reporter, they "conversed in the most friendly way" and every once in a while, Choynski "went through some illustrations in punching while talking to Corbett."[682]

Three weeks later, on July 15, a benefit was held for Choynski at the Mechanics Pavilion in hopes of raising money for his medical expenses. Corbett showed up and boxed a friendly four-rounder with Choynski before 2,000 applauding fans.

Choynski walked away with $1,600 in box receipts — a sum that reportedly bothered Corbett who made less for his victory on the barge.[683]

Yet Choynski struggled with the fact Corbett never gave him a rematch, and his bitterness clearly showed in a private letter to Fleischer in October of 1940. At the time, Fleischer wanted Choynski's reaction to the filming of a new movie based on Corbett's life, *Gentleman Jim*. The Warner Brothers production was being based loosely on Corbett's 1925 autobiography, *The Roar of the Crowd*, and was starring the debonair Errol Flynn as Corbett.[684]

Bitterly, Choynski took the opportunity to tell Fleischer "do you know Nat only two people have asked me why I fought Corbett for $1,000 in private — when club offered us $20,000? My wife and Chinese boy I raised in Chicago. Damn fools says he? Corbett was afraid of me: and he did not want to be whipped by me so in the open. With his mob he could wrangle the fight (if he) was being worsted and a draw would ensue.

He had Sergeant (of) Police in S.F. who sat alongside me . . ."[685]

As for the movie, Choynski wrote, "I have no interest Nat in regards (to) moving pictures of Corbett." Choynski ends the letter in frustration, admitting there's nothing he can do if filmmakers want to say Corbett defeated him four times. That claim — one made liberally by Corbett in his lifetime — bothered Choynski deeply.

The claim simply wasn't true.

What probably bothered Choynski most of all wasn't Corbett's incessant retelling of the barge fight over the years, but the liberal manner in which he retold the story. In addition to his autobiography — an entertaining, yet legacy-preserving endeavor — Corbett gave his story to countless magazines and newspapers. Sometimes, Corbett's tales grew like Jack's beanstalk.

In Corbett's defense, his status as world heavyweight champion made him an international celebrity well beyond boxing circles. His gentlemanly manners, good looks, and ventures into theatre also made him highly approachable, and what boxing champion wouldn't want to talk about a legendary fight in which they emerged the winner?

Corbett simply lived the dream.

Choynski, by contrast, seemed to shun publicity. He was a professional's professional in the ring, and by all accounts, a soft-spoken gentleman outside the ropes. Later in life he returned to school and graduated as a chiropractor in Chicago, where his brother, Maurice, owned a theatre. Joe also lived at various times in Chicago, Pittsburgh, and Cincinnati, where he retired with his wife, Louise.

Louise, a former actress, was a member of a non-Jewish Cincinnati family.

At the age of seventy, Choynski trained young fighters at the Athletic Club in Cincinnati where he was reportedly still "lightning fast" on his toes and with his fists.[686]

Jackie Wilson, James J. Corbett, and Joe Choynski strolling the Atlantic City Board-walk in August 1914. *Courtesy of Christopher J. LaForce*

In the end, he also softened his stance on the *Gentleman Jim* movie, and served as a consultant.[687]

Yet, when emotionally aroused, Choynski could still deliver a knockout blow. In 1942, five month before his death, Choynski was quoted as crankily referring to Corbett as a "bum." Whether Choynski truly made this statement will forever be unknown, but his respect for Corbett and Corbett's respect for him, is without question.[688]

The reality is their relationship was complex. What is known is that whenever Corbett passed through Pittsburgh in his later years he always enjoyed the company of Choynski and his wife at dinner.[689]

On those nights they were surely young again, reliving their prime and the glories they shared in the ring.

* * *

The magic of the 1889 barge battle hardly rested in the recollections of the two combatants. Hundreds of eyewitnesses filtered throughout San Francisco and the countryside to tell the story of that unforgettable June day, and from time to time, various accounts appeared in print.

Participants Ed Graney and Billy Delaney both left colorful anecdotes about what took place between Corbett and Choynski in Fairfax and Benicia.

Delaney, who became a legendary trainer, once said, "You ask me what the greatest fight I ever saw was, and I'm going to tell you that the barge fight between Corbett and Choynski was the toughest I have ever seen or heard of."[690]

Delaney built his own legacy of greatness by training many of the great heavyweights of his day, including Corbett, Jeffries and even Johnson. Delaney was actually in Jeffries' corner the two times he defeated Corbett, but had a falling out with the former champion when he backed out of a fight with Australian Bill Squires.

In 1910, Delaney accepted the controversial offer to train Johnson for his upcoming title defense with Jeffries. Ringside observers claimed Jeffries seemed to emotionally wilt at the sight of his former trainer in Johnson's corner.

When asked why he deserted Jeffries, Delaney bluntly replied, "I quit Jeffries for welching on a gambling debt and running out on the Squires match. I could not conscientiously have any further dealings with Jeffries."[691]

Delaney died two years later at his home in Oakland. He was only fifty-eight.

Graney, ever proud of Choynski, actually called Corbett the greatest fighter he ever saw.

"Corbett standing six feet-one inch, wearing an eighteen-inch collar and sporting a chest like a dry goods box, was something to look at," Graney said in a 1919 interview. "I'm talking about the Corbett of 1889. The Corbett who was twenty-three years old. That was about the time he knocked Choynski out on the barge. Choynski was a great fighter, wasn't he? Corbett beat him two out of three times . . .

"When you saw Corbett fight you saw the kingpin of the ring. Today there isn't a mark on him and he fought the best that ever stepped into a ring."[692]

Graney passed away September 7, 1929, in San Francisco after suffering a stroke. His death prompted a flood of telegrams to the funeral parlor and Graney home from some of the most prominent figures in the business and sporting world.

His billiard hall at 61 Eddy Street served as a headquarters for boxers, fight managers and others interested in the San Francisco sports scene. In earlier years, Graney managed to secure the horseshoeing contract for his blacksmith shop from the San Francisco Fire Department, and became involved with several political figures.

Still, Graney was always best known for having served as Choynski's loyal second on the barge, as well as his illustrious career as a referee. He died at age sixty-one.[693]

Sol Bloom is another eyewitness who left an account of the

barge fight. Bloom, who went on to serve as a United State Representative from New York, dedicated three pages to the legendary fight in his autobiography, *The Autobiography of Sol Bloom.*

Bloom described the Corbett-Choynski rivalry as "a feud of Hatfield-McCoy dimensions," and of the fight, said simply, "I have never seen another to equal it."[694]

The fight left an indelible imprint on many who witnessed its savagery. Benicia hotel owner W.J. Fitzpatrick, who helped construct the makeshift ring, spoke of the

Sol Bloom, who later served as a U.S. Congressman from New York, witnessed the famous barge bout and dedicated three pages to it in his autobiography *The Autobiography of Sol Bloom. Author's Collection* fight publicly in a 1914 interview with the *Oakland Tribune*. He noted how he left "in disgust" at the sight of so much blood.[695]

Images of the blood also haunted former shipyard apprentice John Carty who ditched work that day to watch the fight. Carty gave his vivid account of the gory battle to *Benicia New Era* publisher William Dykes when word reached the tiny waterfront community of Corbett's death in February 1933.[696]

Glory, controversy, and tragedy also followed a number of participants and eyewitnesses.

Blistering editorials dogged Judge William Patrick Lawlor during his confirmation as a California Supreme Court Justice for his role in orchestrating the illegal fight to the finish between Corbett and Choynski decades earlier. One editorial mused:

> *The Bar Association has refused to endorse Lawlor for Judge (John J.) De Haven's position, but it is understood that Corbett and Choynski are willing to shake hands and unite in his support. It is their belief that the judgeship should be put to a physical test and that Lawlor is qualified under Queensberry rules.*[697]

In November of 1914, Californians elected Lawlor Associate Justice of the Supreme Court for a full twelve-year term.

Jack Dempsey, "The Nonpareil," encountered his own ring wars not long after seconding Choynski on the barge. In August 1889, Dempsey was set to defend his world middleweight championship against George LeBlanche. But when LeBlanche tipped the scales over the limit at 161 pounds, the bout was declared a non-title fight.

Dempsey appeared to be on his way to a thirty-second round knockout when LeBlanche let loose his now-infamous "pivot blow," in which he struck Dempsey with the back of his right hand after whirling his body completely around like a kickboxer. The blow — later declared illegal — knocked Dempsey cold.

In 1891, Dempsey finally lost his world championship legitimately to Fitzsimmons in New Orleans. Dempsey, suffering from tuberculosis, battled like a warrior. Fitzsimmons repeatedly knocked him down, and pleaded with Dempsey to quit.

Dempsey refused.

Fitzsimmons finally knocked Dempsey out cold in the thirteenth round, and carried him to his corner.

Ironically, Dempsey only lost three times during his illustrious career — two of those to ring greats Tommy Ryan and Fitzsimmons, who later climbed up in weight to take Corbett's heavyweight crown.

Moses A. Gunst — Choynski's wealthy backer — died even wealthier in 1928 after building a tobacco empire. Gunst recovered nicely after losing a hefty wager on Choynski in 1889, having died a millionaire.[698]

Actor Nathaniel Carl Goodwin, who likely prevented a riot in the Fairfax barn, continued his stellar career, and in the aftermath of the barge battle, began to be recognized for his comedic genius. Between 1912 and 1916 he even acted in a handful of films, including the first full-length feature of *Oliver Twist*. Goodwin died in 1919 at age sixty-one.

Wilson Mizner, the kid who injured his hand trying to board the crowded barge, became a renowned playwright, raconteur, and entrepreneur. He was best known for his plays *The Deep Purple* and *The Greyhound*, and was the manager and co-owner of the famous Brown Derby restaurant in Los Angeles.

Mizner reportedly battled an opium addiction and was involved in several scams. At one point Mizner managed several boxers, undoubtedly inspired by the Corbett-Choynski brawl of his youth. But allegations of fight-fixing followed Mizner who often did little to hide his shady side.

Once, one of his fighters — Stanley Ketchel — was murdered. Wilson reportedly quipped, "Tell 'em to start counting to ten over him, and he'll get up."

Mizner died at age fifty-six on April 3, 1933 — two months after Corbett's passing.

Former Marin County Sheriff John E. Healy died a beloved man in January 1920. The sixty-nine-year-old Healy was eulogized as a man who was "held in very high esteem by every person of his acquaintance."[699]

Referee Patsy Hogan's life careened into tragedy in 1898, only nine years after being the third man in the ring for the memorable barge bout. Hogan's wife filed for divorce in October of that year. A few weeks later an enraged Hogan shot and killed his wife in San Francisco. Hogan, whose real name was Keenan, then tried to stab himself to death, but his self-inflicted wound failed to do the job.[700]

Hogan reportedly went on to fight in World War I, lost his legs in a car accident in Texas, and died penniless in a veteran's home.

Tragedy also struck the Corbett family in the most disturbing manner in 1898.

Patrick Corbett, who had been mentally despondent for two years, awoke at 5 a.m. on a Tuesday morning in August as he ordinarily did and dressed in everything but his shoes and coat. He retrieved his revolver, walked into his master bedroom upstairs and leaned over his sleeping wife, Catherine. The elder Corbett then shot his wife twice in the head.

Patrick Corbett proceeded to place the revolver in his mouth, firing one last fatal shot.[701]

James Corbett received the devastating news while training for an upcoming bout with Charles "Kid" McCoy in Asbury Park, New Jersey. The then-former world champion immediately sent his brother, Harry, a telegram that read:

> *ASBURY PARK, NEW JERSEY (N.J.), August 16, 1898. Harry E. Corbett, 518 Hayes street: Can you keep them until we get home. I cannot believe they are gone till I see them. I am about half crazy. JIM, VERA & TOM.*[702]

Corbett canceled his fight and returned home to be with his family. He also issued a statement to the press in an effort to

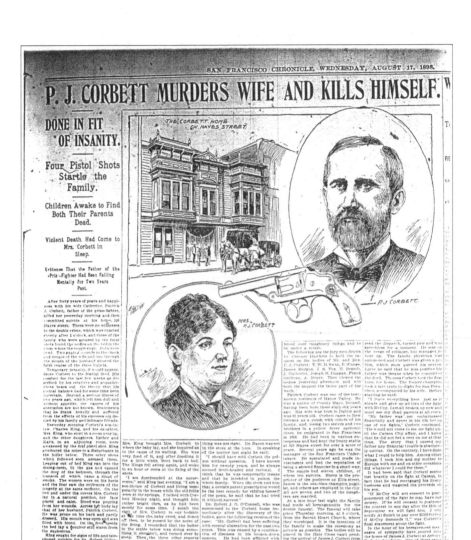

Patrick and Catherine Corbett raised ten children in San Francisco. In 1898, tragedy rocked the family when Patrick murdered his wife before taking his own life. *Author's Collection*

dispel rumors that his father fell into insurmountable debt due to his own financial difficulties.

In 1895, Corbett's personal life played out in a scandalous divorce proceeding with Olive, who learned he was having an affair with Vera Stanwood. Eyewitnesses often saw Jim and Vera together, even registering in the same hotel room as Mr. and Mrs. Corbett. Corbett eventually married Vera after the finalization of his divorce to Olive, but the pain and humiliation of that period of his life was but a shadow to the murder-suicide of his beloved father and mother.

Choynski also endured the loss of his parents in his lifetime, but through natural causes.

Harriett Choynski died in 1928, and was interred next to her husband at Hills of Eternity Cemetery in Colma, California. I.N. died twenty-nine years earlier of throat cancer on January 24, 1899, at the family's Golden Gate Avenue home. He was sixty-three.[703]

The flamboyant I.N. went out with a flare. On his deathbed, Choynski amazingly found enough energy to pen his last message. The message later appeared in print:

> *On Friday morning last, it was just 6 o'clock as we opened our eyes, there stood before us in the open doorway a tall, gray-bearded man, the very picture of Father Time, and he held a huge black sign in his hand, reaching from top to bottom of the door, upon which was written in bold white type, German script, "Marked for death." It was a fine greeting for a pleasant morning; but we opine that the Germans should not have been so cruel, and not have shown themselves so inhuman. We saw all the doctors the evening before, and why not have given us a chance to put our place in order? It is a cruel, wicked world; we had our struggle. Good-by.*[704]

Joe Choynski surely read his father's deathbed farewell with tears in his blue eyes and a smile on his face. I.N. Choynski was defiant and full of fight until the end.

The last survivor of the historic 1889 barge battle might have actually been the famous barge itself. In March of 1933 — in the aftermath of Corbett's death — a report surfaced out of Benicia, stating that "Part of the barge . . . remains afloat in Southampton Bay."[705]

To this day, one local legend persists that a portion of the sunken barge where Corbett and Choynski brawled long ago can still be seen at low tide. Whether this story is true or nothing more than a romantic tale is irrelevant. The fact is the legend lives.

Endnotes

Chapter One — The Legend

1. Choynski is pronounced coy-EN-ski. In his ancestral homeland of Poland, the family name is pronounced HO-en-ski.

2. *Benicia New Era*, 18 February, 1933.

3. Carty was seventeen years old at the time of the Corbett-Choynski fight.

4. *Benicia New Era*, 18 February, 1933.

Chapter Two — The 'Dude'

5. Bloom, Sol. *The Autobiography of Sol Bloom* (New York: G.P. Putnam's Sons, 1948), 24-25; Oscar Lewis. *San Francisco: Mission to Metropolis* (Berkeley, California: Howell-North Books, 1966), 156.

6. Baker, Malcolm E., ed. *More San Francisco Memoirs, 1852-1899: The Ripening Years* (San Francisco: Londonborn Publications, 1996), 251.

7. *Builders of a Great City: San Francisco's Representative Men* (San Francisco, 1891), 58.

8. *Ibid.*, 272-273; William Issel and Robert W. Cherny, *San Francisco, 1865-1932: Politics, Power, and Urban Development* (Berkeley, California: University of California Press, 1986), 27; Lewis, *San Francisco: Mission to Metropolis*, 152-153.

9. Baker, *More San Francisco Memoirs*, 273.

10. *Ibid.*, 233.

11. Levy, Harriet Lane. *920 O'Farrell Street* (Garden City, N.Y.: Doubleday & Co., 1947), 12.

12. Baker, *More San Francisco Memoirs*, 252.

13. *Ibid.*, 229.

14. *Ibid.*, 199.

15. Corbett, James J. *The Roar of the Crowd: The True Tale Of The Rise And Fall Of A Champion* (New York: G.P. Putnam's Sons, 1925), 12; William Inglis. *Champions Off Guard* (New York: The Vanguard Press, 1932), 111.

16. Armond Fields. *James J. Corbett: A Biography Of The Heavyweight Boxing Champion And Popular Theatre Headliner* (Jefferson, North Carolina: McFarland & Company, Inc. Publishers, 2001), 12.

17. *Ibid.*

18. Corbett, *The Roar of the Crowd*, 12.

19. *Ibid.*

20. *Ibid.*, 11.

21. Fields, *James J. Corbett*, 13.

22. Corbett, *The Roar of the Crowd*, 11.

23. *Ibid.*, 12.

24. Nat Fleischer. *Gentleman Jim: The Story of James J. Corbett* (New York: C.J. O'Brien, Inc., 1942), 4. Corbett, *The Roar of the Crowd*, 39.

25. Fields, *James J. Corbett*, 5; *San Francisco Chronicle*, 17, August, 1898.

26. *Ibid.*

27. *San Francisco City Directory*, 1856-1858; Fields, 8.

28. Fields, *James J.* Corbett, 10-11; *San Francisco Chronicle*, 17 August, 1898.

29. *Ibid.*

30. Fleischer, *Gentleman Jim*, 5.

31. *Ibid.*

32. Fields, *James J. Corbett*, 11-12.

33. Corbett, *The Roar of the Crowd*, 4; Fleischer, *Gentleman Jim*, 7.

34. *Ibid.*

35. *Ibid.*, 4-5.

36. *Ibid.*, 6.

37. *Ibid.*, 7.

38. Fields, *James J.* Corbett, 12; Ibid, 9.

39. Corbett, *The Roar of the Crowd*, 9.

40. Fields, *James J. Corbett*, 12.

41. *Ibid.*

42. Fleischer, *Gentleman Jim*, 9.

43. Fields, *James J. Corbett*, 14.

44. *The History of The Olympic Club* (San Francisco: The Art Publishing Company, 1893), 26; Corbett, *The Roar of the Crowd*, 12.

45. Corbett, *The Roar of the Crowd*, 13.

46. *Ibid.*

47. *Ibid.*

48. *Ibid.*, 14.

49. *Ibid.*, 15; *The History of The Olympic Club*, 17.

50. Corbett, *The Roar of the Crowd*, 16-16.

51. Fields, *James J. Corbett*, 10.

52. *Ibid.*, 11.

53. *The Chronicle Telegram* (Elyria, Ohio), 14 February, 1933; Tom Lewis and Joe Choynski, "I Fought 'Em All," *Fight Stories* (October, 1930), 22.

54. Corbett, *The Roar of the Crowd*, 38.

55. 12 June, 1917, *Syracuse* (N.Y.) *Herald*.

56. *Ibid.*

57. *Ibid.*

58. *Ibid.*

59. *Ibid.*

60. *Ibid.*

61. *Ibid.*

62. *Ibid.*

63. Corbett, *The Roar of the Crowd*, 38; Old Timer, "Famous Fights I Have Seen," *Fight Stories* (March, 1929), 57. The author of the article, probably Corbett himself, witnessed the stable sparring session and claimed that, "The blond one (Choynski) went down in a rumbled, unconscious heap."

64. 12 June, 1917, *Syracuse* (N.Y.) *Herald*.

65. *Ibid.*

66. *Ibid.*

67. 12 June, 1917, *Syracuse* (N.Y.) *Herald*.

68. *Ibid.*

69. *Ibid.*

Chapter Three — 'Chrysanthemum' Joe

70. Lewis and Choynski, "I Fought 'Em All," 22.

71. *Ibid.*; *San Francisco Call-Bulletin*, 26 January, 1943; *Modesto Bee*, 26 January, 1943; *The Chronicle* (Elyria, Ohio) *Telegram*, 14 February, 1933.

72. Lewis and Choynski, "I Fought 'Em All," 22.

73. Janet (Choynski) Fleishhacker tape recorded interview 1973-1974, The Bancroft Library, University of California, Berkeley. Fleishhacker was the daughter of Herbert Choynski, Joe's oldest brother; William M. Kramer and Norton B. Stern, "San Francisco's Fighting Jew," *California Historical Quarterly* (Winter, 1974, v. 53, no. 4), 333-346.

74. Lewis and Choynski, "I Fought 'Em All," 20.

75. *Ibid*, 22.

76. Blady, Ken. *The Jewish Boxers Hall of Fame* (New York: Shapolsky Publishers, Inc., 1988), 36.

77. *The Chronicle* (Elyria, Ohio) *Telegram*, 14 February, 1943; Brady, *The Jewish Boxers Hall of Fame*, 29.

78. Singerman, Robert. "The San Francisco Journalism of I.N. Choynski," *Western States Jewish History* (v. 29, no. 2, January, 1997), 8. Singerman

chronicled I.N. Choynski's life in an outstanding three-part series for *Western States Jewish History* – (v. 29, no. 2, January, 1997, 7-48), (v. 29, no. 3, April, 1997, 166-190), and (v. 29, no. 4, July, 1997, 260-282). Singerman meticulously mined for details in order to piece together I.N.'s colorful story, and to date, his research should be considered the authority on the elder Choynski — a legendary figure in his own rite. This author is certainly indebted to such pioneering work.

79. *American Israelite*, 16 October, 1885. I.N. Choynski wrote a column under the title of "Maftir" in the *American Israelite*, and left a number of clues to his ancestry and life sprinkled throughout his writings.

80. *Ibid.*, 16 January, 1885.

81. *Transcript of Appeal*, California Supreme Court, *People v. I.N. Choynski*, filed Nov. 3, 1890, 55 (copy at California State Archives, Sacramento).

82. *American Israelite*, 27 November, 1890.

83. *Ibid.*, 3 June, 1887. Translation found in Singerman's "The San Francisco Journalism of I.N. Choynski," *Western States Jewish History* (v. 29, no. 2, January, 1997), 37.

84. *Ibid.*, 16 November, 1883; 25 February, 1881; 29 June, 1883.

85. Edwin Coe statement, July 11, 1951, I.N. Choynski folder, California Historical Society. In the 1920s, Edwin changed his last name from Choynski to Coe.

86. I.N. Choynski's naturalization papers, dated September 7, 1859, National Archives, Pacific Sierra Region, San Bruno, California, RG21, U.S. Circuit Court, Ninth Circuit, Northern District of California, San Francisco; Singerman, "The San Francisco Journalism of I.N. Choynski," (v. 29, no. 2, January, 1997), 12.

87. Singerman, "The San Francisco Journalism of I.N. Choynski," (v. 29, no. 2, January, 1997), 16; *San Francisco Chronicle*, 25 January, 1899; Lewis and Choynski, "I Fought 'Em All," 21.

88. *The* (San Francisco) *Bulletin*, 12 January, 1924; Stern, Norton B. "Harriet Ashim Choynski: A Western Arrival to San Francisco, 1850," *Western States Jewish History* (v. 24, no. 3, 2003), 24.

89. Janet (Choynski) Fleishhacker interview.

90. *Ibid.*

91. Fleishhacker Family Papers, I.N. Choynski letter to Harriet Choynski, December 14, 1862. The author thanks David and Mortimer Fleishhacker for graciously sharing copies from the private papers of their great-grandparents, I.N. and Harriet Choynski. Original letters from I.N.'s journey to Aurora were preserved by their mother, Janet – Herbert Choynski's only child. Herbert was Joe's oldest sibling.

92. *Ibid.*

93. *Ibid*, I.N. Choynski letter to Harriet Choynski, February 8, 1863.

94. *Ibid*.

95. *Ibid*., I.N. Choynski letter to Harriet Choynski, May 17, 1863.

96. *Ibid*., I.N. Choynski letter to Harriet Choynski, May 23, 1863.

97. *Ibid*., I.N. Choynski letter to Harriet Choynski, June 1, 1863.

98. Singerman, "The San Francisco Journalism of I.N. Choynski," (v. 29, no. 2, January, 1997), 22; Lewis and Choynski, "I Fought 'Em All," 21; *San Francisco Call-Bulletin*, 15 February, 1934.

99. Blady, *The Jewish Boxer's Hall of Fame*, 29; Lewis and Choynski, "I Fought 'Em All," 21.

100. Cowan, Robert Ernest. *Booksellers Of Early San Francisco* (Los Angeles: The Ward Ritchie Press, 1953), 26.

101. *Ibid*., 28.

102. *Ibid*.

103. *Ibid*.

104. *Ibid*.

105. *Ibid*.

106. *Ibid*.

107. *Ibid*.

108. Janet (Choynski) Fleishhacker interview.

109. *Ibid*.

110. *Ibid*.

111. *Ibid*. Janet (Choynski) Fleishhacker said the story was always a favorite among her grandchildren.

112. *New York Times*, 26 January, 1943; *San Francisco Examiner*, 26 January, 1943.

113. Kramer and Stern, "San Francisco's Fighting Jew," 342. Tidbit found in an undated clipping of the *San Francisco Examiner* inside the Choynski file in the newspaper's library. Years later, Choynski also developed an interest in fine antiques, and "possessed some exceptionally valuable ivory." (*San Francisco Call-Bulletin*, 26 January, 1943).

114. Janet (Choynski) Fleishhacker said in her taped interview, "The family was always somewhat ashamed of his being a boxer. It was a disgrace in those days, of course. Well, it's still looked down upon, I suppose, but at this certain period of time it was just a shocking thing to them to have a son who was interested in this." Fleishhacker is partially correct. Harriet did find boxing barbaric, but Joe had great support from his family as Joe's sister-in-law, Florence Coe, remembered. Coe – the wife of Joe's youngest

brother, Edwin Coe – once stated: "Before a fight (Joe's) mother became so upset, behaving like a crazy woman, but the rest of the family overrode her objections." (Kramer and Stern, "San Francisco's Fighting Jew," 343).

115. *The Jewish Conservator* (Chicago), 18 November, 1904.

Chapter Four — Blood Feud

116. *The Syracuse Herald*, 15 June, 1917.

117. *Ibid.*

118. *Ibid.* The fight would take place two weeks after their first tussle in the Corbett stables. (*The* [Elyria, Ohio] *Chronicle Telegram*, February 14, 1933).

119. *Ibid.*

120. *Ibid.*

121. *Ibid.*

122. Corbett, *The Roar of the Crowd*, 39.

123. *The Syracuse Herald*, 15 June, 1917.

124. *Ibid.*

125. *Ibid.*

126. Corbett, *The Roar of the Crowd*, 39.

127. *Ibid.*

128. *Langley's San Francisco Directory* (San Francisco: Francis, Valentine & Co., Printers, 1889), 342. I.N. Choynski and his family lived at 1209 Golden Gate Avenue for many years. Choynski's newspaper and antiquarian bookstore was located at 137 Taylor.

129. *The Syracuse Herald*, 15 June, 1917.

130. *Ibid.*

131. *Ibid.*

132. *Ibid.*

133. *Ibid.*

134. Corbett, *The Roar of the Crowd*, 40.

135. Years later, Corbett would remember that man with amusement, stating, "I have often wondered if that fellow who watched us ever learned afterward the identity of the two boys he saw mixing it that Sunday morning." (*The Syracuse Herald*, June 15, 1917). In his autobiography, Corbett mused, "there he sat, enjoying this free entertainment, little realizing, I suppose, that of those two slugging 'kids' one was later to be a near champion, the other champion heavyweight of the world!" (Corbett, *The Roar of the Crowd*, 40).

136. Lewis and Choynski, "I Fought 'Em All," 22. Choynski remembered about "eight or ten" Corbett supporters he referred to as his "Hayes Valley

gang." Corbett, meanwhile, stated that only his brother, Frank, and buddy, Jack Gallagher, were present.

137. *Ibid.*

138. *Ibid.*, 23.

139. *Ibid.*

140. Corbett, *The Roar of the Crowd*, 40.

141. *Ibid.*

142. *The Syracuse Herald*, June 15, 1917.

143. *Ibid.*

144. Corbett, *The Roar of the Crowd*, 41.

Chapter Five — Rising Star

145. John Sequeira, "Le Preux Chevalier Of The Winged 'O,' " *Olympian* (Date unknown), 6-7. Sequeira's article was found in the James J. Corbett vertical file at the San Francisco Public Library.

146. Corbett, *The Roar of the Crowd*, 20-21; Fleischer, *Gentleman Jim*, 11.

147. Corbett, *The Roar of the Crowd*, 21.

148. *Ibid.*

149. *Ibid.*

150. *History of the Olympic Club*, 25.

151. Corbett, *The Roar of the Crowd*, 23.

152. *Ibid.* Fleischer, *Gentleman Jim*, 11.

153. Dempsey's ring record can be found by logging onto www.boxrec.com.

154. Corbett, *The Roar of the Crowd*, 29.

155. *Ibid.*

156. *Ibid.*

157. *Ibid.*

158. *Ibid.*, 30.

159. *Ibid.*, 31.

160. Corbett, James J. *A Bit Of My Life: Training the Body for Supervitality* (Unknown), 13.

161. *Ibid.*

162. Corbett, *The Roar of the Crowd*, 32.

163. *Ibid.*

164. *Ibid.*

165. *Ibid.*

166. *Ibid.*, 33.

167. *San Francisco Chronicle*, 25 August, 1885.

168. Fields, *James J. Corbett*, 19.

169. Corbett, *The Roar of the Crowd*, 36.

170. *Oakland, Alameda and Berkeley City Directory, 1889-90* (San Francisco: F.M. Husted, 1890), 261.

171. *Ibid.*

172. *Ibid.*, 37.

173. *Ibid.*

Chapter Six — Prodigal Son

174. *The* (Salt Lake City) *Daily Tribune*, 15 July, 1886; Corbett, *The Roar of the Crowd*, 59-60.

175. *The* (Salt Lake City) *Daily Tribune*, 15 July, 1886.

176. *Ibid.*

177. www.boxrec.com.

178. Fields, *James J. Corbett*, 12.

179. *The* (Salt Lake City) *Daily Tribune*, 15 July, 1886.

180. *Ibid.*

181. *Ibid.*

182. *Ibid.*

183. *Ibid.*

184. Corbett, *The Roar of the Crowd*, 53-54.

185. *Ibid.* Corbett also wrote that his marriage with Marie was "later annulled," but in fact they remained married for nine years before getting a divorce (*The Roar of the Crowd*, 46).

186. *Ibid.*, 58-59.

187. *Ibid.*, 59.

188. *Ibid.*

189. *Ibid.*

190. *Ibid.*

191. *San Francisco Chronicle*, 20 July, 1886.

192. *San Francisco Chronicle*, 26 January, 1887.

193. *San Francisco Chronicle*, 27 January, 1887.

194. *San Francisco Chronicle*, 10 March, 1887.

Chapter Seven — Coins

195. Lewis and Choynski, "I Fought 'Em All," 23; *Daily Alta California*, 23

March, 1887; "Choynski Tells Own Story of Corbett Tiffs," undated and unknown newspaper article, circa 1934, San Francisco History Center vertical files.

196. *Ibid.*

197. Lewis and Choynski, "I Fought 'Em All," 23.

198. *Ibid.*

199. *Ibid.*

200. *Daily Northwestern* (Oshkosh, Wisconsin), 14 February, 1933.

201. Lewis and Choynski, "I Fought 'Em All," 23.

202. *San Francisco Examiner*, 26 January, 1943.

203. Lewis and Choynski, "I Fought 'Em All," 23.

204. *Ibid.*

205. *San Francisco Call-Bulletin*, 26 January, 1943.

206. *Ibid.*

207. *Ibid.*

208. Lewis and Choynski, "I Fought 'Em All," 23-24.

209. *New York Times*, 26 January, 1943.

210. *Daily Alta California*, 23 July, 1887.

211. *Ibid.*

212. *Ibid.* The *Daily Alta California* later stated that Choynski fought this bout under the name, "Joe King." (*Daily Alta California*, 26 February, 1889).

213. *Daily Alta California*, 25 July, 1887.

214. *Daily Alta California*, 22 August, 1887.

215. *San Francisco Chronicle*, 8 August, 1887.

216. *Ibid.*

217. Fleischer, *Gentleman Jim*, 16.

218. *San Francisco Chronicle*, 15 August, 1887.

219. *Ibid.*

220. *San Francisco Chronicle*, 28 August, 1887.

221. *Ibid.*

222. *Ibid.*

223. *American Israelite* (Cincinnati), 30 June, 1885.

224. *American Israelite* (Cincinnati), 23 September, 1887.

225. *Daily Alta California*, 24 October, 1887.

226. Corbett, *The Roar of the Crowd*, 9.

227. *Ibid.*

228. *Ibid.*, 9-10.

229. Lewis and Choynski, "I Fought 'Em All," 24.

230. *Ibid.* In Dewitt Van Court's version of the story, he remembered Choynski addressing the official with Brown standing nearby. He quotes Choynski as saying, "That's all right with me, Mr. Brown, but I had to split that ten with Jim Corbett (*San Francisco Chronicle*, January 26, 1943).

231. Lewis and Choynski, "I Fought 'Em All," 24.

232. *Ibid.*

233. *Daily Alta California*, 10 December, 1888.

234. *Ibid*; *Daily Alta California*, 19 December, 1887.

Chapter Eight — The 'Professor'
235. Fields, *James J. Corbett*, 25.

236. *San Francisco Chronicle*, 13 February, 1888.

237. *San Francisco Chronicle*, 26 March, 1888.

238. Fields, *James J. Corbett*, 26.

239. *San Francisco Chronicle*, 23 April, 1888.

240. *San Francisco Chronicle*, 21 May, 1888.

241 *San Francisco Chronicle*, 9 July, 1888.

242. *Ibid.*

Chapter Nine — 'Anyone In The House'
243. *San Francisco Chronicle*, 15 August, 1888.

244. *Ibid.*

245. *San Francisco Chronicle*, 9 July, 1888; Lewis and Choynski, "I Fought 'Em All," 24.

246. *Woodland Daily Democrat*, 7 September, 1928. In 1896, prior to winning the heavyweight championship, Bob Fitzsimmons applied to work at Graney's blacksmith shop, but was told there was no room for him. The Englishman later won a $2,000 bet from Graney after winning a horseshoeing championship. Fitzsimmons won the heavyweight title on March 17, 1897 when he knocked out James Corbett in the fourteenth round. (*San Francisco Morning Herald*, 21 November, 1898).

247. *San Francisco Chronicle*, 15 November, 1888.

248. Lewis and Choynski, "I Fought 'Em All," 24.

249. *San Francisco Chronicle*, 26 January, 1943.

250. Lewis and Choynski, "I Fought 'Em All," 24.

251. *Ibid.*

252. *Ibid.*

253. *Ibid.*

254. *Ibid.*

255. *San Francisco Chronicle*, 26 January, 1943.

256. Lewis and Choynski, "I Fought 'Em All," 25.

257. *Ibid.*

258. *San Francisco Chronicle*, 15 November, 1888.

259. *Ibid.; Daily Alta California*, 15 November, 1888.

260. *Daily Alta California*, 15 November, 1888.

261. Lewis and Choynski, "I Fought 'Em All," 25.

262. *Langley's San Francisco Directory, 1889*, 342.

263. *San Francisco Chronicle*, 26 January, 1943.

264. *Ibid.*

265. *Daily Alta California*, 15 November, 1888; *San Francisco Chronicle*, 15 November, 1888.

266. Janet (Choynski) Fleishhacker interview, 296; Lewis and Choynski, "I Fought 'Em All," 25.

267. *San Francisco Chronicle*, 26 January, 1943; Lewis and Choynski, "I Fought 'Em All," 25.

Chapter Ten — Collision Course

268. *San Francisco Chronicle*, 1 January, 1889.

269. Lewis and Choynski, "I Fought 'Em All," 22.

270. *Daily Alta California*, 29 April, 1889; *Daily Alta California*, 26 February, 1889. Choynski filled in as boxing instructor at the Golden Gate Athletic Club during Con Riordan's absence a few months earlier (*Daily Alta California*, 19 November, 1888). The Irish-born Riordan had a reputation as a scrapper, and was the first boxer to exchange punches with Peter Jackson after his arrival to America in the spring of 1888. The two fought a four-round exhibition in June of that year. (*San Francisco Daily Examiner*, 4 June, 1888; *San Francisco Daily Examiner*, 5 June, 1888).

271. Lewis and Choynski, "I Fought 'Em All," 25.

272. *Daily Alta California*, 26 February, 1889. Meadows traveled with the Peter Jackson contingent from Australia, along with Paddy Gorman. (*San Francisco Daily Examiner*, 13 May, 1888; *San Francisco Call*, 13 May, 1888; *National Police Gazette*, 9 June, 1888).

273. *Ibid.; Daily Alta California*, 27 February, 1889.

274. *Daily Alta California*, 27 February, 1889; *National Police Gazette*, February, 1889.

275. *Chicago Sunday Inter-Ocean*, 3 March, 1889.

276. Lewis and Choynski, "I Fought 'Em All," 25.

277. Ibid., 25; *Oneonta* (N.Y.) *Daily Star*, 2 December, 1924.

278. *Syracuse Herald*, 15 June, 1917.

279. Corbett, *The Roar of the Crowd*, 60-61.

280. *Ibid.*, 60.

281. *Ibid*. Years later, World Lightweight Champion Battling Nelson described Choynski's "wicked" trick in detail in his autobiography, *Life, Battles And Career of Battling Nelson* (Hegewisch, Ill., 1909, p. 118):
"I discovered this deadly punch from watching Joe Choynski. He had a wicked habit of placing his fingers on an opponent's breast while in the clinches of a fight as if to talk to him.
"With the tips of his fingers touching the other fellow's right nipple he would say, 'Now, old fellow, you want to be good.' Then before the word could be said in reply, by the mere movement of the wrist, he would plunge the heel of his left-hand into a man's liver. When a man doubled up from the unexpected pain, Joe would whang [sic] him in the jaw and the fight would be over."

282. *Ibid.*

283. *The Appleton Post-Crescent*, 24 January, 1931.

284. *Ibid.*

285. *Daily Alta California*, 22 April, 1889.

286. *Ibid.*

287. *Syracuse Herald*, 15 June, 1917.

288. *Ibid.*

289. *Ibid.*

290. *Ibid.*

291. Lewis and Choynski, "I Fought 'Em All," 26; *The Chronicle Telegram*, 14 February, 1933; Choynski letter to Nat Fleischer, 11 October, 1940; Undated newspaper, circa 1934.

292. *Syracuse Herald*, 15 June, 1917; *Syracuse Herald*, 21 June, 1917; Corbett, *The Roar of the Crowd*, 61-63.

293. Fleischer, *Gentleman Jim*, 20. Corbett relates a similar dialogue in his autobiography (*The Roar of the Crowd*, 63).

294. Corbett, James J. "A Champion Looks Back," *Sport Story Magazine* (Date unknown), 16.

295. *Ibid.*

296. *Ibid.*

297. Choynski letter to Fleischer, 11 October, 1940.

298. Lewis and Choynski, "I Fought 'Em All," 26.

299. *Ibid.*

300. *San Francisco Chronicle*, 12 June, 1910; Lewis and Choynski, "I Fought 'Em All," 26; *Daily Alta California*, 23 April, 1889; *Daily Alta California*, 24 April, 1889; *Oakland Tribune*, 24 April, 1889.

301. Corbett, *The Roar of the Crowd*, 64; *Los Angeles Times*, 6 May, 1887.

302. Corbett, *The Roar of the Crowd*, 64; *Waterloo Daily Courier*, 2 February, 1895.

303. Lewis and Choynski, "I Fought 'Em All," 27; *Syracuse Herald*, 21 June, 1917.

304. Lewis and Choynski, "I Fought 'Em All," 26; *Marin Journal*, 2 May, 1889.

305. Fleischer, *Gentleman Jim*, 22.

306. *Daily Alta California*, 23 April, 1889.

307. *Ibid.*

Chapter Eleven — High Drama

308. *San Francisco Chronicle*, 29 April, 1889.

309. *Syracuse Herald*, 27 June, 1917.

310. *Oakland Tribune*, 4 May, 1889; *Daily Alta California*, 23 April, 1889.

311. *Ibid.*; *San Francisco Morning Call*, 5 May, 1889.

312. *Daily Alta California*, 29 April, 1889.

313. *Waterloo Daily Courier*, 2 February, 1895.

314. *Ibid.*

315. *San Francisco Call-Bulletin*, 26 January, 1943.

316. *American Israelite*, 23 September, 1887; *American Israelite*, 16 December, 1887; *Daily Alta California*, 30 November, 1887. For further reading on Joe Choynski and his Jewish roots read Kramer and Stern's excellent study "San Francisco's Fighting Jew" in the *California Historical Quarterly* (Winter 1974), 333-346.

317. Corbett, *The Roar of the Crowd*, 65.

318. "Choynski Tells Own Story of Corbett Tiffs," undated and unknown newspaper article, circa 1934, San Francisco History Center vertical files.

319. *Ibid.*

320. *San Francisco Chronicle*, 29 April, 1889.

321. *Ibid.*

322. *Ibid.*

323. Lewis and Choynski, "I Fought 'Em All," 26.

324. *History of Marin County, California* (Petaluma, California: Charmaine Burdell Veronda, 1972), 383-384.

325. *Daily Alta California*, 13 May, 1889; *San Francisco Chronicle*, 13 May, 1889.

326. *Woodland Daily Democrat*, 7 September, 1928.

327. *Daily Alta California*, 12 May, 1889.

328. *Daily Alta California*, 21 February, 1884; *San Francisco Call*, 12 August, 1900; *Daily Alta California*, 13 May, 1889.

329. *Daily Alta California*, 12 May, 1889.

330. *Ibid.*

331. *Daily Alta California*, 23 April, 1889.

332. *Daily Alta California*, 12 May, 1889.

333. *Ibid.*

334. *Ibid.*

335. Corbett, *The Roar of the Crowd*, 36; *Syracuse Herald*, 21 June, 1917.

336. *Syracuse Herald*, 21 June, 1917.

337. *Ibid.*

338. *Ibid.*

339. *Ibid.*

340. Oakland's Eugene S. Van Court, a member of the Olympic Club, remembered a different version of how Delaney came to train his friend. According to Van Court, Corbett's need for a trainer first came to light while the two sat in the dressing room at the Olympic Club prior to his upcoming fight with Choynski.

"I don't know where to get a good trainer," Van Court recalled Corbett saying. "I can find lots of trainers but what I want is a first-class man and they are hard to find."

Van Court claims he immediately thought of Delaney, and invited Corbett to go with him to Oakland. That night the two caught the 5 p.m. boat to Oakland to meet Delaney at his home inside the Galindo Hotel. Corbett and Delaney instantly hit it off, and the rest was history (*Oakland Tribune*, 17 July, 1899).

Van Court's version is completely plausible, although there is no mention of Delaney at Corbett's camp as late as May 10. In all likelihood, Van Court did introduce the two, perhaps as Corbett remembered in his autobiography, *The Roar of the Crowd*, 36-37. He probably then suggested Delaney's services after the announcement of the Choynski fight, although that is simply conjecture.

Regardless, Delaney's fateful encounter with Corbett led to one of the great fighter-trainer tandems in boxing history.

341. *San Francisco Chronicle*, 13 May, 1889.

342. *Ibid.*

343. *Ibid.*

344. *Daily Alta California*, 13 May, 1889.

345. *Ibid.*

346. *San Francisco Chronicle*, 13 May, 1889.

347. *Daily Alta California*, 14 May, 1889.

348. *Daily Alta California*, 31 May, 1889; *Daily Alta California*, 13 May, 1889.

349. *Ibid.*

350. *San Francisco Chronicle*, 19 May, 1889.

351. *Ibid*; *San Francisco Chronicle*, 12 June 1910.

352. *Ibid.*

353. *Daily Alta California*, 20 May, 1889.

354. *Ibid.*

355. *San Francisco Chronicle*, 11 May, 1889; Syracuse *Herald*, 21 June, 1917.

356. *San Francisco Chronicle*, 20 May, 1889.

357. *Ibid.*

358. *San Francisco Chronicle*, 30 May, 1889.

359. *Ibid.*; *San Francisco Daily Evening Bulletin*, 30 May, 1889.

360. *Syracuse Herald*, 21 June, 1917.

361. *Ibid.*

362. Lewis and Choynski, "I Fought 'Em All," 26.

363. Corbett, *The Roar of the Crowd*, 66.

364. *Daily Alta California*, 31 May, 1889.

365. *Syracuse Herald*, 25 June, 1917.

366. *Ibid.*; Corbett, *The Roar of the Crowd*, 66.

367. *Syracuse Herald*, 25 June, 1917.

368. *Ibid.*

369. *Oakland Tribune*, 12 April, 1908.

370. *Syracuse Herald*, 25 June, 1917; Corbett, *The Roar of the Crowd*, 66.

371. Corbett, "A Champion Looks Back," 16.

Chapter Twelve — A Fairfax Barn

372. *San Francisco Daily Evening Bulletin*, 30 May, 1889; *Daily Alta California*, 31 May, 1889. Decoration Day is now known as Veteran's Day.

373. *Daily Alta California*, 31 May, 1889.

374. *Ibid.*; *San Francisco Daily Evening Bulletin*, 30 May, 1889; *History of Marin County, California*, 391. The Pacific and San Francisco yacht clubs both built buildings on the wharf in 1878.

375. *San Francisco Chronicle*, 12 June, 1910.

376. *Ibid.*

377. Jean Secchitano. *The Golden Days of Fairfax, 1831-1931* (Fairfax, California: The Fairfax Certified PTA, 1931), 30.

378. *Daily Alta California*, 31 May, 1889; The Marin County Great Register of 1880. White's Hill was also variously known as White's Valley, White's Arroyo and White's Rancho in 1889. By 1892, the mountain appears to have been generally known as White's Hill, appearing on an official county map by that name (Map of Marin County California, 1892. Compiled from Records and Surveys by George M. Dodge. Copy provided by the generosity of The Anne T. Kent Collection California Room, Marin County Free Library).

379. Map of Austin property from a 1903 railroad survey. Copy provided by Fairfax historian William Sager, who graciously provided this author with information and directions to the site of the Choynski-Corbett fight at Peter Austin's old farm. Today, the farm site is home to the Henry E. Bothin Youth Center (Girls Scout) Camp. There are no longer any signs of Austin's original structures.

380. *San Francisco Evening Bulletin*, 30 May, 1889; *San Francisco Morning Call*, 30 May, 1889. I.N. Choynski was scheduled to appear at a preliminary hearing June 5, 1889, only to have the hearing postponed on a motion from counsel. Oddly, the charges appeared to be dropped as no further documentation of the case has ever surfaced.

381. Corbett, *The Roar of the Crowd*, 67.

382. *Ibid.*

383. *San Francisco Daily Evening Bulletin*, 30 May, 1889.

384. *Ibid.*

385. *Ibid.*

386. *Daily Alta California*, 31 May, 1889.

387. Corbett, *The Roar of the Crowd*, 67-68.

388. *San Antonio Light and Gazette*, 17 February, 1910.

389. Peter E. Palmquist and Thomas R. Kailbourn, *Pioneer Photographers of the West: A Biographical Directory, 1840-1865* (Redwood City, California: Stanford University Press, 2000), 276.

390. *Ibid.*

391. *Ibid.*

392. *Syracuse Herald*, 25 June, 1917; *San Antonio Light and Gazette*, 17 February, 1910.

393. *San Francisco Chronicle*, 26 January, 1943; *Syracuse Herald*, 25 June, 1917.

394. Corbett, *The Roar of the Crowd*, 68.

395. *Ibid.*

396. Corbett, *The Roar of the Crowd*, 68-69.

397. Lewis and Choynski, "I Fought 'Em All," 26.

398. *Ibid.*

399. *Daily Alta California*, 31 May, 1889.

400. Corbett, *The Roar of the Crowd*, 69; *Syracuse Herald*, 25 June, 1917.

401. *Ibid.*

402. *Ibid.*

403. *Ibid.*

404. *Ibid.*

405. *Syracuse Herald*, 25 June, 1917.

406. *Ibid.*

407. *Ibid.*

408. *Ibid.*

409. *Ibid.*

410. Lewis and Choynski, "I Fought 'Em All," 27.

411. *Ibid.*; *Daily Alta California*, 31 May, 1889; Old-Timer, "Famous Fights I have Seen," 58.

412. *Daily Alta California*, 31 May, 1889.

413. *Ibid.*

414. *Ibid.*

415. Old-Timer, "Famous Fights I Have Seen," 58; *Syracuse Herald*, 27 June, 1917; Corbett, *The Roar of the Crowd*, 69-70.

416. Lewis and Choynski, "I Fought 'Em All," 27; Old-Timer, "Famous Fights I Have Seen," 58. The *Daily Alta California* writer reported the knockdown a slip, but even Choynski conceded he had been knocked down in his account of the fight.

417. Old-Timer, "Famous Fights I Have Seen," 58.

418. Lewis and Choynski, "I Fought 'Em All," 27.

419. *Daily Alta California*, 31 May, 1889.

Chapter Thirteen — Sheriff Healy

420. United States Census, Marin County, 1910; *Marin Journal*, 29 January, 1920.

421. *Marin Journal*, 6 June, 1889.

422. *Marin Journal*, 6 June, 1889.

423. *Ibid.*

424. *Ibid.*

425. *Ibid.*

426. *Ibid.*; *History of Marin County, California*, 234.

427. Corbett, *The Roar of the Crowd*, 70; *Syracuse Herald*, 27 June, 1917; Old-Timer, "Famous Fights I Have Seen," 58.

428. *Syracuse Herald*, 27 June, 1917.

429. *Daily Alta California*, 31 May, 1889.

430. Corbett, "A Champion Looks Back," 16.

431. *Reno Evening Gazette*, 24 January, 1931.

432. *Daily Alta California*, 31 May, 1889.

433. *Ibid.*

434. Lewis and Choynski, "I Fight 'Em All," 28; Marin County's 1906 Voter Registration.

435. *Marin Journal*, 6 June, 1889.

436. *Daily Alta California*, 31 May, 1889.

437. *Ibid.*

438. Marin County's 1906 Voter Registration; *Daily Alta California*, 31 May, 1889.

439. Corbett, *The Roar of the Crowd*, 70.

440. *Marin Journal*, 6 June, 1889.

441. *Daily Alta California*, 31 May, 1889; Old-Timer, "Famous Fights I Have Seen," 58; Corbett, *The Roar of the Crowd*, 70.

442. *Daily Alta California*, 31 May, 1889.

443. *Ibid.*

Chapter Fourteen — Benicia

444. *Daily Alta California*, 5 June, 1889.

445. *Syracuse Herald*, 27 June, 1917.

446. *Ibid.*

447. *Ibid.*

448. *Oakland Tribune's* "Benicia," circa 1881, 1. Copy in The Bancroft Library,

University of California, Berkeley, California.

449. Andrew Neal Cohen. *Gateway To The Inland Coast: The Story Of The Carquinez Straight* (Sacramento: The Carquinez Strait Preservation Trust & Carquinez Strait MOU Coordinating Council), 3.

450. *San Francisco Chronicle*, 12 June, 1910.

451. Elliott J. Gorn. *The Manly Art: Bare-knuckle Prize Fighting In America* (New York: Cornell University Press, 1986), 211.

452. *Oakland Tribune*, 6 April, 1913; The *Appleton Post-Crescent* (Appleton, Wisconsin), 24 January, 1931; *Manitoba Free-Press*, 1 January, 1927; Lewis and Choynski, "I Fought 'Em All," 28.

453. Horace Davis. *California Breadstuffs* (Chicago: The University of Chicago Press, 1894), 531; *Oakland Tribune's* "Benicia," 3.

454. *Oakland Tribune's* "Benicia," 4, 5, 9-10.

455. Turner Shipyard vertical file, Benicia Historical Museum, Benicia, California.

456. Excerpts from a taped interview with Eva Chapman Hunt, Felton, California, 1977. Benicia history buffs interviewed Hunt, whose grandfather was Matthew Turner – the shipyard's founder. The tape was later copied by C.T. Hosley February 22, 1987, and excerpts can be found at the Benicia Historical Museum in Benicia, California.

457. Edward Dean Sullivan. *The Fabulous Wilson Mizner* (New York: The Henkle Company, 1935), 33; *The History of Solano County* (San Francisco: Wood, Alley & Co., 1879), 444-445.

458. Corbett, *The Roar of the Crowd*, 71; Sullivan, The *Fabulous Wilson Mizner*, 33.

459. In 1917, Corbett stated that he stayed the night of June 4, 1889 at a cottage belonging to the brother of Wilson Mizner, who later became a celebrated American playwright. Wilson was one of Lansing B. Mizner's seven children, and was 13 in June 1889 (*Syracuse Herald*, 27 June, 1917).

460. *Syracuse Herald*, 29 June, 1917.

461. *Syracuse Herald*, 27 June, 1917.

462. Corbett, "A Champion Looks Back," 16.

463. *Ibid.*

464. *Ibid.*

465. Lewis and Choynski, "I Fought 'Em All," 28.

466. *Syracuse Herald*, 29 June, 1917.

467. *Oakland Tribune*, 19 March, 1914.

468. Lewis and Choynski, "I Fought 'Em All," 28.

Chapter Fifteen — Dawn of Battle

469. *San Francisco Chronicle*, 6 June, 1889.

470. *Ibid.*

471. *Ibid; Daily Alta California*, 6 June, 1889.

472. *Ibid.*

473. *Daily Alta California*, 6 June, 1889.

474. *San Francisco Chronicle*, 12 June, 1910; *Daily Alta California*, 6 June, 1889.

475. *Syracuse Herald*, 29 June, 1889.

476. *Ibid.*

477. *Ibid.*

478. *Ibid.*

479. *Ibid.*

480. *Ibid.*

481. *Ibid.*

482. Corbett, *The Roar of the Crowd*, 72.

483. *Ibid.* In December of 1887 – a month after Choynski's fourth-round knockout of Keneally – the *Daily Alta California* reported: "There is but little possibility of Kenealley (*sic*) and Choynski having a return match, as Choynski wishes to rest on his laurels for a time, when he will again put himself in trim to attend to the heavy-weight championship of the club, which he so ably represents. Kenealley, on the other hand, is very anxious for another chance, and believes he can turn the tables, and will put himself in a course of training different from that which he adopted previous to his last encounter, when he stayed over his furnace almost up to the last hour, and consequently his flesh was in a good condition to show every blow received upon it."

484. Corbett, *The Roar of the Crowd*, 73.

485. *Ibid.*

486. *Ibid.*

487. *San Francisco Chronicle*, 6 June, 1889.

488. *Ibid.*

489. *The History of Solano County*, 438-439; Richard Dillon, *Great Expectations: The Story of Benicia, California* (Benicia, California: Benicia Heritage Book, Inc., 1976), 57. The Dillon ranch house was eventually demolished, and today Dillon's Point is part of the Benicia State Recreation Area.

490. *San Francisco Chronicle*, 6 June, 1889.

491. *Ibid.; San Francisco Chronicle*, 12 June, 1910.

492. *San Francisco Chronicle,* 6 June, 1889; Daily Alta California, 6 June, 1889; *San Francisco Chronicle,* 12 June, 1910.

493. *Daily Alta California,* 6 June, 1889.

494. *Ibid.*

495. *Ibid.*

496. *Benicia New Era,* 19 February, 1933.

497. Dillon, *Great Expectations,* 176.

498. *San Francisco Chronicle,* 6 June, 1889; *Daily Alta California,* 6 June, 1889.

499. *Daily Alta California,* 6 June, 1889; Bloom, *The Autobiography of Sol Bloom,* 100; Old-Timer, "Famous Fights I Have Seen," 59.

500. Bloom, *The Autobiography of Sol Bloom,* 100.

501. Old-Timer, "Famous Fights I Have Seen," 59.

502. Corbett, *The Roar of the Crowd,* 73-74.

503. *Ibid.*

504. *Syracuse Herald,* 29 June, 1917.

Chapter Sixteen — Controversy

505. *Daily Alta California,* 6 June, 1889; *San Francisco Chronicle,* 6 June, 1889.

506. Lewis and Choynski, "I Fought 'Em All," 28.

507. *San Francisco Chronicle,* 6 June, 1889.

508. *Ibid.;* Bloom, *The Autobiography of Sol Bloom,* 100.

509. *San Francisco Morning Call,* 6 June, 1889; *San Francisco Chronicle,* 6 June, 1889.

510. *Ibid.*

511. Old-Timer, "Famous Fights I Have Seen," 59.

512. Corbett, "A Champion Looks Back," 16.

513. *Ibid.; San Francisco Examiner,* 6 June, 1889; *Reno Evening Gazette,* 24 January, 1931.

514. Corbett, "A Champion Looks Back," 16.

515. *Daily Alta California,* 6 June, 1889.

516. *San Francisco Chronicle,* 6 June, 1889.

517. *Ibid.*

518. Corbett, *The Roar of the Crowd,* 75.

519. *Ibid.*

520. *San Francisco Morning Call,* 6 June, 1889; Bloom, *The Autobiography of Sol Bloom,* 100-101; *San Francisco Examiner,* 6 June, 1889; *San Francisco Chronicle,* 12 June, 1910.

521. *Daily Alta California*, 6 June, 1889.

522. *Ibid.; San Francisco Chronicle*, 6 June, 1889.

523. *Daily Alta California*, 6 June, 1889.

524. *Ibid.*

525. *Ibid.*

526. *Ibid.*

527. George Harting appears to have served as the official timekeeper on the barge. The New Zealand native sailed from Australia on the same ship that brought Peter Jackson to America. Upon his arrival Harting, began working as a timekeeper at the California Athletic Club. Decades later, Timothy McGrath recalled T.T. Williams working as the timekeeper on the barge. In all likelihood, McGrath was confused, remembering that Williams kept the first Choynski-Corbett showdown in Fairfax. (*Colorado Springs Gazette*, 2 July, 1910; *Reno Evening Gazette*, 24 January, 1931).

Chapter Seventeen — A Grim Business

528. *Daily Alta California*, 6 June, 1889.

529. *Ibid.*

530. *San Francisco Examiner*, 6 June, 1889.

531. *Daily Alta California*, 6 June, 1889.

532. *San Francisco Examiner*, 6 June, 1889.

533. *Daily Alta California*, 6 June, 1889.

534. *Ibid.*

535. *Ibid.*

536. *San Francisco Chronicle*, 6 June, 1889.

537. Lewis and Choynski, "I Fought 'Em All," 28.

538. *Oxnard* (California) *Daily Courier*, 3 December 1924; Old-Timer, "Famous Fights I Have Seen," 59.

Chapter Eighteen — Slaughterhouse

539. *San Francisco Examiner*, 6 June, 1889; *San Francisco Chronicle*, 6 June, 1889; *San Francisco Morning Call*, 6 June, 1889; Fleischer, *Gentleman Jim*, 25-26. It should be noted that *San Francisco Examiner* reported the fourth as the round that broke Corbett left hand, "catching Joe with a terrible blow on the forehead, knocking his head between his shoulders." The *San Francisco Morning Call* would report that Corbett "sprained his wrist" in the fifth round. Corbett, meanwhile, always maintained he broke the knuckles in his left hand after knocking Choynski down in round three (Corbett, *The Roar of the Crowd*, 76; *Oxnard Daily Courier*, 3 December, 1924; *Oneonta Daily Star*, 26 October, 1925; Fleischer, *Gentleman Jim*, 25.)

540. *Oxnard Daily Courier*, 3 December, 1924.

541. Fleischer, *Gentleman Jim*, 26.

542. *San Francisco Chronicle*, 6 June, 1889.

543. Old-Timer, "Famous Fights I Have Seen," 60.

544. *San Francisco Morning Call*, 6 June, 1889.

545. *Daily Alta California*, 6 June, 1889.

546. *San Francisco Morning Call*, 6 June, 1889.

547. *Daily Alta California*, 6 June, 1889; *Oakland Tribune*, 12 June, 1910.

548. *Ibid.*

549. *San Francisco Examiner*, 6 June, 1889.

550. Lewis and Choynski, "I Fought 'Em All," 28.

551. *San Francisco Examiner*, 6 June, 1889.

552. *Ibid.*

553. *Ibid.*

554. *Ibid.*

555. *San Francisco Morning Call*, 6 June, 1889.

556. *San Francisco Chronicle*, 6 June, 1889; *San Francisco Morning Call*, 6 June, 1889.

557. Corbett, *The Roar of the Crowd*, 78.

558. *Manitoba Morning Free Press*, 17 May, 1911.

559. *San Francisco Morning Call*, 6 June, 1889.

560. *San Francisco Chronicle*, 6 June, 1889.

561. *Manitoba Morning Free Press*, 17 May, 1911; *Oakland Tribune*, 19 March, 1914.

562. Corbett, *Roar of Crowd*, 76-77; *Oneonta* (New York) *Daily Star*, 26 October, 1925.

563. *Daily Alta California*, 6 June, 1889.

564. Lewis and Choynski, "I Fought 'Em All," 29.

565. *Daily Alta California*, 6 June, 1889; *San Francisco Chronicle*, 6 June, 1889.

566. *Daily Alta California*, 6 June, 1889.

567. Fleischer, *Gentleman Jim*, 26.

Chapter Nineteen — Shifting Tide

568. *Manitoba Morning Free Press*, 17 May, 1911.

569. *Daily Alta California*, 6 June, 1889.

570. *San Francisco Chronicle*, 6 June, 1889.

571. *Syracuse Herald*, 3 July, 1917; Corbett, *The Roar of the Crowd*, 79-80;

Oneonta (New York) *Daily Star*, 26 October, 1925.

572. *Syracuse Herald*, 3 July, 1917.

573. *Ibid.*

574. Corbett, *The Roar of the Crowd*, 81.

575. *Ibid.*

576. Fleischer, *Gentleman Jim*, 26; Corbett, *The Roar of the Crowd*, 80-81.

577. Fleischer, *Gentleman Jim*, 26.

578. *Ibid.*

579. *San Francisco Chronicle*, 6 June, 1889.

580. Ibid; Corbett, *The Roar of the Crowd*, 81.

581. Corbett, *The Roar of the Crowd*, 83-84.

582. *Daily Alta California*, 6 June, 1889; *San Francisco Chronicle*, 6 June, 1889.

583. Lewis and Choynski, "I Fought 'Em All," 29.

584. *Ibid.*, 29-30.

585. *Daily Alta California*, 6 June, 1889; *San Francisco Chronicle*, 6 June, 1889.

586. Corbett, *The Roar of the Crowd*, 83.

587. *Ibid*; Lewis and Choynski, "I Fought 'Em All," 29.

588. *Daily Alta California*, 6 June, 1889.

Chapter Twenty — Iron Man

589. *Manitoba Morning Free Press*, 17 May, 1911.

590. *San Francisco Chronicle*, 6 June, 1889.

591. Lewis and Choynski, "I Fought 'Em All," 30.

592. *Ibid.*

593. *Ibid.*

594. *Ibid.*

Chapter Twenty-One — Desperate Courage

595. *Titusville* (Pennsylvania) *Herald*, 30 December, 1930.

596. *San Francisco Chronicle*, 6 June, 1889; *San Francisco Examiner*, 6 June, 1889.

597. *Ibid.*; *San Francisco Morning Call*, 6 June, 1889.

598. Corbett, *The Roar of the Crowd*, 77.

599. *Ibid.*

600. *San Francisco Chronicle*, 6 June, 1889.

601. *Daily Alta California*, 6 June, 1889.

602. *San Francisco Examiner*, 6 June, 1889.

603. *San Francisco Chronicle*, 6 June, 1889; *Daily Alta California*, 6 June, 1889.

604. *San Francisco Morning Call*, 6 June, 1889.

605. *San Francisco Examiner*, 6 June, 1889.

606. Old-Timer, "Famous Fights I Have Seen," 61.

607. *San Francisco Chronicle*, 6 June, 1889.

Chapter Twenty-Two — The Last Stand

608. Lewis and Choynski, "I Fought 'Em All," 30.

609. *San Francisco Chronicle*, 6 June, 1889.

610. *Ibid.*; *San Francisco Examiner*, 6 June, 1889; *Daily Alta California*, 6 June, 1889. Corbett described the knockdown by saying, "Choynski ducked his head almost to my waist-line. I saw a chance and brought my left up in inner-cut fashion and landed on Choynski's chin – not with my hand or my knuckles, but with my wrist." (*Oneonta Daily Star*, 2 December, 1924). Delaney said, "Corbett palmed Joe with a left flush on his face." (*Manitoba Morning Free Press*, 17 May, 1911).

611. *Ibid.*; *Syracuse Herald*, 10 July, 1917.

612. Fleischer, *Gentleman Jim*, 27.

613. *San Francisco Chronicle*, 6 June, 1889; *Daily Alta California*, 6 June, 1889; *San Francisco Examiner*, 6 June, 1889.

614. *Syracuse Herald*, 10 July, 1917

615. Fleischer, *Gentleman Jim*, 27.

616. *Daily Alta California*, 6 June, 1889.

617. *Ibid.*; *San Francisco Morning Call*, 6 June, 1889.

618. *Ibid.*

619. *Ibid.*

620. Corbett, *The Roar of the Crowd*, 88; San *Francisco Chronicle*, 6 June, 1889.

621. *San Francisco Chronicle*, 6 June, 1889.

622. *San Francisco Chronicle*, 12 June, 1910.

623. Corbett letter to Dykes, 17 July, 1928.

624. *San Francisco Chronicle*, 12 June, 1910; *San Francisco Chronicle*, 6 June, 1889.

Chapter Twenty-Three — Final Act

625. *Daily Alta California*, 6 June, 1889; *San Francisco Chronicle*, 6 June, 1889.

626. *Daily Alta California*, 6 June, 1889.

627. Lewis and Choynski, "I Fought 'Em All," 30.

628. *Ibid.*

629. *Daily Alta California*, 6 June, 1889.

630. *Ibid.*

631. *Ibid.*

632. *Ibid.; Langley's San Francisco Directory For the Year Commencing May, 1889,* 1422.

633. *Daily Alta California,* 10 June, 1889.

634. *San Francisco Chronicle,* 6 June, 1889.

635. *Ibid.*

636. *Ibid.*

637. *Marin Journal,* 2 May, 1889. Original article appeared in the *New York Sun.*

638. *Langley's San Francisco Directory For the Year Commencing May, 1889,* 379, 521.

639. *Oakland Tribune,* 6 June, 1889.

640. *Ibid.*

641. Lewis and Choynski, "I Fought 'Em All," 31.

642. *San Francisco Chronicle,* 7 June, 1889.

Epilogue
643. *San Francisco Chronicle,* 12 June, 1910.

644. *Ibid.*

645. *Ibid.*

646. *Oakland Tribune,* 12 June, 1910.

647. *Ibid.*

648. *Ibid.*

649. *Ibid.*

650. *Ibid.*

651. *Ibid.*

652. *Ibid.*

653. *Ibid.*

654. *Ibid.*

655. *Ibid.*

656. *New York Times,* 19 February, 1933.

657. *Ibid.*

658. *Ibid.*

659. *Ibid.*

660. Lewis and Choynski, "I Fought 'Em All," 31.

661. *San Francisco Chronicle,* 10 June, 1889; *Syracuse Herald,* 21 July, 1917.

662. Corbett, *The Roar of the Crowd,* 93.

663. *San Francisco Chronicle*, 10 June, 1889; Corbett, *The Roar of the Crowd*, 94-95.

664. William Inglis. *Champions Off Guard* (New York: The Vanguard Press, 1932), 115.

665. *Ibid.*, 106.

666. *The Modesto Bee and News-Herald*, 26 January, 1943.

667. *Los Angeles Times*, 18 January, 1950.

668. *San Jose News*, 2 February, 1934.

669. *The Modesto Bee and News-Herald*, 26 January, 1943.

670. Nat Fleischer, "Jim Jeffries Talks About Great Fighters of His Era," *The Ring* (October, 1950), 25.

671. *Ibid.*

672. *San Francisco Call-Bulletin*, 26 January, 1943.

673. Lewis and Choynski, "I Fought 'Em All," 31.

674. *Daily Northwestern* (Oshkosh, Wisconsin), 14 February, 1933.

675. Fleischer, *Gentleman Jim*, 25.

676. Corbett, *The Roar of the Crowd*, 88.

677. *Syracuse Post-Standard*, 25 May, 1910.

678. *Wisconsin Rapids Tribune*, 1 February, 1943.

679. *Oakland Tribune*, 12 June, 1910.

680. Lewis and Choynski, "I Fought 'Em All," 31.

681. Fleischer, *Gentleman Jim*, 28.

682. *Daily Alta California*, 20 June, 1889.

683. *Daily Alta California*, 16 July, 1889; *San Francisco Chronicle*, 22 July, 1899.

684. *Gentleman Jim* was released in 1942, starring Errol Flynn as a brash, young Corbett, and Alexis Smith as his love interest.

685. Choynski letter to Fleischer, 11 October, 1940.

686. *New York Times*, 26 January, 1943.

687. Bernard Postal, Jessie Silver, and Roy Silver. *Encyclopedia of Jews in Sports* (New York, Bloch Publishing Company, 1965), 152.

688. *The Coshocton Tribune* (Coshocton, Ohio), 10 August, 1942.

689. Corbett, *The Roar of the Crowd*, 88.

690. *Manitoba Morning Free-Press*, 17 May, 1911.

691. *New York Times*, 26 January, 1912.

692. *New Castle* (Pennsylvania) *News*, 10 September, 1919.

693. *Woodland Daily Democrat,* 7 September, 1929; *The Fresno Bee,* 9 September, 1929.

694. Bloom, *The Autobiography of Sol Bloom,* 99, 101.

695. *Oakland Tribune,* 19 March, 1914.

696. *Benicia New Era,* 18 February, 1933.

697. *Oakland Tribune,* 6 April, 1913.

698. *Oakland Tribune,* 23 June, 1928.

699. *Marin Journal,* 29 January, 1920.

700. *Big Stone Gap* (Wise County, Virginia), 27 October, 1898.

701. *San Francisco Chronicle,* 17 August, 1898.

702. *Ibid.*

703. Stern, "Harriett Ashim Choynski: A Western Arrival To San Francisco, 1850," 27.

704. *San Francisco Morning Call,* 28 January, 1899.

705. *Dallas Morning News,* 9 March, 1933.

Selected Biography

Archival Collections

Anne T. Kent Collection California Room, Marin County Free Library
Marin County, California Map 1892

Bancroft Library, University of California, Berkeley
Janet (Choynski) Fleishhacker Interview.
"Benicia" pamphlet, circa 1881.

Benicia Historical Museum, Benicia, California
Mizner Family Vertical File
Turner Shipyard Vertical File

California State Archives, Sacramento
People v. I.N. Choynski (1890).

California Historical Society, San Francisco
I.N. Choynski Vertical File.

National Archives, Pacific Sierra Region, San Bruno, California
I.N. Choynski's Naturalization Papers.

San Francisco History Center
Joe Choynski Vertical File

San Francisco Public Library
James J. Corbett Vertical File.
Mose Gunst Vertical File.

Private Collections

David and Mortimer Fleishhacker
Fleishhacker Family Papers.

Published Primary Materials
Books and Pamphlets

Baker, Malcolm E., ed. *More San Francisco Memoirs, 1852-1899: The Ripening Years.* San Francisco: Londonborn Publications, 1996.

Bloom, Sol. *The Autobiography of Sol Bloom.* New York: G.P. Putnam's Sons, 1948.

Builders of a Great City: San Francisco's Representative Men. San Francisco, 1891.

Corbett, James. J. *The Roar of the Crowd: The True Take of the Rise and Fall of a Champion.* New York: G.P. Putnam's Sons, 1925.

A Bit of My Life: Training the Body for Supervitality. Publisher and publishing date unknown.

Cowan, Robert Ernst. *Booksellers Of Early San Francisco.* Los Angeles: The Ward Ritchie Press, 1953.

Davis, Horace. *California Breadstuffs.* Chicago: The University of Chicago Press, 1894.

Fleischer, Nat. *Gentleman Jim: The Story of James J. Corbett.* New York: C.J. O'Brien, Inc., 1942.

Inglis, William. *Champions Off Guard.* New York: The Vanguard Press, 1932.

Langley's San Francisco Directory. San Francisco: Francis, Valentine & Co., Printers, 1889.

Levy, Harriet Lane. *920 O'Farrell Street.* Garden City, N.Y.: Doubleday & Co., 1947.

Marin County's Voter Registration, 1906.

Nelson, Battling. *Life, Battles And Career of Battling Nelson* (Hegewisch, Ill., 1909)

Oakland, Alameda and Berkeley City Directory, 1889-1890.

San Francisco Directory, 1856-1858.

The History of The Olympic Club. San Francisco: The Art Publishing Company, 1893.

United States Census, 1910

Newspapers

American Israelite (Cincinnati)
Benicia New Era
Big Stone Gap (Virginia)
Chicago Sunday Inter-Ocean
Colorado Springs Gazette
Daily Alta California (San Francisco)
Daily Northwestern (Oshkosh, Wisconsin)
Dallas Morning News
Los Angeles Times
Manitoba Morning Free-Press
Marin Journal
Modesto Bee
National Police Gazette
New Castle (Pennsylvania) *News*
New York Sun
New York Times
Oakland Tribune
Oneonta (N.Y.) *Daily Star*
Oxnard (California) *Daily Courier*
Public Opinion
Reno Evening Gazette
San Antonio Light and Gazette
San Francisco Call-Bulletin
San Francisco Chronicle
San Francisco Daily Evening Examiner
San Francisco Daily Examiner
San Francisco Examiner
San Francisco Morning Call
San Francisco Morning Herald

Syracuse Post-Standard
The Appleton Post-Crescent
The (Salt Lake City) *Daily Tribune*
The (San Francisco) *Bulletin*
The Chronicle Telegram (Elyria, Ohio)
The Coshocton (Ohio) *Tribune*
The Fresno Bee
The Jewish Conservator (Chicago)
The Modesto Bee and News-Herald
The Syracuse (N.Y.) *Herald*
Titusville (Pennsylvania) *Herald*
Waterloo Daily Courier
Wisconsin Rapids Tribune
Woodland (California) *Daily Democrat*

Articles

Corbett, James J. "A Champion Looks Back," *Sport Story Magazine* (Date unknown)

Fleischer, Nat. "Jim Jeffries Talks About Great Fighters of His Era," *The Ring* (October, 1950)

Lewis, Tom and Joe Choynski. "I Fought 'Em All," Fight Stories (October, 1930)

Old-timer. "Famous Fights I Have Seen," *Fight Stories* (March, 1929)

Secondary Printed Materials
Books and Pamphlets

Blady, Ken. *The Jewish Boxers Hall of Fame.* New York: Shapolsky Publishers, Inc., 1988.

Cohen, Andrew Neal. *Gateway To The Inland Coast: The Story of the Carquinez Straight.* Sacramento: The Carquinez Strait Preservation Trust and Carquinez Strait MOU Coordinating Council, date unknown.

Dillon, Richard, Great Expectations: *The Story of Benicia, California. Benicia, California*: Bennicia Heritage Book, Inc., 1976

Fields, Armond. *James J. Corbett: A Biography of the Heavyweight Boxing Champion and Popular Theatre Headliner.* Jefferson, North Carolina: McFarland & Company, Inc. Publishers, 2001.

Gorn, Elliott J. *The Manly Art: Bare-knuckle Prize Fighting In America.* New York: Cornell University Press, 1986.

History of Marin County, California. Petaluma, California: Charmaine Burdell Veronda, 1972.

Issel, William and Robert W. Cherny. *San Francisco, 1865-1932: Politics, Power, and Urban Development.* Berkeley, California: University of California Press, 1986.

LaForce, Christopher J. *The Choynski Chronicles: A Biography of Hall of Fame Boxer Jewish Joe Choynski.* Iowa City, Iowa: Win By KO Publications, 2013.

Lewis, Oscar. *San Francisco: Mission to Metropolis.* Berkeley, California: Howell-North Books, 1966.

Palmquist, Peter E. and Thomas R. Kailbourn. *Pioneer Photographers of the West: A Biographical Directory, 1840-1865.* (Redwood City, California: Stanford University Press, 2000.

Postal, Bernard, Jessie Silver, and Roy Silver. *Encyclopedia of Jews in Sports.* New York: Bloch Publishing Company, 1965.

Secchitano, Jean. *The Golden Days of Fairfax, 1831-1931.* Fairfax, California: The Fairfax Certified PTA, 1931.

Sullivan, Edward Dean. *The Fabulous Wilson Mizner.* New York: The Henkle Company, 1935.

The History of Solano County. San Francisco: Wood, Alley & Co., 1879.

Articles

Kramer, William M. and Norton B. Stern. "San Francisco's Fighting Jew," *California Historical Quarterly* (Winter, 1974, v. 53, no. 4)

Sequeira, John, "Le Preux Chevalier of The Winged 'O', *Olympian* (date Unknown 6-7.

Singerman, Robert. "The San Francisco Journalism of I.N. Choynski," *Western States Jewish History* (January, 1997, v. 29, no. 2; April, 1997, v. 29, no. 3; July, 1997, v. 29, no. 4)

Stern, B. Norton. "Harriet Ashim Choynski: A Western Arrival to San Francisco, 1850," *Western States Jewish History* (2003, v. 24, no. 3)

Index

233

Author Bio

Ron J. Jackson, Jr. is a bestselling author, historian, and award-winning journalist who has been writing professionally for thirty-three years. He is the author of six books, including *Joe, The Slave Who Became an Alamo Legend*; *Blood Prairie: Perilous Adventures on the Oklahoma Frontier*; and *Alamo Legacy: Alamo Descendants Remember the Alamo*, as well as thousands of articles on sports and history. His work has also appeared in national and regional magazines such as *Wild West*, *True West*, and *Oklahoma Today*.

Jackson began his career in 1985 as a sports writer for *The Reporter* in his hometown of Vacaville, California. He covered everything from world championship boxing to the World Series for the next eleven years before switching to news. Over the years Jackson has interviewed people from all walks of life, including five heavyweight champions, astronauts, a secretary of state, governors, legendary athletes, and working-class heroes.

In addition, Jackson is a member of the Western Writers of America who has worked as a consultant for History Channel and the Houston Arts and Media's award-winning *Birth of Texas Series*. He lives in Binger, Oklahoma with his wife, Jeannia, and their beloved children and granddaughter.